MICHAEL McCANN

BURNT OUT

HOW 'THE TROUBLES' BEGAN

FOREWORD BY TOMMY McKEARNEY

MERCIER PRESS

For my parents
and for a special family
who have made me proud

MERCIER PRESS
Cork
www.mercierpress.ie

© Michael McCann, 2019
Foreword © Tommy McKearney, 2019

ISBN: 978 1 78117 619 1

A CIP record for this title is available from the British Library

Printed and bound in the EU.

CONTENTS

Maps 4

Abbreviations 10

Editorial Note 11

Foreword 13

Introduction 17

1 Orange State in Crisis 22

2 The Evictions Commence 56

3 Derry in the Eye of the Storm 96

4 Ashes to Ashes: Pogrom on the Falls 122

5 From Epicentre to Periphery: Clonard and Ardoyne 163

6 Picking up the Pieces 207

7 Absolving the Establishment 246

Conclusion 267

Notes 273

Bibliography 303

Acknowledgements 310

Index 312

MAPS

NORTHERN IRELAND

(Taken from the Cameron Commission report)

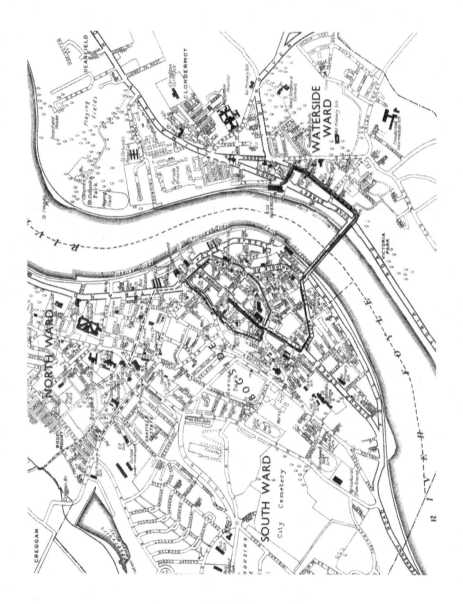

DERRY

(Taken from the Cameron Commission report)

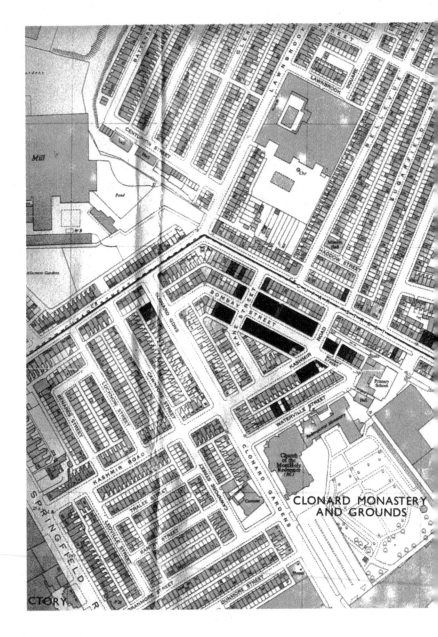

CONWAY AND CLONARD
(Taken from the Scarman Tribunal report)

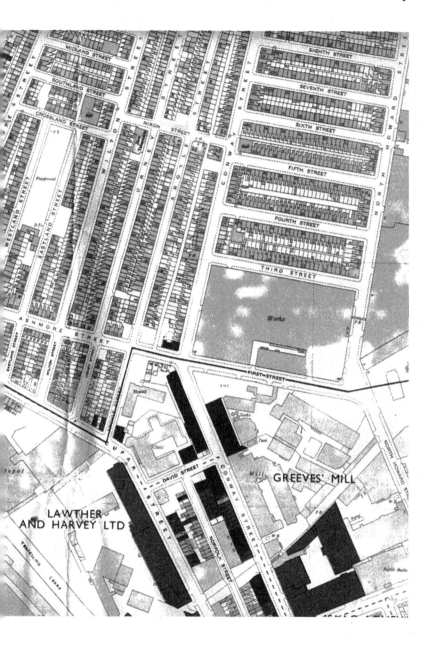

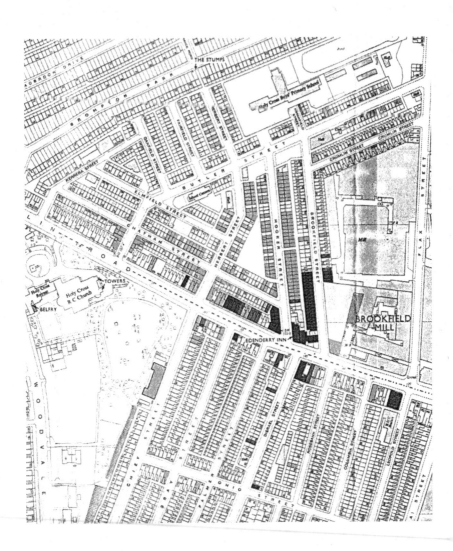

ARDOYNE
(Taken from the Scarman Tribunal report)

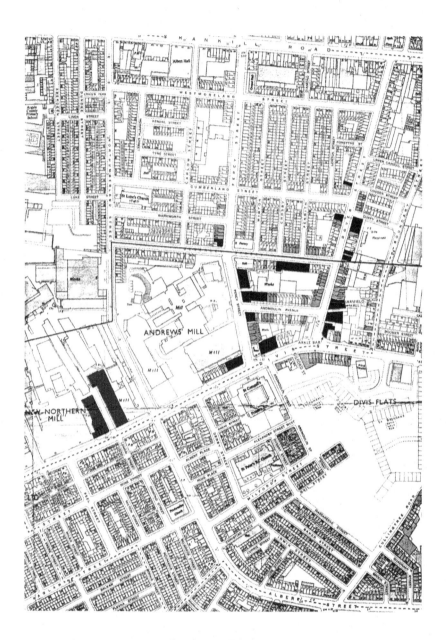

DIVIS STREET
(Taken from the Scarman Tribunal report)

ABBREVIATIONS

CCDC	Central Citizens Defence Committee
DCAC	Derry Citizens Action Committee
DCDA	Derry Citizens Defence Association
DI	District Inspector
DUP	Democratic Unionist Party
GPMG	General Purpose Machine Gun
PD	People's Democracy
GOC	General Officer Commanding
IRA	Irish Republican Army
NICRA	Northern Ireland Civil Rights Association
RUC	Royal Ulster Constabulary
RUCR	Royal Ulster Constabulary Reserve
SDA	Shankill Defence Association
SLR	Self-loading Rifle
UCDC	Ulster Constitution Defence Committee
UDA	Ulster Defence Association
UPA	Ulster Protestant Action
UPL	Ulster Protestant League
UPV	Ulster Protestant Volunteers
USC	Ulster Special Constabulary
UUP	Ulster Unionist Party
UVF	Ulster Volunteer Force

EDITORIAL NOTE

As anyone familiar with the material covered in this book will know, there are problems in imposing any label on the two main communities that together comprise the large majority of Northern Ireland's population. Many but not all Catholics are also nationalists in their political aspirations; most but not all Protestants are also unionists. However, there were then, and are now, substantial numbers of nationalists who are not devout Catholics, and many unionists for whom religion is peripheral to their attitude towards the constitutional question. The polarisation that has characterised the history of the state, and which became especially pronounced in the period discussed in the pages that follow, had little to do with religious differences, though at times (and particularly in the rhetoric of Ian Paisley and his followers) strident objections to Catholic religious teachings featured prominently. Mindful of these problems, I have usually opted to use the terms nationalist and unionist when describing these communities, though occasionally I also use Catholic and Protestant. In general I have used the terms republican and loyalist when describing groups or actions with some formal relationship to political and/or paramilitary organisations, or individuals who figure here as participants in specific organised actions.

My study makes extensive use of the *Scarman Report of Tribunal of Inquiry: Violence and Civil Disturbances in Northern Ireland in 1969*, which is cited in footnotes as Scarman Report. I have also utilised the testimony of hundreds (mostly civilians) who submitted eyewitness accounts of events during the inquiry. These accounts are separate to the Scarman Report and have been cited in footnotes as originating in the Scarman Transcripts.

FOREWORD

TOMMY McKEARNEY[1]

The events of August 1969 in Derry and Belfast were among the most consequential to occur in the history of the troubled political entity that is Northern Ireland. During a forty-eight-hour period over 14–15 August, eight civilians were shot dead – four of them by the local police force, the Royal Ulster Constabulary.[2] Thousands more were made homeless as the result of a concerted incendiary assault led, on occasion, by members of the northern state's police reserves, the Ulster Special Constabulary. The violence was directed against a practically defenceless nationalist population and was carried out by state agents acting in concert with their unofficial supporters. Such happenings would cause tremors in any society. In the North of Ireland, the consequences were profound and lasting.

In the first instance, the lethal nature of the violence effectively dashed hopes for a non-violent transformation of Northern-Irish society and largely sidelined the peaceful civil rights movement. Secondly, the scale of death and destruction meant that the British government was forced to commit its regular army to the region and, with direct intervention from London, Stormont's half century of absolute authority was brought to an end. A third consequence of those traumatic days was to bring another army into Belfast: a split in the republican movement caused by the bloodshed led directly to the formation of the Provisional IRA. The events also had a major impact south of the border, where the reverberations of August 1969 were felt all across the twenty-six-county state. The Dublin government performed a series of contortions as it sought to contain the anger of its citizens, then largely sympathetic to the plight of northern nationalists. Finally, the findings of the official Scarman investigation into August 1969 were skewed in order to exonerate the British state from complicity. Along with the Widgery Report into Bloody Sunday, Scarman's whitewash of state violence after the most traumatic episode in its short and violent history added further weight to the republican argument for breaking entirely with Britain.

Northern Ireland was created in 1920, partly to accommodate a pro-unionist community in the north-east of the island, but more significantly to guarantee the British Empire a physical presence in the strategically important island close to its west coast. A major weakness in the plan was the presence of a large minority in the newly created state that resented the arrangement from the beginning. From the foundation of the Northern Ireland state, this community of Irish nationalists was subjected to structural discrimination in employment, housing and cultural recognition. Crucially, the largest block of nationalists lived in virtual ghettoes in the state's principal city, Belfast. The experience of previous pogroms within living recollection was seared into the folk memory of this tightly knit community.

In January 1967, inspired in part by the black civil rights campaign in the US South, a mixed group of liberals, radicals, civil libertarians and left-leaning republicans formed an alliance seeking reform in Northern Ireland. Unlike previous campaigns in the region, this initiative sought what appeared to many outside the six-county entity to be a modest package of reforms. An infuriating dilemma for the staunchly pro-British Ulster Unionist government was that this new Northern Ireland civil rights movement began with the most moderate of aspirations – a demand that the old order could not easily refuse: British rights for British citizens.

To this day there remains a question as to whether granting a reasonable, democratic package of reform would have changed the subsequent course of history. Had an enlightened Stormont regime enacted a series of reforms, might the nationalist people have warmed to a Northern Ireland based on genuine equality, one that guaranteed opportunity for all its citizens? After all, hard-bitten, ideologically committed anti-partitionist republicans were a minority across the six counties and had not traditionally held real sway among Belfast nationalists in particular.

The answer, of course, is that we will never know, because the opportunity did not arise. What is of more relevance to what happened is whether this option was ever a realistic possibility, given the make-up and nature of the political entity that was Northern Ireland. From its founding, the state's existence was dependent on the promotion of communal identity politics, and therein lay its vulnerability. Unionist dominance hinged on two factors: one, that they remained a majority, and two, their ability to maintain unity within their own ranks. Democratic reform threatened both. Deprived of the ability to discriminate in the fields of employment and housing and thereby compel economic emigration, there was a distinct possibility that the nationalist population would eventually match or even outnumber the unionist community. Moreover, without the advantage of providing preferential treatment to its supporters in the world of paid employment, unionist solidarity and unity could not be guaranteed.

Such calculations were never far from the mind of unionist leaders. They were acutely aware of being in a minority on the island, and aware also by the mid-1960s that the southern economy was then developing from its long decades of peasant poverty. Equally disturbing for them was an ever-present, albeit rarely voiced, fear of English betrayal.

All of which begs the question: to what extent were the bloody events of August 1969 spontaneous? Were they, as some suspect, coldly calculated?

What is now beyond dispute is that senior figures within unionism were concerned even by the cautious steps taken by Stormont Prime Minister Captain Terence O'Neill towards limited detente with nationalists in Northern Ireland and a thaw in relations with the southern government. More sinister still is the fact that, according to a senior loyalist, the late Billy Mitchell, the UVF was resurrected in the mid-1960s with the encouragement of leading unionists in order to stem the perceived drift towards liberalism in Northern Ireland. Add into that the absence of any clear lines of demarcation within unionism as official and unofficial (legal and covert) structures overlapped – all elected unionist political representatives were members of the Orange Order, as were a majority of police officers and civil servants – and it is not necessary to organise a conspiracy, because one was already in place.

The question of how we can best understand the developments that occurred subsequent to August 1969 is one that deserves careful academic scrutiny. Having profited from pogroms in the early 1920s and mid-1930s, did the unionist ruling class tacitly orchestrate the attack on nationalist Belfast in 1969? Why did the British state not then grasp the nettle of reforming an undemocratic regional administration operating in an integral part of the United Kingdom? Were those advocating a purely peaceful civil rights agenda dangerously naive or did they offer the only viable path forward? Did the Provisional IRA's founders cynically exploit a tragic situation or respond to a crisis in the only way possible? In light of the current state of affairs in the Northern-Irish six-county state – marked, it seems, by chronic crisis – an even more intriguing question arises: will history eventually decide that August 1969 in Belfast was, in reality, not just the start of the modern 'Troubles' but also the beginning of the end for Northern Ireland? Whatever the answer to these important questions, Michael McCann has provided us with an invaluable contribution to our understanding of that crucial period, and one which will no doubt inform and enlighten contemporary discussion about the future of this part of the world.

INTRODUCTION

The prominent civil rights activist and founder of People's Democracy, Michael Farrell, once wrote that while 'in most of the world, and even in the rest of Ireland, differences between Catholic and Protestants had ceased to matter much politically ... in Ulster they persisted.'[1] Not only did sectarian divisions persist; in Northern Ireland they constituted the bedrock of the Stormont regime, perceptively characterised by a British journalist as 'rule by the Orange Order through the medium of the Unionist Party'.[2]

The Government of Ireland Act (1920) effectively sanctioned and financed a sectarian state. The years between 1921 and 1969 witnessed one-party rule, underpinned by a Special Powers Act in 1922 and reinforced by a well-armed paramilitary police force. From its seat of power in Stormont, the government entrenched discriminatory policies and practices into the fabric of northern society, reinforcing a system of social, political and economic apartheid which flouted democratic conventions to secure unionist control of local government and the patronage, in housing and employment, which came with it.

When a new generation of young, university-educated Catholics emerged in the late 1960s to challenge the status quo, the state resorted to the traditional methods of repression so successful over the previous half century in containing militant republicanism. On 5 October 1968, for example, the Royal Ulster Constabulary (RUC) battered civil rights demonstrators from the streets of Derry. This time, however, the brutality of the Stormont regime, Britain's nasty little secret, was exposed to a global television audience. Journalist Mary Holland later recalled in the pages of *The Irish Times*:

> ... the shock of what happened ... still sears the memory. As far as we were concerned this was a British city and these were British police.

In 1968 I'd never seen a policeman use a baton let alone charge a crowd of demonstrators, trapped in a narrow street, with such naked eagerness.[3]

Yet it would be wrong to view the Derry march in isolation, or as the trigger to the violence that ensued. The hard-line Protestant firebrand, Ian Paisley, had stoked the sectarian embers in 1964, inciting the Divis Street riots in Belfast. Two years later, he established the Ulster Constitution Defence Committee (UCDC) and the Ulster Protestant Volunteers (UPV), both closely linked to the emerging loyalist Ulster Volunteer Force (UVF). In 1966, two years before the Derry march, loyalists turned ominously towards a sectarian murder campaign, while Paisley orchestrated counter-demonstrations against the emerging civil rights movement, railing against ecumenism, popery and the timid reforms enacted by unionist Prime Minister Terence O'Neill. This book attempts to demonstrate that the rise of militant loyalism in the mid-1960s was a crucial factor in pushing Northern Ireland towards the decades-long protracted conflict that became known as 'the Troubles'.

Paisley's reactionary and incendiary rhetoric worked because he exposed developing fissures in the unionist monolith. O'Neill's measures, though moderate and piecemeal, only exposed the Orange state's incapacity for reform. A cross-class consensus among northern unionists constructed before the First World War, based on relative economic prosperity and held together by the rhetorical glue of anti-Catholicism, appeared by the late 1960s to be unravelling under the weight of new challenges. The Loyal Orders (Orange Order, Apprentice Boys and Royal Black Preceptory) had long acted as the gatekeepers of the Orange state, and the regime's inability to break its relationship with a blatantly sectarian organisation left it badly exposed in an era of social liberalisation and democratic change across much of Europe and America.

During July 1969, however, the loyalist backlash against the civil rights movement took on a familiar character. The lodges marched while, behind them, the forces of reaction prepared to teach Northern Ireland's nationalist minority a lesson – to show them that hard-line unionism still ruled the roost. One month later, Stormont's unwillingness to proscribe the Apprentice Boys' annual parade in Derry on 12 August led to large-scale unrest. Abetted by loyalist militants, the RUC mounted a prolonged assault on the nationalist Bogside. These actions provoked a series of tragic events that reverberated throughout the North, but found fullest expression in the narrow, terraced streets of the unionist citadel of Belfast.

This book analyses the assault on the nationalist community in Derry and particularly Belfast before and after what became known as the 'Battle of the Bogside'. It uses evidence provided to the Scarman Inquiry, established by the British government to investigate the acts of violence and civil disturbance that occurred between March and August 1969, but more significantly, it triangulates this against a host of eyewitness accounts of the horrendous violence and the expulsions of thousands of Belfast's beleaguered Catholic minority. In doing so it challenges the conventional wisdom shared by most professional historians and social scientists who have written about this period and who almost uniformly misrepresent the dynamics of sectarian violence in the tragedy of 1969 and (in the name of 'balance') equivocate in identifying the perpetrators of the pogrom of August 1969 in North and West Belfast. There are complexities to the story related here, but there are unequivocal facts as well, and nothing can be gained by pretending otherwise.

At the heart of this book lies a close assessment of how and why the violence of 1969 began. Through recorded oral histories and primary source material a compelling case is made that the Troubles did not start on 14 August 1969, because the cataclysm visited upon nationalists in the Lower Falls and surrounding areas commencing on that day had been conceived some weeks and months previous. Particular attention will be paid to the central role played by John Dunlop McKeague, a disciple of Paisley, and his Shankill Defence Association (SDA) in orchestrating events from April 1969 onwards.

I also seek to establish how the truth became one of the first casualties of the horrific events of August 1969. The unionist regime's attempted cover-up began just a few hours after the RUC killed nine-year-old Patrick Rooney and while loyalist mobs were continuing their push to drive out vulnerable nationalists. By 18 August Stormont ministers were publicly accusing nationalist victims of burning their own homes and attributing the wider violence to a well-planned republican uprising. Since the earliest attempts to spin the events, this flagrantly absurd version has found its way into many 'objective' accounts penned by academic historians and others. Most accounts fail to mention the number of families made refugees in the violence (1,820), while the greatest sin of omission surely lies in the failure to acknowledge that it was RUC machine-gunners in armoured vehicles who spearheaded the assault on nationalist districts in Belfast – firing indiscriminately into homes, killing one child and injuring countless innocent people. Their reckless actions provided a bridgehead for loyalist mobs, which flooded into the breach to continue the attack on nationalists.

Finally, and significantly, I demonstrate that loyalist violence did not cease in mid-August, but continued to touch North, South, East and West Belfast, swelling the numbers of nationalist refugees. I assess the systematic attacks on Catholic-owned businesses – particularly public houses and off-licences – from April 1969, and illustrate how a heady mix of sectarian bile and looted alcohol fuelled the pogrom. It was in the immediate aftermath of the Belfast burnings that the first British soldier was wounded and then the first RUC man lost his life in the Troubles – both shot by loyalists before the Provisional Irish Republican Army had even been founded. This book challenges and attempts to counter the spurious accounts that have, until now, dominated our understanding of these events, and seeks to establish the basic facts relating to the beginning of the modern Troubles – a conflict born of sectarian violence instigated by the state and its loyalist defenders in the fiery cauldron of August 1969.

1

ORANGE STATE IN CRISIS

ACADEMIC BIAS: THE SPECTRE
OF A RISING REPUBLICAN THREAT

One of the most unbelievable feats in Irish history writing over the past generation has been the largely successful attempt to transform the main victims of the traumatic violence of the summer of 1969 into the chief villains in starting the Troubles. Most of the published accounts of these critical events locate the origins of armed conflict in the North of Ireland not in the failed policies of a discriminatory colonial state, or in the aggressive actions carried out by the substantial paramilitary forces it had at its disposal, or even in the provocations of murderous sectarian mobs, but in the peaceful, mostly symbolic attempts by Belfast's beleaguered nationalist community to mark the fiftieth anniversary of the Easter Rising in the narrow streets of their own ghettoes.

Paul Bew's reference to 1966 in *Ireland: The Politics of Enmity 1789–2006*, led one reviewer to harbour the suspicion that this choice was made to allow Bew to target 'the 1916 celebrations as the fuse that ignited the Troubles'.[1] In this Bew is not alone: several prominent Irish academics point to 1966 and an alleged resurgence of militant republicanism in explaining the source of conflict. In *Northern Ireland Since 1945*, the former Queen's University academic Sabine Wichert emphasised the role of 'rumours of an IRA revival' amidst the republican celebrations of 1966 in aggravating sectarian tensions across the North.[2] Thomas Hennessey's *Northern Ireland: The Origins of the Troubles* recounts Northern Ireland Prime Minister Terence O'Neill's conversation with his British counterpart, Harold Wilson, to claim that 'the passionate celebrations of the fiftieth anniversary of the Easter Rebellion, had led to a "backlash" of ultra Protestant feeling'.[3] Fear of this 'backlash' becomes, in Hennessey's rendering, a rationalisation for Stormont's unwillingness to reform: in considering whether to ban civil rights marches, O'Neill's Minister for Home Affairs, William Craig, 'had to bear in mind how the 1916 commemoration ... had led to a dangerous deterioration in community relations, leading to Protestant extremists taking up arms'.[4] One of the key achievements of ostensibly liberal unionist history writing has, therefore, been its success in embedding the idea that the Easter 1966 commemorations started the North down the path towards the Troubles. But the evidence points in a very different direction.

As it had throughout the history of the Northern Ireland state, the spectre of republican subversion proved an effective device for blocking reform, and Ian Paisley exploited this skilfully in galvanising a new generation of loyalist militants. The reality, however, was that by the mid-1960s the IRA was at the weakest it had been since partition. Its border campaign ('Operation Harvest' 1956–62) had ended in dismal failure, demoralising supporters and establishing a broad consensus among northern nationalists that physical force was ineffective for challenging partition. 'The hoped-for uprising of northern nationalists had failed to materialise,' one recent study acknowledges. 'Some southern republicans had come to realise how little they actually knew about the North and unionism.'[5] This failure led republicans towards a fundamental reconsideration of strategy and tactics, the outcome of which was a rejection of the narrow nationalism and militarist obsession that, except for a brief period in the 1930s, had long dominated the movement north of the border. Establishing Wolfe Tone Societies and Republican Clubs across the north, the republican leadership acknowledged the futility of armed struggle as a vehicle for ending partition, abandoning its short-term perspective in favour of a class-based analysis and popular, anti-sectarian agitation. The IRA posed no

military threat to Stormont in 1966, and its forces were far too weak
and undeveloped to pose a serious political challenge. Two men who
joined the movement in Belfast during the early 1960s describe the
situation at the time:

> I joined the IRA in 1962. The recruitment classes lasted some twelve
> months. The classes were to deter anyone joining the movement. A
> fair number of people started together and when the twelve months
> had finished only three remained. When I became a volunteer I was
> immediately sent to 'D' Company based in the Lower Falls, simply
> because there was no IRA structure in Belfast. The IRA were in
> effect 'history' … What surprised me during this period was that the
> IRA engaged in an indoctrinating programme … The weaponry the
> IRA had were [sic] sold off and the Free Wales Army was buying it
> … many senior IRA men held a mistrust of the direction in which
> the leadership was taking it – namely a political agenda – and the
> IRA was to be made defunct. [In 1966] we found ourselves in a
> terrible situation, because of our protest over political agitation; we
> were looked over and forgot [sic] about. To give the background, I
> had done nothing [in the] movement for years. 1966 was a gesture
> from the movement in order to celebrate the Rising: a few things
> happened, but nothing of significance.[6]

The second man concurs:

> The army [IRA] was doing nothing during these times. They were
> marking time: neither going forward nor backwards. From 1962 and
> throughout the 1960s the IRA did not exist as a fighting force. At
> that point agitation was happening and we were having meetings …
> The older people in the movement wanted change and if the army
> were kept it would be a stumbling block – young men like myself
> began to drift away.[7]

While this sense of drift, reorientation, disarmament and decline features almost universally in the memories of northern republicans active at the time, historians have seemed eager to embrace official perceptions of a mounting republican threat. In reality, however, Stormont ministers conjured the republican threat to deflect from increasingly anxious scrutiny from London.

A short distance from Hastings Street RUC Barracks in West Belfast, the republicans' '48 Club' operated. A regular of the social club claimed that Special Branch officers, who were on first-name terms with many members, openly watched the premises and were well aware what was and what was not happening on the ground. By contrast, the unionist government never seems to have instructed the RUC to monitor loyalist activity and in fact, it seems that loyalists and police already had a growing relationship at this time. On 11 July 1966 the Nationalist MP for Mid-Tyrone, Thomas Gormley, claimed that 'a number of members of the Special Constabulary in Ulster were involved with militant extremists and Protestant Unionist organisations in a plot to overthrow the Ulster Government. It was clear that [loyalist] extremist movements were well armed with Government-owned weapons.'[8] It was suspected by some nationalists that loyalists may have been involved in acquiring additional arms. In Cookstown, the RUC investigated the suspicious robbery of a sub-machine gun, a pistol and a substantial amount of ammunition from the homes of three B-Specials.[9]

Despite clear evidence of an emerging threat from loyalism, Hennessey focuses on activity within the pre-Troubles IRA as evidence of republican manipulation of civil rights agitation, which led to the Troubles.[10] Close examination reveals that much of the analysis and most of the sources he employs are highlighted by the Scarman Tribunal's *Violence and Civil Disturbances in Northern Ireland in 1969*, from which the author paraphrases.[11] One of the documents that Hennessey quotes is an IRA document which claimed that 'we must learn from the Cypriots and engage in terror tactics only'.[12] Crucially, however, Scarman himself acknowledged that these were merely captured draft documents that few republicans had ever discussed, let alone adopted.

This concentration on extravagant republican plots distracts from the widespread, deeply felt outrage over flagrant sectarian discrimination that was the main underlying cause of the conflict. Cameron's *Disturbances in Northern Ireland*, published in 1969, acknowledged widespread discrimination. However, within the revisionist lexicon, the legitimacy of nationalist grievances seems impossible to establish: Roman Catholics merely 'believed themselves to be the victims', they embraced 'a collective perception' that they were discriminated against.[13] In fact, the historiography has largely ignored the findings of Cameron, Scarman and Hunt, all contemporaneous official British inquiries containing evidence emanating from the political establishment but critical of the Stormont regime. Conversely, numerous historians have relied heavily (and largely uncritically) on local newspapers for information. The unionist press argued consistently that the republican marches of 1966 and Terence O'Neill's superficial gestures towards the minority nationalist community heightened tensions and fears within unionism. What is obviously and again quite naturally absent from such publications is a close documentary examination of, or any genuine critical commentary on, the rise of loyalist extremism. Academics largely overlook the sectarianism that was ever-present in the North, and ignore especially the loyalist violence of 1969.

Marianne Elliott attempts to plot a middle path, arguing that '[a]s ever, the extremes fed off each other. Widespread republican rallies for the fiftieth anniversary of the 1916 Rising produced Paisleyite counter-demonstrations and excessive deployment of armed police.'[14] Nonetheless, contemporaneous records reported no trouble resulting from republican commemorations in London, Dublin or across the

North.[15] In reality, it was Paisley's ongoing sectarian speeches, illegal assemblies and marches – which actually preceded republican demonstrations – that drove the unionist government's violent overreaction. This reflexive urge to mete out repression against nationalists reflected the structural basis of the unionist consensus and the insecurity of the Stormont elite. Michael Farrell points out that '[i]n April Paisley forced the government to mobilise the B-Specials for a month and ban trains from the South from coming to commemorations of the fiftieth anniversary of the 1916 Rising, and then denounced them for not banning the parades altogether'.[16] This chronology is affirmed by the London *Sunday Times* Insight Team, who claimed that the 'first challenge to O'Neill came not from the Republicans, nor from the pacific Catholics like the McCluskeys [founders of the Campaign for Social Justice]', but from one of his nominal supporters, Ian Paisley.[17] Indeed, according to the same source, in 1965 O'Neill informed Harold Wilson that while he could 'walk through the Catholic Falls Road area of Belfast without an escort, even with a full bodyguard they could give him no guarantee of security in the extremist Protestant areas'.[18] In his autobiography, O'Neill claimed that he lost the post of prime minister because the Ulster Unionist Party (UUP) 'would never stand for change'; it was loyalist extremists who drove him from office.[19] Put simply, '[t]he old sectarian and anti-Catholic forces within Protestantism and Unionism ruled the day, leaving O'Neill to lament on his resignation in 1969'.[20]

THE O'NEILL YEARS

An ill-founded consensus exists that Terence O'Neill's ascent to power after loyalist hard-liner Basil Brooke resigned in 1963 heralded a sea change in unionism. In fact, O'Neill's appointment was contingent on his membership of the Orange Order. Having taken up office, he subsequently joined the Royal Black Preceptory and the Apprentice Boys of Derry. Appointed by the unionist elite, O'Neill was a member of the landed gentry, a son of a Unionist MP who had served at Westminster, and an ex-British army officer. He succeeded Brooke as leader of a sectarian administration, sanctioned and financed from Westminster; to his credit Patterson admits that in spite of his reputation as an avid reformer 'the dismal truth about O'Neill was that he displayed not the slightest inclination to do anything on this issue [discrimination]'.[21]

Apart from its annual subsidy to Stormont, the British government had largely disassociated itself from Northern Ireland at this juncture. James Callaghan, then (1967) British Home Secretary and future Labour Prime Minister, recalled: 'Not surprisingly, the staff at the Home Office engaged on Northern Ireland was extremely small. Indeed, Northern Ireland was crammed into what was called the General Department, which was responsible for anything which did not fit into any of the major departments ... It covered such matters as ceremonial functions, British Summer Time, London taxicabs, liquor licensing, the administration of state-owned pubs in Carlisle, and the protection of animals and birds.'[22] Occasionally throughout the tenure of the post-war Attlee government and into the mid-1950s, small groups of Labour MPs at Westminster had highlighted the discriminatory practices of the Stormont regime. From 1964, Labour MPs Paul Rose and Stanley Orme raised the same issue, but to no avail. Successive Speakers of the House of Commons, under the influence of Ulster Unionists and Conservatives, rejected any discussion of internal Northern Ireland affairs. Despite its reputation for violence and discrimination, Stormont was granted free rein to oversee affairs in the six-county state.

From its inception as the UUC in 1905, the Unionist Party relied on the Orange Order as a bulwark against concessions and a vehicle for cross-class Protestant solidarity. In his famous 1934 speech at Stormont, James Craig claimed that 'I have always said I am an

Orangeman first and a politician and member of this parliament afterwards ... all I boast is that we are a Protestant parliament and a Protestant state.'[23] Between 1921 and 1969 only three of fifty-four members holding cabinet rank at Stormont were not Orangemen and 'of the remaining ninety-five backbenchers, eighty-seven were members; all Unionists elected to the Northern Ireland Senate between 1921 and 1968 belonged to the Institution, as did fifty-four of the fifty-six Unionist MPs elected to the Westminster parliament – the other two were women.'[24] Even during periods of perceived unionist moderation, the UUP and Orange Order denied Catholics' applications for party membership. Indeed, '[f]or all his talk of bridge-building', Captain O'Neill 'found the question of Catholic membership of Unionism too hot to handle'.[25]

Between 1963 and 1966, O'Neill faced several problems: high rates of unemployment, particularly in the heavy industries which had provided a measure of prosperity for skilled Protestant workers; rising expectations among the Catholic minority for equal rights, and the growing threat of Paisley and the extremists within his own party. 'Within that black reactionary group [Harold Wilson's apt description] were John Brooke, John Taylor, the Unionist MP for South Tyrone; William Craig, whom O'Neill dismissed from his cabinet; Harry West, whom he also dismissed, and [Brian] Faulkner.'[26] After O'Neill met Taoiseach Seán Lemass in January 1965, despite strong opposition from elements of his own party, these difficulties intensified. Faced with widespread unionist dissatisfaction, O'Neill abandoned any inclination to cede the basic reforms demanded by nationalists. Stormont's decision to build a new university at Coleraine instead of Derry, and to name a new model town in mid-Ulster after the staunch unionist and sectarian bigot James Craig, offered powerful evidence that while O'Neill's premiership differed in tone, it remained fully committed to the substance of the traditional unionist programme. This motivated a small group of moderate activists, who had been collaborating in documenting anti-Catholic discrimination, to launch a civil rights campaign, a new development predictably denounced by unionist hard-liners within the government as part of a republican plot. Unsurprisingly, '[f]or many unionists, the civil rights demonstrations from the outset bore the mark of Cain as an essentially nationalist movement'.[27] A large section of the unionist community responded negatively to the Northern Ireland Civil Rights Association's (NICRA) demand for civil rights, and 'the opposition to O'Neill was carried far beyond street protests and counter-demonstrations to obstruct the civil-rights movement' to 'secret caucus meetings in the drawing rooms of Unionist politicians'.[28] Boyd noted:

> In public Faulkner stood a little to one side when Paisley was causing turmoil in Northern Ireland and so making O'Neill's premiership uncomfortable and embarrassing. In private Faulkner was not above plotting with Paisleyites against O'Neill. It was, in fact, revealed that [Desmond] Boal, who is now the theorist of the Orange extremist party, the Democratic Unionist Party, and others met in Faulkner's house to discuss a plan to overthrow O'Neill. Faulkner later denied, when asked about this meeting, if [sic] he had taken part in the discussion. He said he left the room when Boal and his friends were talking.[29]

As early as January 1965 (and therefore well before the republican Easter commemorations), MP for Belfast's Shankill district Desmond Boal joined Ian Paisley, future co-founder of the DUP, in warning against UUP capitulation to those fighting discrimination. Other leading unionists strained to deflect criticism for this from the Stormont regime. Before a civil liberties conference in London in March 1965, John Taylor attempted to shift the blame onto 'the South's hostility to Northern Ireland, IRA attacks, Nationalist

Party propaganda, and the Catholic church's segregatory attitude for keeping alive old sectarian animosities', denying any culpability for his own party or the Orange Order.[30] Nevertheless, the British media's increasing scrutiny of discrimination in local government and in housing allocation in the North deepened unionist anxiety. By the summer of 1966 even the Tory-leaning *Daily Telegraph* pointed out 'that the government in Northern Ireland still presents features which look shocking when viewed from Westminster'.[31]

Unlike Taylor, Stormont Minister for Home Affairs William Craig never concealed his contempt for nationalists, whom he claimed suffered from educational and social deficiencies. 'When you have a Roman Catholic majority ... you have a lesser standard of democracy: rule by the people was not much of an idea if they were the wrong people ...'[32] Craig led the reaction against O'Neill's reforms within the cabinet. In December 1966 he informed a trade union delegation seeking equal voting rights that 'Britain was out of step with Northern Ireland'.[33] Craig regularly banned marches by NICRA, which he frequently characterised as a communist-republican front.[34] Eventually O'Neill grew tired of the backbiting, dismissing Craig from his cabinet on 11 December 1968, after which Craig continued to agitate from the political sidelines.

THE RISE OF LOYALIST VIGILANTISM

Despite his involvement on the fringes of political activity since 1949, Ian Paisley only really came to public attention in the 1960s. Paisley directed his vitriol against Catholicism, ecumenism, republicanism, communism and, indeed, those Protestants he castigated as 'Lundys' and reformers at Stormont.[35] Having denounced the BBC for being 'infested with Papists', the staunchly unionist *News Letter* as 'cowardly' and the *Belfast Telegraph* for its 'lying and treachery', the relentless barrage of sectarian rhetoric pounded out by Paisley

from the early 1960s manifested itself powerfully on the streets
in August 1969. Yet Paisley did not conjure sectarian conflict out
of thin air: Belfast was by then home to a long and deeply rooted
tradition of radical fundamentalist preachers, embodied in an earlier
century by Henry Cooke, who had wielded a domineering influence
on Ulster Protestantism from the late 1820s to his death in 1868.
'It was Cooke,' John Brewer writes, 'who forged the link in the
public's mind between evangelicalism, doctrinal orthodoxy and anti-
Catholicism. "We will fight", said the dying Henry Cooke in 1868 ...
"and this will be our dying cry, echoed and re-echoed, 'No Popery'."
"No Surrender".' Brewer continues, 'Anti-Catholicism at the level of
behaviour therefore often showed itself in violence.'[36]

The Rev. Hugh Hanna ('Roaring Hanna'), a disciple of Cooke,
took up the mantle of sectarian demagoguery after the latter's death.
The years 1857, 1864, 1872, 1886 and 1898 witnessed brutal attacks on
the city's growing Catholic minority. Inflammatory sermons at open-
air gatherings helped stimulate a remarkable growth in Orangeism
and, unsurprisingly, a sharp and often lethal rise in sectarian polarisation. The Rev. Thomas Drew, Orange Grand Chaplain and Church
of Ireland minister on the Shankill Road, claimed at a large rally on
12 July 1867 that the 'lives and property of the Protestants of Ireland
are prey to the despoiling priest', and this kind of rhetoric – drawing
on the tradition established by Cooke and Hanna – became typical
fare in Belfast and beyond, employed annually in July, and especially
in times of high Protestant unemployment and political instability.[37]

From its inception, the Stormont administration relied on special 'emergency' legislation and permanent access to state paramilitary forces – the Ulster Special Constabulary (USC), organised into
A-, B- and C-Specials, an exclusively Protestant and wholly partisan paramilitary force – to deal with the threat from republicans and
forestall potential challenges from an intermittently militant labour
tradition. The regular RUC was itself a partisan force from the outset,

the core of its ranks drawn from the loyalist UVF. The Sir Robert
Peel Orange Lodge, registered with the Grand Lodge of Ireland in
1923, included some 300 RUC men, or ten per cent of the force. Indeed, J. W. Nixon, a district inspector and notorious ringleader of the
Cromwell Club (the loyalist murder gang responsible for the brutal
McMahon murders and the Arnon Street massacre at the founding
of the Northern Ireland state in 1921), held the post of worshipful
master. In April 1923 Stormont Minister of Home Affairs Dawson
Bates attended the Lodge's AGM, making 'a belligerent and highly
political speech', with the political tone of the meeting 'strengthened
by the presence of three UULA [Ulster Unionist Labour Association]
MPs and the secretary of the Unionist Party'.[38] In effect, the unionist
government at Stormont commanded a highly partisan security force
in defence of the Orange State, employing overtly coercive legislation
and regularly overriding basic liberal democratic rights in the process.

Notwithstanding the protection available from regular state
forces, leading unionists also supported extra-judicial loyalist gangs.
For instance, the Ulster Protestant Association, formed in 1920,
essentially carried out a campaign of workplace expulsions and
murder against Catholics. The Stormont administration responded
'not by interning its members under the Special Powers Act, but by
enrolling them in the USC and enlisting their aid in the work of a
newly established Secret Service! Indeed, considerable latitude was
given to Protestant and Orange extremists in the police forces.'[39] To
the extent that the new Northern Ireland state managed to establish
some stability in the years immediately after its founding, the costs
were borne overwhelmingly by working-class nationalists subjected
to vicious assault from state and non-state loyalist paramilitaries
intent on a pogrom:

> Catholics, who were heavily out-numbered and relatively poorly
> armed, were largely on the receiving end of the violence, an estimated

twenty-three thousand of them having been driven out of their homes. During a two-year period nearly five hundred people were killed with over two thousand wounded, but Catholics were killed on a ratio of two to one, even though they constituted only one-third of the population. In fact, the situation is thrown into sharper relief when we bear in mind that, in terms of the areas where most of the troubles took place, the Catholics constituted a mere one-sixth of the population. Indeed, nearly half the Protestants who died were killed by British military fire in riot situations.[40]

Lily Fitzsimmons recounts what happened to her grandfather when he worked in the shipyard during the same period:

My grandfather Charlie Begley married a girl called Marie-Ellen Murphy. They moved to a house in Mary Street, off the Falls Road. In 1922 Charlie worked in the shipyard and in the same year they had their seventh child. It was also a period of unrest against the Catholics in the shipyard. Charlie and other Catholic men decided to go into work together, believing in safety in numbers. They knew the dangers that were there but they had no choice because times were hard, jobs were hard to come by, and when you had a family you had to feed them and clothe them: they had no choice. One morning they had entered the gates of the shipyard when a Protestant man who knew Charlie shouted a warning to him, telling him to watch themselves: that a crowd was waiting for them. When they got further into the yard they were pelted with nuts, bolts, lumps of metal and spanners. The loyalist mob chased them and my grandfather was caught. My grandfather was beaten so badly he received severe head injuries; his teeth were kicked down his throat. He was dragged over to the water and thrown in. The mob threw everything on top of him and other Catholic men. My grandfather went under the water, but somehow he was pulled out [and] taken to hospital with serious multiple injuries. A short time later my grandfather died from his injuries, aged 38. Less than a year later my grandmother Marie-Ellen became ill and was taken to the City Hospital where she died, aged 36. Their seven children were left orphaned.[41]

In 1931, in the face of growing agitation induced by the Great Depression, the unionist elite founded the Ulster Protestant League (UPL) to thwart attempts by labour and left-wing militants to unite workers across the divide. Farrell points out that 'government speeches became more sectarian and violence escalated up to the riots of 1935'.[42] Sir Basil Brooke, Stormont Minister for Labour J. M. Andrews and Senator Joseph Davison, Grand Master of the Orange Order, implored employers to hire only Protestants and expel Catholic workers. The small Catholic business class, particularly victuallers, represented a particular target for loyalist mobs, which launched concerted attacks against Catholic-owned pubs; this pattern would be repeated in August 1969. Like its predecessor, the UPL carried out sectarian attacks and murders, killing ten people and burning fifty-six homes after an Orange march in York Street on 12 July 1935. Budge and O'Leary noted that the Minister of Home Affairs, Dawson Bates, first banned all processions, then capitulated to a demand by the Orange Order to exempt their processions, culminating in riots lasting three weeks and rendering 400 (mainly nationalists) homeless.[43] Ironically, fleeing nationalists sought refuge in newly built houses in Glenard, Ardoyne – houses initially built for Protestant families. Although the 1935 sectarian riots, instigated by prominent figures at Stormont, were among the most violent episodes ever experienced in Northern Ireland, together the unionists and the British government effectively blocked demands for a Royal Commission inquiry.

John McGreevy recounts what happened to his mother in this area:

My mother came from the Docks area – Sailor Town. Her maiden name was Holden. Around 1934–5 the trouble had been very bad in Sailor Town, York Street and Lancaster Street areas. Film newsreels have recorded the trouble at the time, so there is a record of this. Buck Alec, the famous loyalist gunman, was very active at the time. A Catholic man was shot in North Thomas Street. My mother lived in North Thomas Street, and this was a mixed street [in that both Catholics and Protestants lived there]. Around this time my mother was shot in the neck when she was expecting me. She was coming home one night and she reached my grandmother's doorway. I could not tell you who shot her, but I know the people shouted over to her, 'Your bastard will never be born', and they fired at her. My mother survived because it was not a serious injury.[44]

In the House of Commons the usually verbose Nationalist MP Joe Devlin bluntly summarised the predicament facing his constituents in Belfast: 'If Catholics have no revolvers to protect themselves, they are murdered. If they have revolvers, they are flogged and sentenced to death.'[45]

These deep-rooted traditions of loyalist vigilantism, endorsed since the founding of the state by official unionism, combined with a toxic legacy of sectarian street-preaching to elevate the public career of Ian Paisley. In December 1956 Paisley joined the UPL veteran Ernie Lusty and fellow UUP member Albert Thoburn at the founding meeting of Ulster Protestant Action (UPA) at UUP headquarters. Others attending included Johnny McQuade, Charlie McCullough, Frank Millar and Billy Spence, the brother of Gusty Spence, later a leading figure in the UVF. One academic tracing the lineage of extreme loyalism argues that it was underpinned by fears among Protestant fundamentalists that any concessions to the Catholic minority would enhance the threat of a takeover by a monolithic, aggrandising church at Rome. 'These believers were an important element in groups like the Ulster Protestant League (founded in 1933) and Ulster Protestant Action (founded in 1959). But [they] did not confine themselves to religious issues. Arising during economic recession, they also demanded job reservation for Protestants and drew much support from shipyard men, unemployed and marginal workers.'[46] Paisley became the first leader of the UPA in 1959, later the Protestant Unionist Party – formed 'to resist ecumenism in the province' and undergoing another name change in 1971, to the Democratic Unionist Party.[47] In June 1959, on the Lower Shankill Road, Paisley's supporters in the UPA launched a wave of anti-Catholic violence unseen in Belfast for over a decade, with nationalist homes and businesses attacked on the Shankill. An excerpt from Paisley's speech at the time points to a direct connection between his sectarian rhetoric and the subsequent violence:

You people of the Shankill Road: what's wrong with you? Number 425 Shankill Road – do you know who lives there? Pope's men, that's who! Forte's ice cream shop, Italian papists on the Shankill Road! How about 56 Aden Street? For ninety-seven years a Protestant lived in that house and there's a Papisher in it. Crimea Street, Number 38! Twenty-five years that house has been up, twenty-four years a Protestant lived there but there's a Papisher there now.[48]

In 1964 Paisley sparked vicious rioting in Divis Street that lasted for a number of days. His threat to lead a loyalist mob into nationalist-dominated Divis Street to remove an Irish tricolour in a shop window of the Republican Club raised tensions dramatically, but in this case the RUC determined to pre-empt Paisley by assuming the burden of carrying out his mission themselves. Predictably, serious rioting erupted between the RUC and nationalist youth when the police waded through a crowd to smash the shop window and remove the offending flag. Four bloody nights of rioting ensued, with many police officers and hundreds of men, women and children injured, and damage costing thousands of pounds caused. Farrell noted that the Divis Street riots 'served to focus British attention on the Northern Ireland situation at the very time when a new Labour government was coming into office'.[49]

Paisley's power and influence among disaffected loyalists was on a steady upward trajectory following the so-called Tricolour Riots. In early 1966 loyalists attacked a number of schools, homes and Catholic-owned businesses across Belfast, daubing 'Fenian Bastards' and 'Up the UVF' on public houses owned by nationalists. The UVF apparently sent threatening letters to Catholics living in the Glenbryn housing estate in North Belfast, a fate also shared by visiting BBC reporter Cliff Michelmore. Clearly intent on raising tensions between his followers and the nationalist minority, and in the process undermining O'Neill, in February Paisley demanded that the administration name a new bridge after Edward Carson, enlisting the UVF founder's son to assist him in challenging O'Neill. In the same month Paisley declared that 'Every Ulster Protestant must unflinchingly resist these leaders and let it be known in no uncertain manner that they will not sit idly by as these modern Lundys pursue their policy of treachery. Ulster expects every Protestant in this hour of crisis to do his duty.'[50] Less than two months later, in April, Paisley launched his *Protestant Telegraph* in response to criticism that *The Revivalist,* the newspaper of the Free Presbyterian Church, had become too political. The *Telegraph* 'provided its loyalist and fundamentalist readership with a regular and often bizarre diet of anti-Catholicism, sometimes heavily laced with sexual innuendo. It became an outlet for bigotry, insecurity, ignorance, frustration and latent violence.'[51]

In March 1966, a month before the Easter Rising commemorations, a group of loyalists on the Shankill Road re-formed the UVF. The UVF gang immediately issued a warning declaring that it would defend Northern Ireland and eradicate the IRA. Two months later, on

7 May, the gang attacked and firebombed a Catholic-owned public house in Upper Charleville Street, critically injuring a seventy-seven-year-old Protestant, Matilda Gould, who died the following month. On 28 May they entered the Clonard area off the Falls Road and murdered an innocent Catholic, John Patrick Scullion. By 26 June the same gang had murdered a young Catholic barman, Peter Ward, and injured his two friends in Malvern Street off the Shankill Road. The UVF's rabid sectarianism attracted an expanding membership and 'by the Summer of 1966 there were rural cells in South Antrim, Portadown, County Armagh, and Pomeroy, County Tyrone'.[52]

Arrests quickly followed and O'Neill banned the UVF under the Special Powers Act. One convicted Ulster Volunteer, Hugh McClean, told police that he 'was asked did I agree with Paisley, and was I prepared to follow him. I said that I was.' Later he lamented that he was 'terrible sorry I ever heard tell of that man Paisley or decided to follow him. I am definitely ashamed of myself to be in such a position'.[53] Paisley condemned the murderers, denied any connection with loyalist extremism and criticised O'Neill for not proscribing the UVF earlier. Responding, O'Neill quoted Paisley's speeches at the Ulster Hall, where he 'thanked all those who had marched that day and specifically mentioned the UVF by name' (17 April), and a resolution from 'ex-servicemen ... now comprising four divisions of the UVF' (16 June) to question 'the extent to which Mr Paisley can properly claim ignorance of the activities of the UVF'.[54]

In April Paisley, together with Noel Doherty, '[t]he driving force behind the construction of a political vehicle for Paisleyite politics', established the twelve-man UCDC, whose objective was to uphold the 'Protestant constitution' and force O'Neill from office.[55] Paisley was made chairman on 22 May 1966, the same month the UPV emerged, a more sinister group linked with UCDC and organised along military lines under the old UVF motto 'For God and Ulster'. Interestingly, the UPV encouraged membership amongst the USC, yet excluded RUC men. The UPV provided the backbone of Paisley's entire movement. Some of its members were later convicted for conspiracy to commit explosions.

Acquainted with Paisley since the mid-1950s, Noel Doherty was a printer who had established the Puritan Printing Press in 1966 to produce the *Protestant Telegraph*. Both men established the UCDC and UPV, with Doherty – already a B-Special – setting up cells within the UPV. 'We already had government-issued .45 Webleys and government-issued Sten guns,' Doherty later recalled, 'so we thought, "Why not have our own – under the floorboards", and that's what we started to do.'[56] Doherty then became associated with fellow Free Presbyterian Billy Mitchell, later a leading UVF member convicted for a vicious double murder. On 21 April 1966 Paisley brought both men to Loughgall to meet with local Free Presbyterians, including several B-Specials, before driving to another meeting in Armagh. Doherty was introduced by Mitchell to a local quarryman and UPV member, Jim Marshall, who would be able to supply him with gelignite. Doherty and two UVF men from the Shankill – Desmond Reid and George Bigger – collected this the following month. Doherty became 'the intermediary through whom members of Loughgall UPV supplied gelignite to the Shankill UVF'.[57] Paisley subsequently disowned Doherty, changing the locks on the latter's printing operation when, in October 1966, Doherty and two others were convicted on explosives charges. The spurned Doherty later acknowledged that Paisley's disowning 'was worse than the two-year gaol sentence'.[58]

THE RISE OF PAISLEY

On 6 June 1966 Paisley organised a rally in Belfast against ecumenism and the 'Romeward trend' within the Presbyterian Church, leading a march to the General Assembly. Serious violence ensued as the (illegal) march passed the predominantly nationalist Markets area en route to the city centre: mayhem erupted when the Paisleyites broke through RUC lines, 'calling the police Nazis and Northern Ireland a police state'.[59] His supporters then swarmed into Fisherwick Place in Belfast city centre, abusing the dignitaries of the Irish Presbyterian Assembly as 'Romanists', 'Popeheads' and 'Lundys', while their leader lambasted the moderator by loudhailer, bellowing that 'They can go to Rome if they wish, but they will not take Ulster with them.' The Stormont administration responded by charging Paisley and six others (including two clergymen) with public order offences. Paisley and the two clergymen were sent to Crumlin Road Gaol on 20 July for refusal to pay their fines.

Paisley settled comfortably into this new role of loyalist martyr. Outraged by his imprisonment, thousands of loyalists 'rampaged through the centre of the city breaking shop windows, stoning the Catholic-owned International Hotel and going to Sandy Row where they tried to burn down a bookie's shop which employed Catholics'. The authorities placed a three-month moratorium on demonstrations in Belfast, giving 'the RUC power to break up any gathering of three or more people'.[60] Bruce argues that '[w]hether or not the procession from the Ravenhill Church and the barracking of the Presbyterian Church Assembly had been to constitute a direct challenge to the government, things were moving rapidly in that direction ... there is no doubt that the imprisonment was a major breakthrough for both religious and political Paisleyism. Different sorts of supporters reacted in different ways. The young urban loyalists took to the streets.'[61] Paisley claimed 'on the Sunday before imprisonment, that it might be his last religious service since the government had declared war on Protestantism, making it clear that he was prepared for martyrdom like other Protestant martyrs. If his life "has to go", he announced, "it will go in that cause".'[62]

Paisley's prolonged campaign helped resurrect deep-seated anti-Catholic sentiment among many loyalists, sustaining the sectarian tensions that normally emerged and subsided again annually during the summer marching season over an extended period. His incessant agitation was central to generating a deep reservoir of bitterness, and it was entirely predictable that this would eventually spill over into sectarian violence. Buckland writes that although at times 'the consequences did alarm him, as when his oratory was said to have inspired Protestants to kill Catholics', Paisley was never deterred 'from keeping up a torrent of invective against opponents and seeking to confront them on the streets. His oratory may have been subtle but many of his hearers simply thought that victims were being pointed out to them.'[63]

Paisley had established the UCDC as an organisational home for his anti-reformist 'O'Neill Must Go' campaign. The subsequent establishment of the Protestant Unionist Party heralded his entrance into electoral politics, and brought militant loyalism into the mainstream. One study commissioned by the University of Lancaster in 1966 estimated that Paisley had the support of 200,000 people out of a population of 1.4 million. The Protestant population numbered approximate 900,000. Another found that a quarter of Protestants disapproved of O'Neill's meeting with Lemass; half opposed ecumenism; and 'a substantial body of Protestant opinion was opposed to O'Neill's policies', with Paisley boasting that 'there are 200,000 people in Ulster who think as I do'. Although a clear majority of Protestants seemed unperturbed by O'Neill's approach, a substantial and growing minority were turning to Paisley. Paisley's 'imprisonment had won hundreds of new converts, attracted by his political message as much as by his fundamentalism. Over the next two years the number of Free Presbyterian churches virtually doubled, and in Belfast he made plans to build a huge new church up the Ravenhill Road to accommodate the growing crowds.'[64]

Speaking from an Orange Lodge in Enniskillen in July 1966, James Hamilton, the Marquis of Hamilton, MP for Fermanagh

South–Tyrone, claimed that Paisleyism operated 'on calculated hatred' and that 'there is no room whatsoever for such [a] wicked, outdated and un-Christian mentality. The mentality was completely divorced from all right-thinking Protestants.'[65] Concurring, Basil Kelly, QC and MP for Mid-Down, addressed an Orange demonstration on the Twelfth describing the 'Paisley movement as the new enemy of the new Ulster.' But O'Neill's indecisiveness on how to respond to civil rights demands allowed deep polarisation to take root, and in this situation the momentum seemed to be moving in Paisley's direction.[66]

The extremism on open display in Paisley's rhetoric and in the actions of his followers made them an easy target, and in important ways the easy castigation of Paisleyism diverted culpability away from the deep wells of sectarian bigotry that the Northern Ireland state had drawn upon for its entire existence. The *Daily Mirror* asserted, with reason on its side, that Paisley's popularity rested on peculiarities intrinsic to the Northern Ireland status quo: 'In England Paisley would be laughed into swift oblivion. In Ulster, stoking all the fires of bitterness and dragging patriotism by the hair behind him, he is a significant force who after ten years crying in the wilderness has suddenly found himself at the very forefront of Ulster politics.'[67] The *Daily Telegraph* was more succinct in attributing the cause: 'the recent outcrop of Protestant violence was itself a foreseeable reaction to the politics of an Ulster Government more liberal and enlightened than any of its predecessors. It is the move towards rapprochement with the South – last year's visit from the Prime Minister of the Republic and the trade union talks ... which has set Protestant extremists alight.' However, the newspaper criticised the Stormont government for its discriminatory practices. 'No doubt, as a group of socialist MPs sympathetic to Roman Catholic causes are at present engaged at pointing out, Government in Northern Ireland still presents features which look shocking when viewed from Westminster. Shameless

Gerrymandering designed to preserve Protestant Unionist majorities in local elections is one of the features.'[68]

During July 1966, as part of his 'O'Neill Must Go' crusade, Paisley visited Belfast, Ballymoney, Claudy and the Caddy Road near Randalstown, where he declared that 'they would march to O'Neill's house' at Ahoghill. Evidence that his continuing campaign against ecumenism and political reform was inflaming Orange opinion was on clear display when Orangemen barred two leading Ulster Unionists, Nat Minford and Phelim O'Neill, from speaking at the Twelfth field in Cullybackey, and Roy Bradford, Unionist MP for Victoria, was harangued and kicked by a crowd at an Orange demonstration in Kilkeel. O'Neill responded to the abuse he and his colleagues were subjected to by insisting that 'if there was one way to endanger the constitution of Northern Ireland, it was by violence, by abuse, and the gun'.[69] Paisley had succeeded in fragmenting unionist unanimity.

Paisley's followers also targeted other Protestant ministers. Because he delivered an anti-Paisleyite speech two years previously, Rev. Robin Williamson, a Non-Subscribing Presbyterian, received over 200 hate letters and scores of calls threatening his life. O'Neill expressed disappointment at poor 'support received from Protestant clergy for cross-border initiatives'[70] and in one case admitted that with 'a few shining exceptions, the Protestant clergy were too frightened to give a welcome to the [Lemass] meeting in case they offended some of their flock'.[71] In September 1966, 'under pressure from their constituency association', extremists in the ranks of the Unionist party would conspire to remove O'Neill.[72]

While a spike in sectarian attacks on nationalists during the summer marching season was far from unusual, Paisley's efforts gave them a new and more sinister intensity in 1966. Nationalist MP Harry Diamond, who received a death threat from the Shankill Volunteers, declared Paisley 'the author of and inspirer of all evil of the last couple of months in Belfast'.[73] On 25 June loyalists attacked houses in Ardmoulin Avenue between the Shankill and the Falls Road. In nearby Cranmore Street, loyalists drove crippled man Thomas McGuire and his wife from their home under gunpoint. In the same area, another Catholic resident was beaten up and stabbed, and the home of Leo Martin was set on fire. Indeed, the UVF and a group called the Sandy Row Revenge Squad pursued an active campaign in the Sandy Row area against Catholic-owned businesses, warning proprietors 'not to come back or else'.[74] An estimated 10,000 people witnessed Paisley opening the Orange arches in Brussels, Boundary and Wilton streets off the Shankill Road.[75] In the same area and directly after the festivities, mobs expelled two Catholic families from Penrith and Northumberland streets. In the former case, hundreds watched as the Loughran family left their home under police guard. Terence Loughran, who had bought the house just eighteen months earlier, said 'there is nothing to do but to move out ... the next time it might be a brick or a bomb through the window'.[76]

On the Eleventh Night, loyalists attacked the Clarke family home in Little Distillery Street off the Grosvenor Road and smashed the windows of their neighbour, Mary Taylor, a widow and mother of five. Likewise, Robert Donnelly and his wife were hospitalised after an assault on their home at 73 Frenchpark Street off the Donegall Road. Across the city, in East Belfast, a gang smashed the windows of O'Hara's grocery shop at 246 Newtownards Road. The owner wondered 'why anyone should have a grudge against me ... My brother died a few weeks ago. His windows were put in on election night [on the Shankill Road], and a short time later a petrol bomb was thrown at the shop.'[77]

Along with other concerned businessmen, John Donegan formed the 'Catholic Front' to rehouse families from vulnerable areas. Donegan claimed that 'there have been dozens of cases of victimisation of

Catholics which had not been publicised and no voice had been raised about them. No MPs have made a mention of these incidents.'[78]

Owen McDonald lived at the time in 11 David Street, between the Shankill and Falls roads, in a home that he and his family were burned out of several years later. He recalls the increasing campaign of sectarianism directed against him and others from the mid-1960s onward:

> David Street was a nice street to live, but every weekend we were tortured. If you stood at your door, you would have been beat up. Sam Hughes next door was standing at his door one day and he got a terrible hiding. When I went to report it to the police the police never did anything about it. After the countless times I had my windows broken on Saturday afternoons after the crowds were leaving Distillery football ground, I went to the police to complain. The police arrived at 11.30 a.m. and asked me where the footballers were now. I told them that the trouble did not start until after the supporters were leaving. One morning when I woke up there was paint over our doors and windows, and [also] our neighbours, and in other streets including Leeson Street … It was not Catholics that did it.[79]

Opposite Conway Street, off the Falls Road, was Balaclava Street, a broad street that hosted many street activities for the local children. Children played games such as football, handball, cricket, rounders and hopscotch, though their playtime activity was frequently interrupted by loyalist football supporters coming through the area on their way to and from matches. Eamon McGonigle recalls:

> I can remember a Saturday afternoon we were all pulled in. I was ten or twelve years of age. I remember us all being called in at a certain time on Saturday, which was about one o'clock, half one,

and we all had to go into the scullery, to sit in the scullery while the crowds walked down Balaclava Street and onto the Grosvenor Road. I can remember the police bringing them [loyalist football supporters] down [the street]. You could hear the crowds going past the window, the cheering and the chanting of 'The Billy Boys'. But I always remember thinking to myself: why are we stuck here? We could have been out playing football. I remember my daddy going to the window: something had happened and he looked out to see what was wrong, and a bottle came through the window.[80]

Paddy Carlin, a shipyard worker, had similar experiences. In 1966 Paddy moved next door to Jim McCourt's Electrical Shop on Leeson Street, which ran between the Falls Road and the Grosvenor Road:

I was sixteen years old at the time, and my first recollection was of the sectarian violence from the Linfield supporters. Football matches were played on a Wednesday night at Grosvenor Park, and when Linfield were playing their supporters would come down Roden Street en masse and throw stones without any reason at the Catholic houses, and shops on the Grosvenor Road. Along with the stones came the sectarian abuse, songs and filthy language. They could have come down Excise Street and Burnaby Street, because it was a shorter walk to the ground, but this was deliberate. They carried stones in their pockets. Everyone knew to stay away from that part of the road. When a game was being played, the streets emptied. Where we lived was our home, but it was also a shop with large windows, which were expensive to replace. We learned after many broken windows to have boards made up, and on the days of the games – Saturdays included – we boarded the windows along with our neighbours. This was not a new experience for the people of Grosvenor and surrounding streets: this had been going on for years, and I would blame in the main the Linfield supporters from the Donegall Road and Sandy Row for this. They did what they liked. After 1969, all that finished: they never came back.[81]

Kevin Kennedy lived in Granville Street, situated between Leeson Street and Grosvenor Road. Kevin recalls:

The two big teams were Linfield (Blues) and Glentoran. Trouble would have started when Linfield supporters arrived for the matches. The Glentoran supporters weren't too bad because they arrived from the city centre end of the Grosvenor Road and returned that way. But the Linfield supporters came from the Shankill direction and made their way to the ground through Catholic streets. I seen before the matches they would have been drinking in some of the bars around the Falls, and going in and out of the bookies, having a bet. There were large crowds of them, and they would have done what they wanted. 1963 was a bad time in the area as a result of trouble on the pitch at Distillery. The trouble then spread onto the surrounding streets, with windows in Catholic houses being broken, and local Catholic residents being beaten. One Wednesday night in 1967 the Blues were playing at Windsor Park, and when the match was over they made their way onto the Grosvenor Road and into the Catholic side streets. A mob of them arrived in McDonnell Street; they systematically broke the windows of the houses as they were moving up the street. I remember Jim Haughey coming out of his house in McDonnell Street, and he began to fight with them. A young girl who lived in McDonnell Street was chased and knocked down by a bus in Albert Street. The next time the Blues played, the local men had had enough and were prepared to defend themselves, but the Blues supporters never showed, and we believe that the police had warned them to avoid the area. They got away with murder; they did what they wanted to do. There were never any police around. The only time any local resistance was shown [by us] was towards the last years of the 1960s.[82]

The historian Geoffrey Bell – a Protestant raised in Belfast – confirms that the RUC generally ignored the intimidation carried out by 'Protestant working-class youths of west Belfast who carry huge Union Jacks and wear blue scarves tinged with red and white as a badge of distinction', leaving their victims to pay for repairs. He describes one of the regular sources of trouble:

> Midway through the 1960s things started to go wrong – for the fans the decline of Linfield was one more affront, one more assault from the forces of darkness. Despite the setbacks on the football field the fans still marched like some victorious army from Linfield's home ground in south-west Belfast to the Shankill Road, the capital of Protestant Ulster, after every home game. The parade has led to more than one riot in recent years [1966–71], yet it has now become as traditional as the Orange marches themselves, and no 'true Blue' Linfield fan would think of travelling the mile and a half to the Shankill any other way ... That is what the Protestant culture is all about: Protestant supremacy, Protestant ascendancy. The Linfield team is merely a part of that ascendancy. The belief in it protrudes into every aspect of contemporary Protestant working-class life: the team, the songs, the humour. The over-riding message is the excellence of the Protestants. As the recent loyalist song puts it: 'Proud and defiant, With folk self reliant, A Loyalist giant, That's Ulster.'[83]

Brendan Hughes, who joined the IRA in 1969 after the devastating attacks on nationalist homes in West Belfast, described his experience as a child in the predominately Protestant Blackwater Street, off the Grosvenor Road:

> There was one old woman, she was in her nineties – Mrs McKissick – and every time I walked past her door she would spit on me; every Sunday she would shout – this is a woman sitting outside her front

door, bigoted old woman – 'Did you bless yourself with the Pope's piss this morning?' But around the July period that got worse.[84]

Similarly, Paddy Carlin experienced sectarianism at home and in the workplace:

In 1966 a man called Tommy Hunter, a Catholic from Corby Way in Andersonstown, asked me if I wanted a job in the shipyard. At first, I thought he was joking, but he said he wasn't, and the following Monday morning I went with him to the shipyard. When I began work in the shipyard, I started off as a 'hammer boy' in the blacksmith shop. In the shipyard, I went from there into the burners, welders and traders; they amalgamated into the steelworkers.

In the beginning the men I met and worked with were very friendly, especially in the blacksmith shop. When I first started it was coming up to the July holidays and because I had just started I had no holiday money to get. The men very kindly had a collection for me and made up two week's wages.

I can't explain it, but every July after that I experienced sectarian behaviour from the majority of my Protestant workmates. From when I began work in 1966 until the 'Troubles' started I had no problems with my Protestant workmates, except for each July, and the first of July was regarded as the mini-Twelfth – the start of hostilities. The banners went up and then the flags around the shipyard, and in the blacksmith shop everything was covered in Union Jacks. I worked the hammer for six blacksmiths and my hammer was decked out with the flags. At the time it didn't bother me. After the July holidays the atmosphere had changed again and we went back to normal as if July had never happened. But after the July holidays one year, this particular Protestant man said to me, 'Paddy you should have been up to the field on the "Twelfth", we give the Pope a right kicking.' My reply was that he deserved it because he shouldn't have been there. He was so angry at my response to him that he tried to hit me, and only for the other men there he would have. He thought his comment would have annoyed me, and when he saw it didn't he was furious.[85]

THE POLITICS OF REPRESSION

Various historians have described the mid-1960s as 'the O'Neill Years', yet Paisley's continuous attacks on O'Neill's administration rocked official unionism's relationship with its working-class base, who were themselves suffering from the collapse of staple industries and open to easy explanations for their declining status. In addition, the emerging civil rights movement highlighted the discriminatory and sectarian nature of O'Neill's administration.

There is a perception of the civil rights agitation still widely disseminated by unionist politicians – and too often accepted by journalists and professional historians – that depicts the emerging movement as a republican and communist conspiracy, an IRA 'Trojan horse', with its sectarianism masked by calls for equality. In fact, the movement demanded justice for all who suffered from social deprivation and, despite its internal differences, seemed united in its determination to exclude any attempts to raise the 'constitutional question'.

Northern Ireland's unionist elite had long relied on sectarianism to divide and weaken the working classes, even though many of the unionist working class were little better off than their nationalist counterparts. When journalist Peter Taylor asked Ulster Volunteer Billy Mitchell if, as a working-class Protestant, he was 'supposed to feel superior ... that's what the politicians were telling you', Mitchell replied:

Yes, those they called 'politicians'. We were election fodder. They'd come down every four or five years with their 'kick the Pope' bands and we were happy enough to cheer them on. They'd wave their Union Jacks and flags at us and wind up my parents and people like that. At the end of the night, we went back to our ghettoes and they went back to their big houses. Then we didn't see them for another four or five years. We didn't realise it at that time. It's taken years for us to evolve this sort of thinking.[86]

O'Neill's administration began tentatively introducing reform only under pressure from the British government – which was itself responding to the civil rights protests – and was motivated at least partly by the threat that the non-sectarian Northern Ireland Labour Party might begin to peel away its support among Protestant workers. A radio interview given by O'Neill just after his resignation on 28 April 1969 underlined his condescension towards the nationalist community:

It is frightfully hard to explain to a Protestant that if you give Roman Catholics a good job and a good house they will live like Protestants, because they will see neighbours with cars and TV sets; they will refuse to have eighteen children. But if a Roman Catholic is jobless, and lives in a most ghastly hovel he will rear eighteen children on National Assistance. If you treat Roman Catholics with due consideration and kindness they will live like Protestants, in spite of the authoritarian nature of their church.[87]

Nonetheless, some academics indulge in a form of wistful naiveté regarding the period. Wichert argues without foundation that, from the perspective of the 1970s, 'many Catholics looked to the almost golden age of the 1960s'. Such assertions do not come close to reflecting the acute sense of historic grievance felt among Belfast's nationalists, growing in tandem with civil rights agitation into outrage from the mid-1960s onward. Indeed, in her concentration on high politics and changes in the economy at large, Wichert seems oblivious to the unwillingness of nationalists to tolerate any longer the institutionalised sectarianism they had endured – often in impotent and resigned silence – for much of the history of the Northern Ireland state.

The Stormont administration began the 1960s without any notion of moving on from traditional sectarianism. The early decade witnessed the end of an IRA campaign, but also the emergence of revived loyalist militancy, manifested most notably in the rise of Paisley. This resurgence, driven by a sectarian reaction against calls for moderate reform, spawned a range of extremist loyalist groups who, well before the 1966 commemorations, had started down the path of sectarian violence. From the mid-1960s, the UVF carried out numerous bombings and shootings, and widespread intimidation, and had embarked on a low-level campaign of murdering Catholics. Even before the eruption of large-scale pogroms in the summer of 1969, it was responsible for dozens of sectarian expulsions in Belfast alone and was implicated in the attempted assassination of Terence O'Neill. In all of this, its position was strengthened by the presence of an ambivalent state – one that perhaps was occasionally embarrassed by the flagrant bigotry of its staunchest defenders, but which had, in fact, been founded upon sectarian violence. By the late 1960s, the armed forces charged by the Stormont administration with upholding law and order – the RUC and B-Specials – brutally attacked peaceful demonstrators, and connived in a pogrom against nationalist communities in Derry and in West and North Belfast carried out by organised loyalists inspired by a decade of Paisley's venomous rabble-rousing. Eight people lost their lives and at least 1,820 families fled their homes in fear in August 1969. For many thousands of nationalists, the 1960s was no 'golden age' but a decade of intensifying sectarian hatred.

Many of the published accounts regarding the start of the modern Troubles point to republican celebrations of the fiftieth anniversary of the Easter Rising as crucial in precipitating the descent into chronic violence. These have identified the correct year, perhaps, but the wrong culprit – projecting backwards the establishment's attempt to single out the Provisional IRA as the instigator of the conflict. Elliott, for example, argues that extremists on both sides were responsible for generating the subsequent violence. Alluding to events in Clonard after the burning of Bombay Street, she claims that 'the Protestant mob believ[ed], with some justification, that they were being attacked by gunmen from within the monastery's precincts'.[88] In a narrow sense Elliott is, of course, correct: loyalists were being held off by two local men armed with shotguns. However, Elliott omits from her narrative the fact that Clonard residents were trying to defend themselves, having already been subjected to horrific violence from loyalist gunmen and petrol bombers, who had just burned out dozens of nationalist homes and killed a fifteen-year-old child on the boundary of the church grounds.

Following the IRA's abandonment of armed struggle after the humiliating failure of Operation Harvest, political violence in the half decade before August 1969 was almost exclusively the preserve of loyalist extremists and the state security forces, with membership often coterminous. The northern state presented a one-party administration incapable of contemplating serious reform. The most fundamental problem in existing accounts of the origins of the modern Troubles, now tied to a version of 'shared history' that tends towards absolving elites of any culpability for violence, lies in their evasion of the state's historic role in maintaining sectarian divisions. These antagonisms were by 1969 deeply rooted: indeed they had exploded in horrific violence at the founding of the Northern Ireland state in 1921–22, and again in 1935. Despite this troubled history no serious attempt had been made to resolve the underlying problems. Indeed,

Stormont had long experience in responding to demands for reform with the blunt force of repression, and it was inclined this way in 1969 no less than it had been previously. In the face of a new and powerful challenge, Stormont doubled down on the structural inequalities, with entirely predictable results.

2

THE EVICTIONS COMMENCE

Tensions across Northern Ireland increased dramatically during the early months of 1969, with violent scenes from marches and demonstrations broadcast across the world. Between April and August 1969, however, loyalist violence spread against the working-class, nationalist population in general, directed especially at those living in mixed or majority-Protestant areas. Government officials bear some responsibility for amplifying tensions, though it was Paisley's supporters who carried out much of the violence at ground level.

The earlier history of the Orange state set the geographical boundaries around which these new tensions would play out. Particularly in Belfast, the violent pogroms of the 1920s and 1930s had essentially corralled the nationalist community into clearly defined districts, or ghettoes. With the establishment of the welfare state and particularly during the 1950s and 1960s, members of the growing nationalist community gradually spilled out from the over-crowded Lower Falls into predominantly Protestant streets leading to the Shankill Road. During the same period rural Catholic businessmen acquired licensed premises within the Shankill and Crumlin Road areas. By the late 1960s both areas contained small but growing nationalist minorities whose presence unsettled loyalists. Charlie Toner, whose family was burned out of its Cambrai Street home and who saw its licensed business put to the torch between 2 and 4 August 1969, recounted how his family 'got on with everyone all year round except during the marching season in July. At that time of the year there was always a bit of hostility. You were made to feel as if you were not wanted and didn't really belong.'[1]

A clear pattern of premeditated and escalating attacks upon the civil rights movement precipitated a general descent into chronic conflict, although this receives limited attention in scholarly assessments of the origins of the Troubles. Curiously, while records from the period show that a single individual – John McKeague, a disciple of Paisley and co-founder of the SDA – was involved in orchestrating this campaign in Belfast and beyond, his name is almost completely absent from mainstream accounts, his seminal role in bringing on the Troubles in 1969 almost completely ignored.

Paisley's manipulation of primitive sectarianism within an element of the Protestant community appealed to McKeague's fanatical anti-Catholicism. By 1966 Paisley had assembled an army of fundamentalist supporters, amongst them loyalist paramilitaries in the form of the UCDC and UPV. McKeague effectively replicated Paisley's organising at local level, building his own army: the SDA. On the Shankill Road he manipulated loyalist insecurities to galvanise sectarian sentiment, which in turn found expression in violent attacks on the nationalist community. Like others in and outside of Stormont, McKeague viewed the civil rights movement as a republican Trojan horse, with the broad nationalist community as its army. Between April and August 1969 he initiated a campaign of murder and expulsion against nationalists, seizing on perceived Protestant vulnerability to incite violence at every opportunity. McKeague's campaign began with attempted expulsions of nationalist residents from Unity Walk flats in Belfast and escalated by August to a large-scale pogrom against vulnerable Catholic families across the city. In the process the SDA expanded to a membership of thousands – completely unimpeded by government officials or the uniformed forces of law and order.

NICRA – A STRUGGLE FOR CIVIL RIGHTS

The, now celebrated, civil rights march in Derry on 5 October 1968 partially exposed the weakness of the coercive apparatus of the unionist government. The Special Powers Act, passed in 1922 to suppress nationalist dissent, appeared ill-equipped for the age of tele-vision, as pictures of RUC brutality against peaceful demonstrators at the march on that day reached a global audience.[2] Nevertheless, the Orange Order actually blamed the civil rights movement for initiating the violence: '[U]ntil 1968 and the civil rights marchers, there had been an easily recognisable improvement in community relations in the Province and a growing prosperity which was obvious to all.'[3]

The work of professional historians has largely reinforced this argument, attributing renascent sectarianism and the re-emergence of violent republicanism to the rise of the civil rights movement. A. T. Q. Stewart of Queen's University Belfast set the interpretive pattern when he claimed that the 'political atmosphere in Northern Ireland was extremely bad, worse than it had been since 1922, *as a consequence of the accelerating Catholic civil rights agitation which had led to clashes with the police in 1968*' [emphasis added].[4] 'Once the civil rights movement assumed a militant, and to all intents and purposes, a sectarian form in 1969,' he continued, 'the entire escalation of the conflict was easily predictable.'[5] By this sleight of hand 'neutral' scholars lent their authority to a deeply conservative establishment consensus that labelled the civil rights movement sectarian and blamed the victims of state and vigilante violence for whatever bru-tality came their way. There is a remarkable convergence, therefore, between the unionist establishment's partisan condemnation of the civil rights movement and the admonishing tone of university-based historians and political scientists. Together these have served as a bulwark against an international consensus that the Irish civil rights movement challenged real injustices, widespread discrimination, gerrymandering and other undemocratic policies.

As tensions escalated throughout late 1968 and into 1969, the unionist establishment vigorously condemned the movement. Ministers publicly vilified the membership and their activities and, at times, openly incited violence against them – bolstered by sensational claims that the strings were being pulled by republicans, communists and Romanist malefactors, or an incongruous combination of all of the above. Most academic historians have been unable to summon the will to challenge these facile characterisations – at times contorting themselves to offer up rationalisations for loyalist violence. Some academics have challenged the civil rights movement's very *raison d'être*, downplaying unionist discrimination or dismissing the movement as propagandist. Roy Foster claims, for example, that while the 'allocation of housing became the flashpoint – levels of inequality were no longer as spectacular as claimed'.[6]

Steve Bruce echoes unionist propaganda from the period by highlighting the 'involvement of committed republicans and nationalists in the civil rights movement' as justification for repression. '[M]any of those involved in the civil-rights protests,' he insists, 'were every bit as "sectarian" as their Protestant opponents.' He also contends that 'many [of the] civil-rights marches, were deliberate exercises in coat-trailing'.[7] Bruce appears to be contriving a reading of the period that justifies state and loyalist repression. According to this logic the very presence of republicans in a movement that peacefully challenged discrimination against a community *of which republicans formed a sizeable element* calls into question its legitimacy. That such an absurd approach can be taken seriously by scholars committed to 'bias-free' scholarship tells us a great deal about the function that mainstream scholarship plays in deflecting criticism of the status quo.

The echoing of the unionist line not only underplays levels of deprivation and discrimination, but is contradicted by the unequivocal findings of the Cameron Commission. The Cameron Commission's brief was to 'report upon the course of events leading to and the immediate causes and nature of violence and civil disturbances … on and since 5th October 1968'. Led by Lord Cameron, in September

1969 it published its report which acknowledged that NICRA was 'justified' in its complaints regarding 'the allocation of houses, discrimination in local authority appointments, limitations on local electoral franchise and deliberate manipulation of ward boundaries and electoral areas'. Indeed, Cameron stated, 'decisions already taken by the Northern Ireland Government since these disturbances began' confirmed the veracity of NICRA's analysis.[8]

Although NICRA organisers were not naive about the possibility of a violent response to their actions from the state, they did not anticipate the scale of opposition and violence that would be unleashed by the Paisleyite UPV and other loyalist paramilitaries against the movement. On 9 October, four days after the Derry march, a Paisleyite counter-rally induced the RUC to obstruct a peaceful student march to Belfast's City Hall. This led to a sit-down protest by the students lasting several hours, after which they reassembled at a meeting in Queen's University. As participant Michael Farrell recalled, 'That night they set up the People's Democracy (PD), a loose activist body committed to civil rights reform, but with a tough Young Socialist hard core. It was to become the dynamic driving force of the civil rights movement.'[9] Cameron acknowledged that the PD attributed the radicalisation and growth of NICRA to Paisley's belligerence and the Stormont administration's repression in Derry on 5 October:

If the object ... was to drive the Civil Rights movement into the ground by a display of force and firmness in the ministerial order, it signally failed. The principal result of this operation, widely publicised – was the opposite, [and] led directly to the formation and development [of] People's Democracy.[10]

The ex-cabinet minister and privy councillor, William Craig, stated that the Cameron Commission had emerged from 'a weak inept

Government and cannot be justified. I do not wish to have any part in it.'[11] Paisley viewed it 'as a betrayal of the Ulster people to the rebels'.[12] Brian Faulkner resigned in reaction to the implementation of the commission's recommendations, highlighting among other things the machinery for dealing with grievances against local authorities, and also in protest against O'Neill's introduction of reforms; he told unionists he 'did not accept that the minority had suffered grave social injustice ... It is a nonsense to talk of Roman Catholic ghettoes and second-class citizens [when] the government had acted fairly and generously towards the Catholic minority.'[13] Indeed, while unionist rejection of the commission's findings is reflected in much historical writing since, for the most part historians and social scientists themselves have ignored the findings.

Not all unionists dismissed the commission findings, however. Several months after O'Neill had resigned from government, a Church of Ireland clergyman gave him his views on the Cameron findings:

I always thought the word 'discrimination' was part of Nationalist propaganda until I read the Cameron report. Now I realise more clearly than ever what you were trying to do. If Lord Cameron had done no more than open the eyes of a typical, decent Anglican clergyman, brave, moderate but uninformed, he would have performed a useful service. In fact, of course, he did more. His report became one of the textbooks upon which reform could be based.[14]

The Cameron Commission's report documents an escalating series of loyalist attacks that followed in the wake of 5 October. On 23 November 1968, in Dungannon's Market Square, a PD meeting was attacked and broken up by loyalist extremists 'including Major [Ronald] Bunting, and ... the behaviour of these people was violent and irresponsible'.[15] Less than two weeks later, 300 loyalists attacked another civil rights meeting in the town. On this occasion, police blocked the loyalists' progress, thereby averting a major incident, though the confrontation contained one ominous feature: a loyalist gunman opened fire, narrowly missing a press cameraman. As Bouton points out, this was 'the first shot to be fired since the UVF murders of 1966; the first of many in the slow slide towards civil war'.[16]

On 30 November 1968, in nearby Armagh, police rerouted a civil rights march because Paisleyite counter-demonstrators – armed with sticks and cudgels and led by Bunting – had blocked the road. Although they took no action against the armed mob, Cameron admitted that the RUC 'could not guarantee the physical safety of the [NICRA] marchers against the obvious menace of unlawful violence'.[17] Loyalist placards posted before the march contained a 'friendly warning' to 'Ulster's Defenders' to 'board up your windows; remove all women and children from the city on Saturday 30th November. O'Neill must go.' Other notices read, 'For God and Ulster, SOS, to all Protestant religions, don't let the Republicans, IRA and CRA make Armagh another Londonderry.' On the morning of the march, Paisley's supporters breached 'a police cordon of the city centre by knocking down a wall in an alleyway'.[18] Police roadblocks stopped vehicles making their way to town, recovering 'two revolvers as well as 220 other weapons, such as bill-hooks, pipes hammered into sharp points and scythes … The [loyalists] standing in Scotch Street and Thomas Street [were] seen to be carrying weapons such as sticks and large pieces of timber. Dr Paisley carried a blackthorn stick and Major Bunting a black walking stick. The police inferred from the results at the roadblock that some firearms were being carried among the crowd which had gathered.'[19] Having received a three-month sentence for unlawful assembly at Armagh on 27 January, Paisley and Bunting addressed a 300-strong crowd, with the former issuing an ultimatum to O'Neill's administration: 'Change your policies or you will have a Protestant uprising on your hands.'[20]

Beginning on 1 January 1969, Bunting had instituted a four-day-long campaign of violence and harassment against PD's Selma-inspired march from Belfast to Derry, a campaign ably assisted by members of the B-Specials. This culminated in savage attacks on peaceful marchers at Burntollet on 4 January, where 'several hundred Loyalists hurled rocks and bottles and then charged, armed with clubs and iron bars. It was an ambush.'[21] The daughter of Paddy Devlin, MP, was 'knocked unconscious from a blow on the head and fell into the river. She was rescued by other marchers and brought back to the bank.'[22]

Tellingly, O'Neill ignored the premeditated violence carried out by loyalists (including police) and reserved his condemnation for the unarmed, peaceful demonstrators attempting to 'destabilise' Northern Ireland. 'The march to Londonderry planned by the so-called People's Democracy was from the outset ... foolhardy and irresponsible ... Some of the marchers and those who supported them in Londonderry itself have shown themselves to be hooligans ready to attack the police and others.'[23] Unionist Reg Empey claimed that the 'general coverage of events since October has shown a distinct bias against the Government and in many cases, especially from England and abroad, showed a distinct lack of knowledge ... elements exist in the [civil rights] movement bent on destroying Northern Ireland and a greater number determined to overthrow the Unionist administration'.[24]

In his sympathetic account of the B-Specials, Arthur Hezlet alleged that:

There is no doubt that the extremists in the Civil Rights movement had as one of their aims the discrediting of the police. This they hoped to achieve by intense provocation leading to retaliation, which could be presented on television and in the Press as police brutality. They were successful in discrediting the RUC in the riots in Londonderry in January and April [1969], although the incidents were enormously exaggerated.[25]

By contrast, in their publication *Burntollet*, based on extensive interviews, Egan and McCormack placed the blame for the events there on loyalist aggressors. One local man recalled:

'About ten o'clock I came out of the gates with another man and walked down the bridge [at Burntollet]. A group with white armbands had gathered. One was handing out sticks. This fellow said to us, "Are you here to help us boys?" I asked what was needed, and was told the Civil Rights march was on its way. So I said I thought the police would be able to manage them. I remember well what he replied, "The police are staying out of it today. We can welt the hell out of them with no interference." Later I learned who this man was.' The individual identified is a member of the Special Constabulary.[26]

Egan and McCormack concluded:

The attack was organised locally by representatives of the Orange Order and the Special Constabulary, in close collaboration with some members, at least, of the Royal Ulster Constabulary. It may well be that local branches of the clandestine organisation known as the Ulster Volunteer Force were involved. But the overlap of personnel between these organisations render such distinction of purely academic significance. The police force on duty, as a whole, knew of the place and approximate magnitude of the attack. Specifically, or by clear indication, the members of the force learned that they were not expected to resist or arrest attackers. Those responsible for organising protection led the march to a trap. Five people were prosecuted. These were victims largely irrelevant to the organisation of the onslaught.[27]

The acts of violence perpetrated upon the marchers at Burntollet by loyalists and B-Specials were not enough for some in the UUP. Terence O'Neill pointed out that he received a call from Robin Chichester-Clark, who told him that he and his brother (James, South Derry MP and chief whip of the UUP) had watched the march through their constituencies, and asked O'Neill to go on air and announce the ordering out of the B-Specials. 'He said that he and his brother both felt that unless this was done the Protestant backlash would be too dreadful to contemplate.'[28] To his credit, O'Neill refused.

The night before the Burntollet ambush, Paisley and Bunting had overseen a loyalist rally in Derry's Guildhall, after which sectarian rioting broke out, with the RUC making repeated baton charges into the nationalist Bogside. The following night, as the exhausted PD marchers made their way back into Derry, loyalists attacked them, and this was followed by further police incursions into the Bogside. Members of the RUC, 'many of them apparently drunk, went on the rampage in the Bogside breaking windows and doors and beating up people'.[29] When investigating this event Cameron reached 'the unhesitating conclusion ... that a number of policemen were guilty of misconduct which involved assault and battery, malicious damage to property ... and the use of provocative sectarian and political slogans'.[30] James Callaghan regarded these findings as 'a pretty cool account [of] a major breakdown in discipline, of a kind which would not have been tolerated in a British police force. Altogether 163 people were treated in hospital after that weekend.'[31] Richard Rose noted that 'civil rights MPs appealed to the Home Office to act, but their appeals were politely turned down'.[32]

On 6 February the newly appointed RUC inspector general, Anthony Peacock, immediately issued a press release blaming the civil rights movement for the disturbances. He reiterated unionist claims of IRA involvement in the civil rights campaign and complained that NICRA's activities had placed considerable pressure on his force.

He then claimed that there was 'no evidence of an armed Protestant force'.[33] Both Harry Diamond, MP for Falls, and Sheelagh Murnaghan of Queen's University criticised Peacock's public reference to IRA participation, complaining that it constituted a political statement on the eve of the general election which was due to take place on 24 February in Northern Ireland.[34] Peacock's remarks prompted Gerry Fitt, MP for West Belfast, to remark that since 5 October, 'many calls have been made for an impartial inquiry into activities of members of the RUC. I believe now that the most searching inquiry should be made into the political affiliations of the present Inspector General.'[35]

The events at Burntollet not only illustrated co-operation in the orchestration of violence between RUC, B-Specials and loyalists, but also revealed the inherent sectarianism of the unionist administration. This was further demonstrated by the resignation of a number of hard-liners over O'Neill's attempt at reforms, and calls for his own resignation from others over the same issue.

On 19 April, another riot broke out in Derry, and the RUC again forced the rioters into the Bogside, saturating the area and remaining there until ordered out by the Minister of Home Affairs. They charged into William Street and broke down the front door of the Devenney home. Once inside, they beat family members including the father, Sam, who died of his injuries three months later. These actions confirmed the impression – among Bogsiders and the wider nationalist community – of the RUC as a sectarian force, empowered by the unionist government to suppress nationalist agitation. Regarding the murder of Samuel Devenney, 'the RUC reported that it carried out a wide-ranging investigation which had almost completely negative results about the assault on Devenney'.[36] Rose described the findings as 'politically convenient for Stormont, in view of the low morale of the RUC at the time'.[37] The Devenney family nonetheless received damages from a Northern Ireland court, a 'politically embarrassing' result 'both for Stormont and London'.[38]

Throughout this period Terence O'Neill's position became increasingly untenable. This was partly due to the incessant attacks from Paisley and to the firebrand's decision to challenge O'Neill in his own constituency during the crossroads election of February 1969. In February, Paisley told a group of supporters, including the Young Conquerors band, that O'Neill was 'a traitor, a tyrant, and a viper' intent on bringing back the 'darkness of priestcraft'. 'The press is against me,' he continued. 'The TV is against me. The Old Devil is against me.' He ended with the loyalist battle cry 'No Surrender'. The scene provoked the response, 'Il est bizarre, n'est-ce pas?' from one perplexed French journalist.[39]

O'Neill finally resigned on 28 April 1969, following a series of loyalist bomb attacks. These potentially lethal operations had been carried out in March and April by the UVF in the hopes that they could be pinned on the IRA bogeyman. By so doing they aimed to force O'Neill's departure and secure the release of Paisley and Bunting, who had been jailed on 25 March. 'Together,' Peter Taylor contends, 'these organisations, with the UPV and UVF at their heart, conspired to get rid of O'Neill. If political pressure would not force him to stand down, then a few well-placed explosions might, especially if the IRA was thought to be behind them.'[40]

Paisley's *Protestant Telegraph* quickly blamed republicans for the bombings: 'This latest act of IRA terrorism is an ominous indication of what lies ahead for Ulster[:] IRA barbarism, especially sabotage and ambush. Loyalists must now appreciate the struggle that lies ahead and the supreme sacrifice that will have to be made in order that Ulster will remain Protestant.'[41] The *Telegraph*, meanwhile, laboured to implicate the Dublin government in the bombings. This was a deliberate deflection, as Boulton acknowledges: 'Whatever doubt remains, the participation of members or supporters of the UCDC, the UPV and the Free Presbyterian Church is effectively proven. A link with the proscribed UVF is quite clear.'[42] O'Neill himself was suspicious of the bombings, telling one incredulous senior police officer: 'Don't … put it out of your mind that these explosions may be the work of extreme Protestants' – a possibility dismissed by the officer, who insisted that 'loyalists would never destroy their own country'.[43]

The loyalists' covert bombing campaign, accompanied by an inept – almost laughable – attempt to blame the IRA, nevertheless had the effect of reinforcing the existing but unsubstantiated impression amongst grass-roots loyalists that NICRA was little more than a republican front.

JOHN McKEAGUE AND THE SDA

In April, community leaders from the Shankill Road area called a meeting in Tennent Street Hall, ostensibly to address poor housing conditions. During the meeting Mina Browne, UPA member and a Free Presbyterian, introduced the assembly to John McKeague, later described as 'one of Belfast's most notorious leaders. Blond hair, clamped jaw, tense, he always exuded menace and an angry intolerance, looking and behaving like someone who would have been a suitable recruit to Hitler's SA'.[44] Originally from Bushmills, on Antrim's north coast, McKeague – 'lean, sleazy and snake-like, his eyes slightly sunken' – had moved with his mother to 140 Albertbridge Road in East Belfast in June 1968.[45] A member of the Orange and Black institutions, McKeague was also a member of Paisley's Free Presbyterian Church and of the Willowfield unit of the UPV. Encouraged by Paisley's vitriolic speeches, the misinformation being disseminated from Stormont, and the biased reporting of the unionist press, McKeague became involved in militant loyalism, rising 'to prominence in loyalist circles in the [mid] 1960s as a flag-bearer for Paisleyism' and entering 'the ranks of conspiratorial Unionists', forging links with the Shankill UVF.[46]

Mina Browne was the person most instrumental in McKeague's involvement with the SDA and introducing him to wider loyalist circles in the west of the city. Browne had made a name for herself in 1963 when, as a supporter of Gusty Spence's Shankill UVF and a part-time cleaner employed by Belfast Corporation, she organised protests over the corporation's decision to include Catholics on the list of school cleaners. On 6 June 1966 she was one of the six people arrested with Paisley during the disturbances caused by the march to the Presbyterian General Assembly. Earlier she had sent Unionist MP Nat Minford an anonymous threatening telegram on behalf of the Shankill UVF after Minford denounced Paisley as a 'big wind bag' and a 'bloated bull frog'. Unfortunately for Browne, a postal clerk included her address on the telegram. Stormont appointed a four-man committee to establish the facts, which concluded that her answers were 'carefully rehearsed', 'evasive' and 'untruthful' and did not accept her evidence that she was solely responsible for the telegram. Despite this, no action was taken against her or against the 1st Shankill Division of the UPV–UVF. Boulton claims that the first secretary of Paisley's UCDC, Noel Doherty, was the actual author of the telegram.[47]

By the end of the Tennent Street Hall meeting, the SDA had been established, with McKeague as its chairman and Fred Proctor his deputy. With Browne's help McKeague had hijacked a meeting called to address poor housing and social deprivation, twisting demands for social justice to his own sectarian ends. Bruce describes McKeague as a 'man who could only be a part of a movement if he led it'.[48]

Over a short period McKeague's energetic involvement on the Shankill coincided with a dramatic rise in militant loyalist organisation. Within weeks of its emergence, the SDA had upwards of 2,000 members, organised into vigilante groups bearing armbands emblazoned with 'SDA'. Despite this, one senior RUC officer later attempted to diminish the impact of the SDA, informing Scarman that he considered it a small group of men.

In one of the few accounts that acknowledges the role of the SDA in the later troubles, Kevin Kelley notes that these '[n]eighbourhood-based organisations … announced that they were going to defend Protestant localities from "republican attacks". In reality, however, these bands of club-carrying toughs were raiding vulnerable Catholic areas rather than guarding against incursions that the IRA had no intention of initiating.'[49] In fact, within weeks of its formation, McKeague's SDA had advanced from clubs and crude hand weapons to equipping themselves with firearms and explosives.

Intimidation of Catholics continued throughout April. Some living precariously on side streets around the Shankill reported receiving 'bullet[s] in an envelope marked UVF' ordering them from their homes, while slogans warning 'Fenians get out or be burned out' appeared on gable walls. On 23 April, three Catholic families fled their homes in Dover Street, while a loyalist crowd gathered outside Mrs O'Hara's shouting 'Fenians get out or we'll burn you out'. Four days later, another mob threatened Catholics in Manor Street, North Belfast, while loyalists planted three sticks of gelignite and a clock on the windowsill of a Catholic church in Saintfield, County Down. On 27 April the mainly Protestant workforce at the ICI factory in Carrickfergus organised a petition stating that 'too many Catholics were getting in'. In the Oldpark area of North Belfast two Catholic families received 9mm bullets with a message from the UVF stating, 'Get ready to flit or else the next one will be through your head.'[50] On 29 April police reported that the (Italian) Catholic female owner of the Venice Café on the Crumlin Road received a letter warning that 'if she did not shut her café she would be burned out'. Throughout this period, which witnessed a steady rise in organised loyalist intimidation, Stormont used its emergency powers to counter the non-existent IRA threat, deploying the British Army to guard installations and allocating £59,000 to call up the Special Constabulary.

McKeague, who viewed the UVF as the army of the loyalist

people, was an admirer of Gusty Spence, the Shankill leader jailed for his part in sectarian murders in 1966, and he co-operated with Spence and the Shankill UVF during the latter half of the 1960s. Despite this, during three days testifying before Lord Scarman at the Scarman Tribunal, McKeague consistently denied UVF membership and any involvement in the UVF–UPV bombings in March and April. He did reveal to Scarman that he had 'been friendly with some people who got involved' in 'using explosive substances to destroy or damage public utilities'.

One effect of these bombings, McKeague told Scarman, was that Paisley 'dropped me like a hot cake'.[51] We know that McKeague had been an admirer of Paisley and they met at least once. In January 1969, when the RUC arrived to arrest Paisley at his Beersbridge Road address, they discovered him in conference with McKeague. After the bombings, however, various actions by McKeague led him to be viewed as an embarrassment and he was discarded by Paisley over time.[52]

By May 1969 trouble had erupted between nationalists and the RUC in Ardoyne and 'Catholic families had been forced to flee their homes on the "other" side of the Crumlin Road as loyalist intimidation began to make its presence felt'.[53] McKeague exploited this conflict to expand the SDA's influence, claiming that they had 'hundreds joining our organisation every week'.[54] On 15 June he organised a successful counter-demonstration against a march to Belfast city centre organised by the nationalist Connolly Association. From the steps of the Linen Hall Library, he proclaimed, 'Loyalists of the Shankill, we have a great victory here today. We have prevented the Connolly Association holding a parade past the unholy ground where James Connolly spoke from, many years ago.'[55]

Senior RUC officers submitted evidence to Scarman relating to the SDA and attempted to downplay its influence and increasing membership on the Shankill Road, claiming that the RUC looked upon the SDA as 'McNamara's Band'. However, despite a steady escalation of inflammatory speeches and increasing violence, the force took no action against McKeague or his vigilantes. The 1969 marching season saw a dramatic rise in tensions, with speakers on the Twelfth railing against the perceived threat from republicans and Romanists. Belfast's Fire Brigade recorded increased petrol-bomb attacks on Catholic-owned homes and property in Disraeli, Shannon and Geoffrey streets, while McKeague played on the fears of Protestant families on the Ardoyne side of the Crumlin Road.[56] According to Boulton, 'Intimidation intensified over the next week, with McKeague, in his own words "organising swaps" – the exchange of homes between Catholics and Protestants stuck on the "wrong" side in interface areas. "The inflammatory leadership of the SDA provided by Mr McKeague," pronounced the Scarman report, "must have encouraged the bullying and expulsion of Catholics, even though he stoutly denied it".'[57]

During July the SDA moved on isolated Catholic families on the Crumlin Road. 'From mid-July, Protestant crowds were gathering virtually every night, often organised by John McKeague and John McQuade, later an MP in West Belfast. Catholics began to be burnt out of their homes, despite the close presence of the RUC.'[58] 'On at least one occasion,' Boulton notes, 'nearly forty policemen stood by while Protestants burned down a Catholic house.'[59] One RUC sergeant reported that 'the Protestant section on the left side of the Crumlin Road assumed a new character from the Twelfth of July onwards ... We had crowds assembling there, not entirely local crowds, but from all over Belfast', and with 'Mr McKeague on the scene ... it certainly made the task of the police in that area a lot more difficult when they arrived there.'[60]

The threat of sectarian intimidation and violence had hung over the nationalist community since the state's inception, especially around 12 July, but also at times of heightened tensions, such as

July 1969. Belfast woman Ethna Byrne worked in a clothing factory off Belfast's Donegall Road. She recalled how that July she and her workmates became 'trapped in work. The Catholic workforce inside the factory was informed that a Protestant mob was outside waiting for us. The reason it started was there was [sic] objections by the Catholic girls about the flags and emblems that were increasing every day around our machines.'[61]

Eileen McGonigle recollected how in the same month, in a factory close to Belfast's city centre, Protestant workers draped red, white and blue bunting over Catholic co-workers' machines – including her own. 'We didn't mind if they kept their red, white and blue buntings up on their machines, it made little odds to us, we just resented the fact that they could just stick it up on our machines without asking us.'[62]

Also that July, McKeague directed his growing ranks in launching a campaign of systematic intimidation against the nationalist residents of the Unity Walk flats. During the early hours of the morning of the Twelfth, men playing drums and flutes woke residents abruptly from their sleep. Residents estimated that fifty bandsmen were gathered and playing sectarian tunes, accompanied by another group (including a number of RUC men) who shouted sectarian slogans. A resident claimed that when he called on police to quieten the bands, they replied that 'if I didn't like it I could [move] down South' and 'it was their day and they are the people and if you don't like it you know what to do'. A short time later another group of men stopped, faced the flats and commenced playing sectarian tunes. Four RUC men who were present ignored residents' complaints and the band members remained until five o'clock in the morning. Scarman concluded that 'the bands which passed the flats on this occasion were made up of people from Sandy Row area who had been celebrating around the bonfires in the Shankill Road and were returning to Sandy Row'.[63]

At approximately eight o'clock that morning, the RUC head

constable positioned eighteen men at Unity Walk; they were with-drawn after a morning march passed without incident. That even-ing, however, a crowd of 100 loyalists who had been drinking in the Naval Club, only yards from Unity Walk, poured onto North Street, onto which Unity Walk opens. According to a female resident, the crowd approached the flats shouting 'Fenian bastards' and vowing: 'We will get the Fenians out of the flats.' The situation deteriorated further when one of the Orange Lodges entered North Street and then marched towards the flats. The crowds grew larger as the bands approached, and aggressive sectarian taunting filled the air: residents became alarmed when a large element of the crowd shouted 'Burn the Fenians out.' Head Constable Kyle pointed out to the Scarman Tribunal that things became worse when a number of Scottish bands arrived and behaved in a provocative manner, with quite a few of them using very abusive language. 'Whether this had anything to do with the fact that there was the allegation that it was the Scottish band that had created the disturbance in the early hours of the previ-ous morning, it might have been.'[64]

On 16 July, loyalists attacked and firebombed St Matthew's Catholic church on the Newtownards Road in East Belfast. On 18 July, the News Letter claimed that rioting in Derry between nationalist youths and the RUC was offering a pretext for attacks against Catholics living in vulnerable districts in Belfast. 'The backlash of Londonderry's Bogside bitterness was felt in the Oldpark district of Belfast last night when Roman Catholic families evacuated their homes in the face of threats,' its headlines declared. The Corrigan family of Louisa Street, off Oldpark Road, reported how 'a car with two men came to their house on Tuesday night and told them "to get out or be burned out"'.[65] The Burns family of Cromwell Street suffered a similar fate. John and Mary Cunningham were evicted from their Palmer Street home. Timothy Angland and family moved to Manchester after a series of attacks on their Geoffrey Street home.

A former British soldier and civil servant of twenty-six years, Edward McCrossan of Finbank Gardens witnessed his home attacked by loyalists using bricks and paint, with 'Up Paisley' and 'UVF' daubed on his walls and door. Mr Vivian Simpson, MP for Oldpark, protested to RUC officers about their failure to protect homes from attack. In response the RUC claimed they did not have sufficient numbers to deal with the situation. One Saturday in July, writing appeared on many walls on the Shankill Road urging loyalists to go to Disraeli Street. Several hours later police reported that 250 loyalists had gathered at Disraeli Street waiting for instructions.

In Dungiven an Orange march led to two days of riots in the course of which sixty-six-year-old Francis McCloskey was killed during a police baton charge. Dungiven also saw 'a platoon of B-Specials' fire 'over the heads of a Catholic crowd coming out of a dance'.[66] Concerned about the activities of the B-Specials, civil rights leader Bernadette Devlin and independent nationalist MP John Hume travelled to London to meet Lord Stonham and British Home Secretary James Callaghan. Devlin and Hume demanded the disbandment of the B-Specials because of their use of firearms against civilians, and Devlin further pointed out that the RUC had shot civilians in Derry. Two days later, Ivan Cooper, MP for Mid-Ulster, accused the B-Specials of 'deliberately contravening the Minister of Home Affairs' recent order on carrying of firearms, firing pot-shots in order to terrorise, carrying of arms while not in uniform, and general conduct tantamount to mutiny'.[67] He concurred with Devlin that a platoon of B-Specials had fired 100 shots without provocation in Dungiven on 13 July and that B-Specials had fired sten-guns at innocent bystanders from a passing car. One ex-B-Special and UVF man bragged that in his area 'we did more or less what we liked ... knew all the RCs and kept close watch on them. Sometimes some of the lads gave them a roughing up – I'm not saying this went on a lot, but the politicians never complained then.'[68]

As violence spread beyond West and North Belfast, Paisley and McKeague both took full advantage of tensions within the two communities. On 2 August the *Protestant Telegraph* warned of a 'Papal Conspiracy':

> The Orange parades must be a warning to those who have come to believe that Romanism has changed. The Church of Rome is still the greatest enemy of our country. Its progress can only mean the growth of superstition and slavery and the return of the dark days from which we were rescued by the Glorious Protestant Revolution.

On the same day McKeague primed SDA members on the Lower Shankill Road, leading an assault on Unity Walk. These mainly nationalist flats, which the Belfast City Corporation had built to replace derelict housing in the Carrick Hill area, were one of McKeague's and the SDA's main targets. Completed in 1967, the flats sat at the junction of Upper Library Street and the Lower Shankill Road, commonly known as Peter's Hill. From the outset, McKeague was incensed that the corporation had 'put rebels on our doorsteps' and said that he organised demonstrations on the Shankill. At the Scarman Tribunal, he argued that Unity Walk represented a vulnerable point on the Shankill and complained that nationalists had received flats ahead of local Protestants: 'these [Catholics] have greatly increased in numbers and [the Corporation] have given this territory over to them completely and these rights have not yet been given to the Protestants'.[69]

Boulton, however, argues that McKeague's real objective in his targeting of Unity Walk 'was the preservation of the Protestant purity of the Shankill by an insistence that redevelopment take place within the existing, time-hallowed borders of the "loyalist" ghetto, and that families displaced be rehoused in the same area'.[70] Sarah Nelson concurs, claiming that unionists also increased their involvement in nascent community organisations like the Shankill Redevelopment Association (SRA), highlighting the insistence of a unionist teacher and SRA member that the call for mixed housing was a republican conspiracy: 'One of our planks was opposition to integrated housing. The RCs [Roman Catholics] had been taking over new districts, like the bottom of the Shankill. What they do is, they get enough votes to elect a nationalist councillor, then eventually an MP ... then gradually they will take over the whole of Northern Ireland.'[71] Exploiting this paranoia, McKeague used the SDA to intimidate the nationalist residents of Unity Walk.

Serious trouble broke out at the flats on 2 August after a Junior Orange march, when loyalists stoned the flats, breaking windows. Eyewitnesses alleged that a man carrying a union flag led a group of loyalists into the courtyard, where hand-to-hand fighting ensued between residents and loyalists. Belfast man Frank McCullagh, a member of the Hertfordshire Constabulary, passed the incident with his wife and recalled that the flats 'were surrounded by a hostile Protestant mob, shouting sectarian abuse, and throwing missiles'.[72]

RUC deputy commissioner for Belfast Samuel Bradley told Scarman that he placed his men just above Unity Walk to stop an angry loyalist mob attacking the complex. He claimed that false rumours had spread among loyalists that nationalist residents had abused children on the Orange march as it passed the flats. He called to the crowd through a loudhailer that the reports were untrue, but 'They did not believe me':

It built up from there. They were coming and coming. They built up a weight of numbers I could not hold. So I directed my men to the best of their ability to seal off the flats and allow no person to enter. At the same time, I [asked] for reinforcements ... This was an angry mob, fully bent on entering Unity Flats, and I knew very well that if they had got in – I was annoyed certainly about the windows which were broken, but I was more annoyed if this crowd had got into Unity Flats there would have been murder.

At the time, Belfast police commissioner Harold Wolseley insisted that there was 'no evidence of an attack on the Orangemen, apart from catcalling'.[73]

McKeague, who had played a prominent role in stirring up trouble throughout July, directed the loyalist mobs in their assault on the Unity Walk flats on 2 August. Indeed, it was believed that he had been the source of the rumours about the fictitious attack on the marching children, and he later admitted to the Scarman Tribunal that he ordered his SDA members back to the flats. Less than an hour later, while police remained present, a mob was attacking the flats with missiles. A crowd emerging from a public house on the corner of Boyd Street and Peter's Hill swelled the mob to over 2,000, which then charged Unity Walk from various directions. A number of loyalists parted from the main body, invading Kent Street and smashing in the windows of nationalist residents. Hours later, a Catholic resident of Chief Street reported to the police that he'd witnessed McKeague inciting a Protestant crowd on the Crumlin Road. Despite an RUC officer's remark that 'we know all about it', no arrests were made and no action was taken. Four hundred loyalists then attacked nationalist homes, burning shops in Chief Street and an off-licence in Ohio Street.[74] Anthony Dunham of Leopold Street witnessed nationalists fleeing before a mob of Shankill loyalists, who chanted 'Burn, burn, burn'.[75] The following day loyalists attacked and beat Dunham himself, whom an RUC officer glibly advised, before the beating, to 'move on'. Some weeks later his wife discovered her furniture for sale in Smithfield Market: their home had been wrecked.

Within the flats complex itself tensions erupted between vulnerable residents and the police, and fighting broke out between residents and the RUC and a number of B-Specials, who had been assigned to bolster the RUC presence at the flats. Frank McCullagh witnessed events unfolding: 'I saw several people dragged out from the flats ... When they came into vision, several officers were using their truncheons, striking those [residents] over the head and over the top of the body.'[76] Catherine O'Rourke told Scarman that a B-Special had attacked her brother, striking him and dragging him, with his clothes torn off, including his anorak and shirt. When she intervened, she too received rough treatment and ended up being thrown into an RUC vehicle. A few minutes later, two more residents joined her, including Patrick Corrie, who was knocked unconscious after a number of truncheon blows to the head. Rather than take him to the nearest hospital, the RUC drove to Tennent Street RUC Station, where they pulled Corrie out first and left him on the ground until, an hour later, he was sent for medical treatment. He remained unconscious until his death several weeks later, with the post-mortem revealing 'three skull fractures sustained, involving five separate areas of brain damage'. The Scarman Tribunal found that 'Mr Corrie died from injuries inflicted by a policeman striking him on the head with a baton', with Scarman insisting that it was 'inexcusable that the Land Rover did not go at once to the hospital'.[77]

The RUC's actions on the day were subject to a stern rebuke from Scarman: 'The entry into the flats by policemen dressed in riot gear, without any apparent necessity and at a time when the flats had been under attack by a Protestant crowd, was open to misunderstanding by residents of the flats, whose only crime [was the] throwing of stones at their attackers.'[78] Although they had seemed reluctant to offend loyalist mobs in mid-July, the fierce violence of 2 August 'put an abrupt end to the RUCs "wink and nod" relationship with SDA militants'.[79]

The Orange Order conducted its own inquiry into the Unity Walk incident, with the *Belfast Telegraph* admitting that even here the Orangemen found 'no evidence of an attack on [the] procession of Junior Orangemen'. This did not impede Martin Smyth, a UUP member, Presbyterian minister, Deputy Grand Master of the Orange Order and chaplain to the Belfast Committee of the Apprentice Boys of Derry, from blaming the trouble of the previous months on 'Republican and anarchist factions whose chief aim was to encourage unrest.' Smyth claimed that when 'Roman Catholic families were moved into Protestant districts, Protestant families often wondered if they were to be moved out of their own localities.' He admitted, 'Some Protestants in certain areas were "going mad", and doing things which in their saner moments later they would regret.'[80]

Despite attempts by some unionist councillors to quell the unrest, McKeague continued to call the shots on the ground. Attempting to explain the depths of rage among his followers, McKeague later told Scarman that 'it was rumoured among the crowd that a tricolour had been displayed and the police had been attacked [by residents] and one had been killed'.[81] During the disturbances of 2 August, egged on by such rumours, loyalists launched 'a full-scale attack' on Unity Walk. The RUC strengthened their force by bringing up armoured vehicles and blocking entrances to the flats to prevent another incursion. Loyalists then turned on the RUC, resulting in police casualties. As we have already seen, RUC Deputy Commissioner Bradley was of the opinion that had the crowd got into the flats 'there would have been murder'. Blocked from assaulting the flats, a mob of around 150 loyalists then attacked nationalists on the Crumlin Road. Arriving on the scene, RUC Head Constable Anthony Owens heard the mob chanting, 'We are the people' and 'Let's wreck the Popeheads'; he believed they were moving on to target nearby Hooker Street.[82]

Anticipating further attacks, the RUC resumed their position outside Unity Walk on 3 August. Bradley estimated that a crowd of 300–400 loyalists constructed barricades on the Shankill, attacking police lines with bricks, stones and petrol bombs. He told Scarman that the viciousness of these attacks on the police was connected with police baton charges the night before. A barrier-breaking vehicle, a water canon and Land Rovers were used in an attempt to disperse the crowd, which responded with more stones, petrol bombs and sticks of gelignite. Bradley led at least four charges against the crowd.[83] An outraged McKeague claimed the RUC 'baton charge came as a surprise to the Protestant people – in many cases it is the Protestants who have got the rough hand of the law.' Rioting intensified, with 200 RUC men facing off against more than 3,000 loyalists intent on laying siege to Unity Walk. Amid the violence, Paisley's assistant, Major Bunting, approached the police, assuring them that if they withdrew to the side roads, 'I will go back and try to get this crowd to disperse.' Bunting was rebuffed by District Inspector Gilchrist, who recalled that he 'had seen the mood of this crowd [and] had no intention of withdrawing my men'. According to Gilchrist an elderly man then approached him and claimed that 'they are going to attack the flats, and some have gone to get their guns'.[84] Many residents, terrorised and with their homes destroyed, had already fled for their safety.

McKeague and the SDA then turned their attacks on the RUC. McKeague boasted to the Scarman Tribunal that:

> They brought up their armoured cars and proceeded to batter into the barricades ... Then when the barricades were broken down the people spread into the side streets and every armoured car that went up and down that road received a battering. Both from the right and the left of the road. Then the police seemed to be mounting an ambush in that they were coming down from the top of the road and immediately people went to that area to stop this happening and as the night wore on there was an incident when an armoured car was proceeding over the cross section at Agnes Street and Shankill when what seemed to be a banger of some description went off and I think it cooled them down and after that everything ceased.[85]

McKeague was correct in claiming that rioting halted after the attacks on RUC armoured cars. However – as he is likely to have known – the devices thrown at the armoured cars were not 'bangers' but gelignite blast bombs. The RUC confirmed that blast bombs thrown from side streets had damaged a Humber armoured vehicle and a Land Rover. Later that evening, the RUC discovered a quantity of gelignite sticks and detonators in Marlborough Street. Few accounts published since emphasise the point that it was loyalist extremists who perpetrated the first bomb attacks on the RUC on 3 August 1969.

McKeague led a delegation to RUC headquarters demanding the removal of the force from the Shankill, explaining that he took refuge in a house belonging to an SDA member because the police were driving recklessly in the side streets of the Shankill. 'It was intimated to the police that the people of the Shankill Road did not want any member of the RUC on the road after what happened,' he testified before Scarman, 'and we got the information through to the authorities that we were not having the RUC on the road, they would be in danger of their lives.' The SDA issued a bitter warning. 'Never again,' Boulton observes, 'would the people of the Shankill have any confidence in the RUC – whose proper duty, it seems, was to stand by and watch the loyalists dismantle Unity Flats brick by papish brick'.[86] McKeague wanted the B-Specials and his SDA to replace the RUC. Paisley and the *Protestant Telegraph*, however, declared their full support for the RUC. Paisley also led a delegation to the Minister of Home Affairs, Robert Porter, calling on the minister to deploy the B-Specials in strength in order to restore public order. Among its other effects, the tinderbox of tensions was generating sharp tensions between rival loyalist factions.

The truth is that Paisley's apparent change of heart reflected his desperation to seize on an issue that could be seen to distinguish his UCDC from McKeague's SDA. He was becoming uncomfortably aware of the growth of a rival 'loyalist' leadership on his right flank.

The UCDC issued a terse statement declaring that it and the UPV 'wish to state that the Shankill Defence Association is in no way connected with them, and that John McKeague in no way represents either the views or policy of our movement'.[87]

This was the context in which an extraordinary situation developed in the early hours of 4 August on the Shankill Road. Five separate organisations patrolled the Shankill: B-Specials, the SDA, the Orange Order, the Royal Black Preceptory and – until McKeague demanded their removal – the RUC. Head Constable Kyle told the Scarman Tribunal that he and Detective Inspector (DI) McGimpsey 'walked up the Shankill Road and we spoke to members of the USC and members of the Orange Order', who realised 'they had been used by the hooligan element for the purpose of either getting their own back at the police or looting'.[88] Deputy Commissioner Bradley praised the Orange Order, which, he recalled, 'came out wearing their collarettes and patrolled the Shankill Road each night to prevent any incidents as far as possible'.[89]

Following two days of loyalist violence and destruction, large swathes of the Shankill lay in ruins, with almost every shop attacked and many looted. 'In some cases children were seen handing out goods of all kinds – from groceries to furniture. Small boys climbed into broken shop windows and handed out goods, which were carried off mainly by women.'[90] Unsurprisingly, McKeague blamed the looting on nationalists, claiming that 'as time wore on it seemed to be organised. Many of the cars were seen to leave the area and proceed across the main artery of the Shankill Road towards the Falls area and towards the Crumlin Road.'[91] Curiously, the SDA issued a statement directly contradicting McKeague's bizarre claims, condemning the 'looting of premises by so-called loyalists' and appealing to the people of the Shankill 'to return looted property'.[92]

In his obsession to expel nationalists from the Unity Walk flats, McKeague had ravaged the Shankill. 'When the devastation of the Shankill Road could be viewed and assessed under "cease-fire conditions" in daylight today,' *The Times* reported, 'it became clear that the damage by the weekend rioting and looting that accompanied it had exceeded anything that could be estimated from behind last night's blazing barricades. Hardly a shop in the mile-long road has a window unbroken.'[93]

From Monday 4 August, McKeague and the SDA seized control of the Shankill and removed the RUC. He later boasted before the Scarman Tribunal of having driven 'up and down the Shankill Road with a loudhailer on the van telling the people to remain calm and that the B-Specials were on the road and as far as we were concerned we had security'.[94] Boulton writes, 'Scores of McKeague's men swapped their crash-helmets and armbands for a police uniform, and long before any IRA "no-go areas", the Shankill became an independent self-policing enclave.'[95] McKeague toured the Shankill from his Wilton Street headquarters, reinforcing the message that they were up against an imminent threat from republicans. '[W]e have been campaigning against the activities of a section in our country who line up with members of the IRA,' he told Scarman. 'It is quite common knowledge that the members of the IRA were in control of the Falls Road area and if we could not term these people as rebels, I do not know what you could term them as.'[96]

McKeague's relentless hyping of the republican threat reinforced the paranoia stirred up by Paisley a couple of years earlier. Through such agitation, substantial numbers of Protestants living in the Shankill came to see their Catholic neighbours as the enemy. His influence could also be seen in the Ardoyne area, inciting many loyalist attacks on Catholic-owned homes. Before 2 August, Tennent Street RUC Barracks had received a series of complaints from Ardoyne nationalists expelled from their homes. Night after night loyalist crowds gathered at Disraeli Street under McKeague's direction, attacking residents in Hooker Street. The RUC formed a barrier in an attempt to prevent loyalist incursions, launching 'baton charges against Protestant crowds trying to enter Catholic territories', with fierce clashes in Disraeli Street, 'where crowds kept forming up and trying to advance through police barricades. Catholic families in nearby Bray Street complained that gangs of Protestants had attacked their homes and tried to set them on fire.'[97] Frustrated with their failure to burn nationalists from their homes, loyalists torched a Catholic-owned bookmaker's shop on the Protestant side of the Crumlin Road.

Early August witnessed the expulsion of more nationalists in Belfast. Loyalists forced the Scott family from their Cosgrove Street home, and the *Belfast Telegraph* reported more than two dozen Catholic families evacuating majority Protestant areas 'to neighbourhoods of their own faith' after being 'driven out by threats of sinister men'.[98] On 4 August loyalists systematically attacked nationalists in Columbia, Rosebank, Bray, Leopold, Oregon, Byron, Palmer, Ohio and Chief streets. Three days of organised violence cleansed the small Catholic population from the Shankill side of the Crumlin Road.

The RUC at Tennent Street received appeals for protection from isolated nationalists and owners of licensed premises. Catholic-owned pubs became conspicuous targets for loyalists, with attacks focused along the Crumlin Road in North Belfast. Toner's off-licence at Cambrai Street had been attacked on 2 July and took more damage on 2 August when a mob surrounded the premises chanting 'Fenians get out'; the RUC was compelled to withdraw for their own safety and the premises was burned to the ground. The same day, loyalists attempted to loot and burn McMahon's in nearby Bray Street. At Hillview Street barman Bernard Gormley found himself confronted by a 100-strong loyalist mob, led by an acquaintance who ordered him to close his premises. When Gormley refused, the leader of the gang shouted to the crowd, 'Get him he's a Fenian', but the publican was saved from serious assault when Protestant neighbours came to his aid. The crowd lingered, however, threatening Gormley – in the presence of the RUC – that 'If you don't close down we'll be back and burn you out.'[99]

Between 2 and 16 August, loyalists either damaged or destroyed every Catholic-owned licensed premises in the area. On the north side of the Crumlin Road only the Protestant-owned public house managed by A. McCann and Company remained. It stood directly opposite the ruins of the Catholic-run Alderman Bar.

After getting away with the attacks on Unity Walk and winning the battle for supremacy between the SDA and the RUC on the Shankill, McKeague felt confident enough to be able to dictate terms to the beleaguered residents of Unity Walk. SDA vice-chairman Fred Proctor arranged a secret meeting at the Kensington Hotel between the SDA, led by McKeague (and including Mina Browne), and a delegation of residents from Unity Walk. McKeague demanded that nationalist residents be removed from the front block of flats (to be converted into an office block) and from the flats facing the Shankill, where they would be replaced by loyal Protestants. Regarding the latter, McKeague was concerned that 'if there was any flag waving from that particular area it would be the flag of the country, the Union Jack'. The Unity Walk representatives rejected the proposal, advising the SDA that they would get 'not one stone in Unity Walk Flats'. What remains intriguing about the entire negotiation, however, is that McKeague had been granted an audience with Unionist Prime Minister Chichester-Clark just before the 'negotiations'.[100] McKeague claimed that he fully informed Chichester-Clark 'what we were going to do and what our intentions were', and that his plans had received the Prime Minister's 'blessing'.[101] In the whole history of the Northern Ireland state there can hardly be a more revealing example of the collaboration between street-level extremists and the ruling Orange elite. On 6 August Chichester-Clark gave a broadcast in which he condemned sectarian attacks and hoped 'that many of those concerned can be made amenable to the law'. But just before his appeal he had met with McKeague and the SDA, the main instigators of the violence and intimidation in Belfast.

The final irony of course is that throughout the period, Stormont ministers were doing their best to convince the world media that the deepening crisis was the fault of the IRA, which, they insisted, was planning attacks on the state.

Tensions escalated steadily after the confrontation at Unity Walk. Paisley's plans for a protest march in Newry on 16 August only added to the strain, though it was overshadowed by a looming confrontation in Derry, where the annual Apprentice Boys' march was scheduled to take place on 12 August. James Callaghan, grasping the severity of the crisis and the likelihood for an explosion, sought to prohibit all future marches, but he was restrained from doing so by Chichester-Clark, who convinced him that preventing the Apprentice Boys' Parade from going ahead would produce outrage among loyalists, 'ruin him politically and ensure that he was succeeded by Brian Faulkner, who was even further to the right'.[102] As Brian Feeney rightly points out, 'Unionist leaders don't "pander" to the worst elements in their community. They provide the model for the worst elements.'[103]

AUGUST 1969: TENSION BUILDS TO BOILING POINT

Although Shankill Road residents suffered the same appalling conditions as their nationalist neighbours, this shared social disadvantage did not automatically engender much political solidarity, and in the context of growing sectarian polarisation could be exploited by demagogues. 'To the Shankill tenant watching Divis Flats being built from his [*sic*] rat-infested house,' one study notes, 'it seemed traditional [unionist] leaders were not even sharing their new-found wealth, but giving it all to the traditional enemy, the "rebels".'[104] As summer turned to autumn in 1969, Paisley's incendiary bombast both reflected and dramatically heightened such loyalist anxieties.

This volatile situation was exacerbated by John McKeague's leadership of the SDA, which shattered any enduring goodwill there may have been amongst the marginally mixed working-class enclaves perched between the Shankill and the Falls Road in West Belfast. McKeague effectively fanned the flames of sectarian antagonism in some of the most impoverished interface areas in North and West Belfast. More than any other individual he was responsible for masterminding a terror campaign against innocent men, women and children – both Catholic and Protestant – in the process creating a human displacement crisis on a level not seen in Belfast since the early 1920s.

Aggravating matters was the RUC's failure to check the ascent of the SDA. The police chose repeatedly to remain passive in the face of escalating scenes of sectarian violence and criminality. Despite the fact that many local police officers faced loyalist intimidation, between April and August 1969 senior RUC officers in North Belfast continually appeased McKeague and his boisterous mobs, turning a blind eye to expulsions along the interfaces, and in some cases callously dismissing individual cries for help. Likewise, Stormont ministers, including Prime Minister Chichester-Clark, issued public condemnations of sectarian violence while at the same time facilitating closed-door negotiations with McKeague and other loyalist extremists.

Paisley's provocative declaration before a 2,000-strong loyalist crowd on 5 July in Bessbrook that he would march on the mainly nationalist town of Newry on 16 August intensified fear still further. 'Let me tell you, friends, he who laughs last laughs longest. The day for the Protestants to take over the town of Newry has come and, as the Orangemen took over Dungiven, we shall take over the town of Newry.'[105] By early August Paisley had become the Pied Piper of

Protestant extremism. On 2 August, the day of the McKeague-led assault on Unity Walk flats in North Belfast, he published a chilling and calculated threat: 'Ulster as a Protestant political unit will be the scene of events worse than those of 1912, 1920s, 1930s and the 1950s,' his *Protestant Telegraph* insisted. '[W]e await armed and premeditated. "Armed and premeditated".'[106] Simultaneously, McKeague was leading his own devoted followers around the Shankill in the same direction.

McKeague had learned from Paisley how to organise and exploit sectarian fears; he now sought to employ this experience in energetically promoting and egging on the most extreme sectarian elements. 'I was on the streets every day, every evening,' a former UVF member recalled about this period. 'McKeague told a street meeting that "papishers" in their midst should be given a one-way ticket to the Republic.'[107] SDA members toured the Shankill area, identifying and then marking Catholic-owned homes with sectarian graffiti. Once branded, McKeague directed the evictions – looting and destroying targeted homes and the meagre possessions they held. RUC indifference to the ongoing evictions directly encouraged the SDA to develop a policy of rehousing Protestants in homes from which Catholics had been expelled. Turning a blind eye to McKeague's nightly parades, where he incited Shankill residents against their nationalist neighbours, RUC commanders in Tennent Street Barracks couldn't muster a response when, repeatedly, McKeague toured the area on the back of a pick-up truck, using a loudhailer to canvass support, and ignored his incendiary street-corner oratory, often laced with threats. McKeague's nightly addresses warned against imminent attack from the Falls Road, swelling the ranks of the SDA and stoking fear and outrage across the wider Shankill area. Local B-Specials paraded nightly, adding to the climate of paranoia and anxiety that would later fuel a sectarian purge.

On 5 August, the Ardoyne Citizens Action Committee sought

aid from the Andersonstown Housing Action Committee to re-house refugees. Gerry Fitt, MP, claimed that the UVF had expelled twenty-one nationalist families from their homes. A member of his audience claimed that 'the RUC had become the message boys of the UVF and had accompanied Paisleyite extremists when they visited Catholic families to order them out'.[108] Loyalists warned a woman in Leopold Street: 'If you [and your daughters] are not out inside an hour you will be shot.' When she sought help from two RUC officers who witnessed the threat, they advised her 'that it would be better for her to leave'. For Fitt, this incident highlighted the collapse of authority: 'We have two members of the RUC whose duty it is to protect its citizens, standing by and hearing a murder threat without taking action whatsoever against either man. This certainly proves my point that law has completely broken down in the North.'[109]

Despite a statement from Belfast's RUC Commissioner, Harold Wolseley, that the police were committed to 'protect[ing] the lives and property of the citizens', sectarian attacks in the areas dominated by McKeague continued unabated. Fearing for their lives, disabled woman Mrs McAlea and her daughter fled their Rosebank Street home. Similarly, a loyalist mob intimidated Mrs Leeson and her four children from Ruth Street. Mrs Liddle fled her Earl Street home, recalling that 'once a brick came through her living room window she had to go'. Mr and Mrs Marshall were attacked at home in Rathlin Street by a group of loyalists.[110] The same happened to the McMillans in Oregon Street, who were told by two RUC officers as they fled that they had 'better get out because they could do nothing'. By 7 August over sixty families were seeking re-housing.[111] The Sharpe family took flight from their Ballymena Street home when three cars pulled up outside and told them to 'get out or you will be burned out'. The RUC could not help as 'they had no time'.[112]

In many cases Protestant neighbours and friends were horrified by the purges, but felt powerless to intervene. Loyalists who expelled seventeen Catholic families from Columbia Street also threatened Protestant neighbours who objected. 'We asked for police help against the eviction gangs who came from another area, but they were unable to provide it. The gangs told me that I would be burned out if I tried to help the Catholics.'[113] One Leopold Street resident wrote to the *Belfast Telegraph*, 'As a Protestant I am ashamed of people who call themselves Protestants after what I witnessed in Leopold Street, where I have resided for the past twenty-five years – people being evicted from their homes on the Sabbath day by a mob singing party tunes. Has the law lost all control that it cannot afford such unfortunate people protection?' Another resident declared she was 'ashamed to call myself a Protestant. What has become of the Protestants of the Shankill after the disgusting events of the past weekend? I can only say I am truly ashamed to call myself a "Protestant". It is a sad day for Belfast that her name should be blackened in the eyes of the world by the hooliganism and brutality I witnessed on Sunday.'[114]

One Protestant, who had known McKeague on a first-name basis, seemingly accepted the reality of loyalist intimidation:

We had Catholics living in our street and I got on with them fine. They had a wee laddie about the same age as mine and they played together. My lad was always in their house and they would come into us. When the trouble started, they got a couple of bricks through their windows and there was a mob gathering outside. I didn't recognise them. I went to get John [McKeague] and said, 'You've got to come up. There's a house with kids in it that's going to be burnt out.' And he came up and talked to the men and we stopped them burning it. They moved of course, but they didn't get hurt.[115]

The evictions continued, with one Catholic man [who wished to remain anonymous] describing his family's terrifying experience: 'We were determined to stick it out until we saw the crowd coming up the Shankill Road. There must have been thousands; the street was black with them. Our Protestant neighbours are heartbroken to see us leaving,' he added. 'But what could they do? Those who helped were threatened.'[116]

The Civil Rights Association held a meeting in Andersonstown on 8 August that censured the RUC for its 'passive acquiescence in the face of serious crimes during last weekend's disturbances'. The police had 'failed to give protection to people threatened ... Although many people had appeared before the courts for looting [shops on the Shankill], the people guilty of intimidation, threats to murder and arson had not been charged.'[117] Indeed, while the numbers of refugees surged, Stormont ministers and senior RUC officers at Castlereagh remained ambivalent about the escalation of violence developing across North and West Belfast. Despite widespread print media coverage, one RUC officer claimed that from 1 July until 12 August 'he had no experience in the district of "actual and real intimidation". He was, however, aware of rumours going around.'[118]

It was entirely predictable that the crunch would come at the Apprentice Boys' march on 12 August, when, after recurring clashes in Derry since October of the previous year, thousands of Orangemen from all over the North came to parade through the city and around the walls overlooking the nationalist Bogside. The occasion was a direct celebration of the Ulster plantation and of Protestant ascendancy, serving as a yearly reminder to Derry's nationalist majority that they were not the masters even of their 'own' city.[119] Chichester-Clark's refusal to ban this march demonstrated the centrality of the Loyal Orders to official unionism. The governor of the Apprentice Boys, Dr Russell Abernethy, insisted that 'It would be a crime against the memory of the Apprentices and the continuity unbroken ever since, to interfere with the procession.'[120]

Despite the increasing volatility of the situation and in the face of pressure applied by Harold Wilson's British government, the RUC had continued throughout the late summer of 1969 to uphold the loyalist prerogative. As a result, when the day of the scheduled march arrived, one-third of the entire police force, fully equipped with armoured vehicles, assembled on the edge of Derry's Bogside to enforce a loyalist march. Thousands of Apprentice Boys and loyalists descended on Derry, a town with such high unemployment that it perhaps best epitomised the undemocratic nature of the Northern Ireland state. Tensions were already raw in the run-up to 12 August, but the arrival of McKeague and the SDA on the scene almost guaranteed that violence would erupt.

Seeking to expand his influence and to spread the sectarian polarisation out beyond Belfast, on the morning of 12 August, McKeague travelled along with 140 SDA members to Derry to observe the Apprentice Boys' march. On arrival, they went to William Street and, having taken photographs, continued on to Waterloo Place – a short distance from the Bogside – where they met with members of Paisley's UPV and other loyalists. Waterloo Place had 'been the scene of fierce clashes between youths and police', and in nearby Bishop Street sharp confrontations had taken place between 'Roman Catholic and Protestant mobs'. McKeague later told the Scarman Tribunal that he and his men left Derry before the violence erupted. When he arrived back to the Shankill, a supporter informed him that nationalists in Derry had rebelled and were attacking the police. McKeague was outraged, claiming 'what had happened in Londonderry could certainly happen in Belfast'. He quickly convened a meeting at his Wilton Street headquarters, where it was agreed that SDA vigilantes should be equipped with firearms and that the organisation would 'compile a register of local people with gun licences, and anyone with any legal shotgun was asked to have this available to stop infiltration into the area.'[121]

'A TRUE LOYALIST'

Between April and August 1969, a dramatic reorganisation had been imposed on the Shankill Road. Under the guise of 'defence,' McKeague had armed and mobilised the growing ranks of the loyalist SDA. Playing on unionist fears, through public and private speeches and malicious sectarian rumour McKeague systematically incited attacks by one part of the city's working class on another. He generated fear, panic and division among many living on the Shankill, which in turn produced violence that irreparably damaged the area's commercial life.

McKeague declared himself a true loyalist and an upholder of the reformed faith – in the service of his queen, country and constitution. Nevertheless, he repeatedly undermined unionist prime ministers, condemning leniency towards nationalists and any tendency towards reform that might benefit the working classes across the divide. He targeted the RUC when they belatedly attempted to defend innocent nationalists and accused the force of disloyalty – and of brutality against his supporters – when they intervened, belatedly, to prevent a bloodbath at Unity Walk. He demanded, and Chichester-Clark granted him, the RUC's removal from the Shankill.

The paradox deepens when McKeague returned from Derry only to be informed that nationalist youth were now involved in rioting against the police – the same RUC his mobs had attacked and attempted to murder just days before. Now he executed an abrupt about-turn, denouncing Derry's Bogsiders for treachery and rebellion for their attacks on the very same force. He and his men intimidated both Catholic and Protestant neighbours from their homes, shattering lifelong friendships. Within several weeks of his arrival on the Shankill, he turned neighbours against one another and orchestrated the burning of nationalist-owned homes and businesses. Finally, all of this took place in open view and with the full knowledge of the whole of the Northern Ireland state apparatus. Neither Stormont ministers nor senior RUC officers seemed to have the stomach for containing the rapidly escalating sectarian tensions. Northern Ireland was caught in a downward spiral, and by the middle of August nationalists in Ardoyne and the Falls had paid a heavy price.

3

DERRY IN THE EYE OF THE STORM

Belfast was not the only city suffering in the summer of 1969. In Derry, the Orange Order marches in July brought yet more strife and misery to the city's nationalist community. Attacks on nationalist-owned homes before, during and after the march, and the subsequent clashes between the RUC and nationalist youths demanded a community response. Ahead of the upcoming Apprentice Boys' march on 12 August, meetings were held throughout Bogside and Creggan between nationalist representatives and residents to find common ground in defusing the threat of violence descending on the nationalist community. On 20 July the Derry Citizens Defence Association (DCDA) was established, consisting of a committee of forty, many of whom had migrated from the previously established Derry Citizens Action Committee (DCAC) which had been set up after the assault on civil rights marchers in the city on 5 October 1968. Seán Keenan, the newly elected chairman of the DCDA, explained to Scarman why the organisation was established and outlined its main objectives:

> Since 5th October inevitably the troubles always seem to get into the Bogside and people were beaten back into the Bogside there and the people of that area suffered a great deal. They had their windows smashed. They had their doors kicked in. They had beatings. I think it shows what the patience of the people of the Bogside area was when it was not until the 20th [July] that they decided to set up a Defence Association ... Meetings were held all over the Bogside area and the

Creggan area and we appealed to the people to keep the peace …and [organise] defence.[1]

Meanwhile, nationalist residents subjected to sectarian attacks in Naylor's Row demanded assistance. According to John Hume 'quite an amount of damage had been done to their homes. They showed me the stones [that] had broken their windows … the roof in one house broken and one lady [said] she had opened her door and stones had come through and struck her …'[2] The curate at St Eugene's Catholic church, Fr Vincent Mulvey, recounted a telephone discussion between himself and the manager of Derry's Development Commission on the issue on 16 July, in which he'd emphasised 'that they had a serious problem in Naylor's Row; the residents there had complained about attacks on their homes in the past, the most recent being on the night of 12 July.[3] Mulvey emphasised the danger to residents ahead of 12 August. 'The general fear, so far as I could assess it, was that some strangers in the city would endeavour to cause trouble for the Bogside people.'[4] As a result, the Housing Association made available apartments in Clarendon Street, accepting five families from Naylor's Row.[5]

In his evidence to Scarman, the Westminster Labour MP Kevin McNamara conveyed the palpable fear in Derry's Bogside surrounding the Apprentice Boys' march on 12 August 1969, particularly for residents living on its fringes, where numerous homes were secured with hardboard, planks and wire. The Apprentice Boys had demanded their march; now the nationalist majority of Derry feared the consequences. According to John Hume several residents had 'received anonymous letters before 12 August threatening that they would be burned out'.[6] Residents in Eglinton Place also sought help, and in the run-up to 12 August organisers 'had to put stewards on there at night to satisfy those people that they would not be touched'.[7] McNamara claimed that this anxiety represented a 'fear, based upon past events, of what might be the conduct of the police if they entered the Bogside ... [Residents] spoke about events in January and the fear they had that they would be subject to the same sort of treatment.'[8] Many nationalist residents on the edges of the Bogside fled their homes, afraid of impending attacks.

The loyalist and police presence in the Maiden City only heightened nationalist insecurity. Bernadette Devlin explained to Scarman:

> If I could have understood any legal reason or human reason why the police wanted into the Bogside, if I could have seen any reason why the police should have been there, it would have been quite easy to an extent for the police to come in if they had behaved like a police force, and if they had formed up as policemen and simply walked as policemen through the barricade. If they had done that in the very beginning way back in January people would have looked on them at least as a police force. Behaving as they did, just storming up to the barricade trying to hit whoever they could and hurling abuse across at people, they were treated for what they behaved like, just ordinary hooligans who were attacking the area in which people lived. Therefore people felt that it did not matter whose Royal Ulster Constabulary they were; they were just a band of people who had a grudge against the Bogside, whose pride had been hurt by the Bogside, whose superiority or reputation had been insulted by the Bogside and they wanted their revenge.[9]

Some 20,000 Apprentice Boys and loyalist followers (including those from the SDA) descended on Derry on the morning of 12 August. According to the RUC, the SDA or 'Shankill Road rough crowd' arrived just after noon 'in a Belfast Corporation bus [and] parked at Foyle Road'.[10] To compound the fears of Bogside residents, thousands of Paisleyites from across the six counties also arrived. The

RUC Inspector General dispatched 700 men to the city – 'a fifth of the entire full-time strength of the police in Northern Ireland'.[11] This force was augmented by the almost wholly Protestant Police Reserve of 300 men, equipped with armoured support vehicles and water cannons.[12] The Bogside had had ample first-hand experience of RUC brutality since the NICRA march of 5 October 1968. Lord Cameron later found, for example, that during one police incursion into the area in January 1969, 'a number of policemen were guilty of misconduct which involved assault and battery, malicious damage to property ... giving reasonable cause for apprehension of personal injury among other innocent inhabitants, and the use of provocative sectarian and political slogans'.[13]

Predictably, violence erupted on 12 August when young people from the Bogside clashed with loyalists in the city centre. Although the General Committee of the Apprentice Boys had pledged to control its members, just in advance of the march 'a few Apprentice Boys tossed coins from the City Walls towards small knots of [nationalists] below. It was a gesture of contempt,' Scarman acknowledged, 'which can only have inflamed feeling in the Bogside.'[14] One witness told Scarman, 'I saw pennies thrown down by men who were obviously taking part in the parades who were wearing Orange sashes and wearing bowler hats.'[15] In the early afternoon a crowd of loyalists marched on Butcher's Gate and proceeded to confront a nationalist crowd. Bogside teenagers reacted by throwing stones, and these missiles were then returned. Leading a contingent of nationalist volunteers, John Hume and Eddie McAteer failed in an attempt to contain the situation. Seán Keenan later pointed out that they had great difficulty in recruiting parade stewards after many of them had been assaulted by police in July: '[T]hese stewards had been batoned and hosed and eventually they just dropped away, they could no longer stand it. They said, "What's the use of trying to steward here, you're just treated as troublemakers."'[16]

As the march proceeded towards Butcher's Gate, police officers and a loyalist mob co-operated in an attack on nationalists. Seemingly unconcerned with the gathering of an angry loyalist mob to their rear, the RUC Reserve Force (RUCR) charged nationalist youths, chasing them into the Bogside. A further platoon of RUCR members was then dispatched into Waterloo Place. At 3.30 p.m. '[s]ome Protestants emerged from Great James Street and, as the police withdrew into Sackville Street, an exchange of stone-throwing developed between the two groups of young men'.[17] Thirty minutes later, five armoured Land Rovers and an additional cohort of RUCR arrived.

'The supporters of the Apprentice Boys now became restless,' Scarman later concluded, 'a considerable crowd of them gathered in Guildhall Square and began throwing stones.'[18] A British Army Intelligence Officer claimed that this continued for two hours.[19]

By five o'clock, a Humber armoured vehicle had demolished a makeshift nationalist barricade in Little James Street, and an RUC baton charge followed close behind. When the RUC advanced into William Street towards Rossville Street, 'some [Protestant] civilians accompanied them, throwing stones and using catapults'. Indeed, Scarman found, some police actually encouraged this behaviour, while others 'were themselves throwing stones'.[20] The armoured vehicle then drove through several streets, demolishing small barricades as it went, which only exacerbated nationalist anger against the RUC. 'Against orders from HQ, the RUC made their first charge into Bogside, followed by a Protestant mob.'[21]

Despite the 'reservations' of RUC County Inspector Mahon, the RUCR District Inspector William Hood sent a further 200 reservists to the edge of the Bogside.[22] At approximately 7 p.m. they assembled in the company of hundreds of loyalist civilians. Moments before the police armoured vehicle blasted through the quickly assembled barricade, police radio transmissions intensified between commanders on the ground and those overseeing the operation from Victory Barracks. One RUCR commander, clearly agitated, claimed 'he had approximately 200 men [and] *enough supporters* to eat that place' [emphasis added].[23] He went on to urge an aggressive incursion: 'Let's go into Lecky Road and polish them off … Let's go in and polish them off.'[24] The *Sunday Times* Insight Team described the situation precisely:

> Around 7.15 p.m. on the evening of 12 August the police attempted to penetrate the Bogside. It transformed the disturbances from being an incident engaging a handful of police and a few youths into a war between the residents of the Bogside and the RUC. It represented an attack which the residents had feared and for which they had prepared ever since the police incursions of 4 January and 5 April – on the last of which Samuel Devenney and his family had been beaten. And the police behaviour was reminiscent of those two previous 'raids'. They were shouting 'IRA scum' and 'Fenian bastards' as they began their charge, and they batoned several bystanders, including a uniformed first-aid man.[25]

The bitter sectarianism permeating the ranks of the RUCR exploded in an orgy of punitive violence directed against the Bogside. Residents watched in horror as armoured vehicles rampaged along footpaths into Rossville Street and Lecky Road attempting to run down locals, including Eddie McAteer, MP. 'I could see … members of the RUC and civilians, some of whom were waving Union Jacks,' one resident recalled. 'Now the civilians … were coming in amongst the police. They were chanting: "We are, we are, we are the Billy Boys".'[26] *Guardian* journalist Harold Jackson recalled seeing 'three constables searching for stones and handing them to the [loyalist] youths who fired them from their catapults, while two policemen directed the mob towards the nationalist crowd: "Give it to them strong lads" … "At least they are back where they belong" [in the Bogside].'[27]

Scarman concluded there was 'no doubt that a substantial number of men, mostly very young, and of the Protestant faction, followed the police into Rossville Street and threw stones not only at the Bogside crowd but at the maisonettes'.[28]

In desperation, DCDA members gathered and decided to establish a headquarters in Paddy Doherty's home at 10 Westland Street. 'I do not think that I had any great control over events in the Bogside,' Doherty told Scarman. 'That there was a headquarters, that there were people there who would make decisions, I think was known to some people, but certainly not to the general populace.'[29] Dramatic decisions were made, Doherty revealed to the Scarman Tribunal: 'I think we had about £79 and the £79 was given out to buy petrol to prepare petrol bombs. We were also evacuating many people at this stage as well out of the area.'[30]

The fierce response that these punitive incursions into the Bogside provoked have to be understood in the context of a concerted attack by the forces of 'law and order', backed by loyalist partisans, against an unarmed nationalist community. Moreover, this was the third major attack within a year, with the previous incursion having left an elderly man dead at the hands of the RUC. Bernadette Devlin, MP, revealed how police radio communications confirmed the fears of those on the ground: '"I've enough men to settle that place once and for all." Order from HQ: "You will do as you are told." Reply: "I will do what I like."'[31] Photographer Clive Limpkin recalled that it 'wasn't the RUC's stoning or rare petrol-bombing … that shocked [but] their hate that really stunned'.[32] James Gibson O'Boyle, reporting for the small-town Pennsylvania Pottstown *Mercury*, observed RUC armoured cars smashing into Rossville Street, followed quickly by over 100 RUC men and loyalist civilians. He watched as loyalists pelted nationalist homes with stones, breaking windows as they went, after which the mob 'then turned on the photographers calling them "Fenian bastards" and started stoning the photographers'.[33] As residents watched, the RUC combined with loyalists in an attempt to seal off the Bogside. Fr Vincent Mulvey suggested that the episode marked a point of no return for nationalists in Derry:

> I would say that [the assault] brushed aside any hope of moderation or any hope of restoring calm … There was what I would call an apparently complete unanimity in opposition to the police force. In fact, then and later that night, and over the next few days, the determination was so unanimous that I would only regard it as a community in revolt rather than just a street disturbance or a riot.[34]

The Bogside reacted by attempting to repel the attackers with everything at their disposal. As the RUC withdrew from the nationalist crowd in Rossville Street, two of them drew their personal weapons. One RUC constable, watching as his sergeant removed his revolver and pointed it at the nationalist crowd, drew his own piece, shouting, 'Shoot, Sergeant, for Christ's sake shoot'.[35] The Bogsiders withdrew from the armed RUC men for good reason: a month earlier, the police had opened fire with live rounds, wounding one man.[36]

By 7.30 p.m. nationalists from surrounding districts had reinforced the defences in anticipation of renewed hostilities. As the swelling mob of loyalists massed behind RUC lines in Sackville Street, Little James Street and Great James Street – now seething with frustration at their failure to take the Bogside – nationalists quickly erected barricades in anticipation of another assault. The RUC and their loyalist 'supporters' were determined to break through, and such was their determination that the RUC opted to deploy a new weapon that had never yet been used on the streets of the UK – CS gas.[37]

On 11 August, just hours before the Apprentice Boys' march, the RUC Deputy Inspector General, Robert Graham Shillington, had drawn up operational instructions for the use of this gas. An hour before the first salvo of gas was fired on 12 August, Shillington arrived in Derry from Belfast, where he met several district inspectors. He then viewed two burning buildings and a serious riot in Sackville Street. Shillington claimed that 400 nationalist rioters were firing petrol bombs and stones at the RUC, while 200 loyalists threw stones at the Bogside crowd. 'Having made that assessment', he recommended the use of CS gas to the Minister of Home Affairs, Robert 'Beezer' Porter.[38] Just before midnight on 12 August, Shillington ordered DI Hood to direct CS gas solely against the Bogside. The attack that followed – which saw the gas dispersed indiscriminately – engendered widespread panic, as it permeated every home, affecting young, old and disabled alike. Associated Television director John Goldschmidt recalled that 'we filmed the events which led up to the police invasion. It was so frightening I shall never forget it … We had a frightful time filming in the gas. I was sick several times. Eventually we got some masks to protect our eyes.'[39]

The RUC then began throwing gas grenades out of moving vehicles as they penetrated Rossville Street. Bernadette Devlin and John Hume appealed for help to the British parliamentary under-secretary in London, Lord Stonham. Devlin recounted how 'it was just going off pop, pop, pop, pop for about ten rounds, saturating the place. It was also being used as ammunition in itself and fired into the crowd of people.'[40] Stonham and the British Home Office were also being regularly updated by military intelligence on the ground. The British Army had been deployed covertly on the streets ever since the loyalists' short-lived bombing campaign in April. Intelligence officers remained with RUC officers throughout the forty-eight hours of conflict in Derry. Despite witnessing the events on the ground, military advisers failed to intervene.

Before the firing of gas into Bogside, at approximately 11.30 p.m., the RUC had shot retired shopkeeper Dennis Harley as he checked on the safety of his sister-in-law in William Street. Harley had a bullet removed from his buttock.[41] In the same attack another Bogside resident, John Campbell, was also shot.[42] The RUC quickly issued a statement denying that its men were involved in this incident. 'As far as we can confirm,' they insisted, 'there were no shots fired last night by police.'[43] However, forensics later confirmed that both men had been shot with the 9mm bullets used in RUC- and USC-issue Sterlings. Nevertheless Scarman concluded that 'the evidence is too scant to permit any findings as to who fired or in what circumstances'.[44]

It became obvious from an early stage of the invasion into the Bogside that elements within the RUC had lost control and were determined to exact revenge on nationalists. Indiscipline, criminal and sectarian behaviour became the order of the day.

The Knights of Malta had established an emergency hospital in the Candy Corner shop on Westland Street. Dr Raymond McClean recounted how patients 'were certainly showing signs of eye irritation, but many of them were also showing alarming respiratory symptoms, to such an extent that many had to be carried into the treatment area and were almost unable to take a breath at all'.[45] He claimed that the nature of the injuries indicated that CS gas cartridges had struck people directly. 'One patient ... had been hit in the face by a gas canister. I lifted his nose and the entire organ was almost separated from the rest of his face and the bony structure below.'[46] Independent Television News (ITN) reporter Bernard Hatfield claimed 'that tear gas was fired, it seemed to me, at a person rather than into the crowd so it would burst by the person ... they were firing at somebody'.[47] Hatfield could find 'no person with overall control, no person giving the sign that CS gas should be used at a certain time. It seemed to me that they left it to the will of the men with the gun.'[48]

Within forty-eight hours the RUC had fired 1,091 cartridges and 161 grenades into Bogside. The large amount used indicated 'that the police were using it "unnecessary and indiscriminately" ... many of them "seemed to regard their tear-gas pistols as a form of personal artillery".[49] Other members of the press reported a similar experience to Hatfield's:

> Some members of the Ulster police far exceeded strict instructions given to United Kingdom police by the Home Office about the way they could use CS. The gas has never been used before in the UK to control riots ... Dozens of eye-witnesses agree that some police officers were hurling CS grenades and firing cartridges with frenzied abandon ... In some cases they fired directly at individuals, and at one point they caused a panic by firing at a Roman Catholic crowd over the heads of and from behind a Protestant crowd who were attacking with petrol bombs.[50]

The RUC had requested gas from early March 1969. The Ministry of Defence in London urged that CN gas, which the RUC already possessed, should be discontinued, recommending CS gas as a safer replacement. Between 14 and 16 July the British Army instructed the RUCR on the use of gas and respirators. Shillington justified the resort to CS gas on this occasion on the grounds that Bogsiders might otherwise enter the city centre and destroy shops and businesses, and that they threatened the safety of his men. But a week before the Battle of the Bogside, senior RUC officers had reported the worst riots in Belfast in decades – the loyalist attacks on the Unity Walk flats – in which RUC lives had been put in danger. Yet in the face of several consecutive days of burning, looting and the firing of gelignite and petrol bombs at the RUC on Belfast's Shankill Road, no senior RUC officers ordered the use of CS gas on loyalists. The disparity in treatment reinforces the impression that the RUC – including senior officers – were determined to teach the Bogsiders a lesson on the high price of disloyalty. In this, CS gas became one of the main weapons in their armoury. *The* [London] *Observer* noted that:

There appears to have been no attempt in these cases to use just enough CS to disperse the crowds. Yet when, a few weeks ago, the Home Office gave the Royal Ulster Constabulary permission to stock CS in place of its obsolete stores of conventional tear gas (CN), the Stormont Government was asked to give an undertaking that CS would be used 'only in grave emergency and then under strict control'. A 'grave emergency' was defined as a situation in which the only alternative is to open fire. Another issue is the amount of CS used, and how the Ulster police managed to get hold of such enormous stocks. In the past few days, several hundred spent cartridges have been counted lying about the streets ... These quantities appear to have been far in excess of the stocks held by police forces in England and Wales, and are thought to have been obtained from Northern Ireland Army Headquarters.[51]

Justice Scarman identified the seriousness of the dispute over the resort to CS gas, pointing out to Inspector Mahon: 'In some parts of the world C.S. gas is used to put a crowd off balance before you go in and shoot them up ... during its use in Vietnam,' he noted, 'people had died as a result.'[52]

Dr McClean, who had served with the Royal Air Force, testified about the immediate and potential long-term effects on Bogside residents. CS gas 'was basically chlorobenzene and malonic acid. Chlorobenzene is well known in industry as a severe liver, kidney and central nervous system depressant. This increased my worries at the time.'[53] A report in *The British Medical Journal* 'referred to reports of brain, liver and kidney damage following exposure to C.S. gas'.[54] On Wednesday 13 August, McClean attended an emergency meeting at the West End Hall, 'probably over half a mile away from [the entrance to the Bogside] where the barricades were'. Unable to see or breathe properly himself, he identified 'the most urgent thing to discuss' as 'this concentration of gas in the area'.[55] So severe was the intensity of the gas that the meeting was convened elsewhere. Dr McDermott, a GP, confirmed to *The Observer* the impact the gas was having on the community and especially on children: 'As many as 60 and maybe 100 babies living in the areas where the gas was thickest are suffering from diarrhoea, and … this outbreak was very probably caused by CS … All tests done so far rule out any other cause.'[56]

The situation in the first forty-eight hours of the upheaval in Derry shocked the watching world and the Taoiseach of the Republic of Ireland, Jack Lynch, came under intense pressure to issue a forceful public response. Through contact with nationalist leaders, his own Minister for Agriculture, Neil Blaney, supported by an Irish Military Intelligence officer, Captain James Kelly, kept Lynch fully informed of developments on the ground, including the attempted police and loyalist incursions into the Bogside and the area's saturation by CS gas. Bernadette Devlin requested gas masks and urgent medical aid. On Wednesday evening, 'in a move scarcely paralleled in the Republic's history, the cabinet, after a review of all that had happened and was likely to happen in Derry and elsewhere in Northern Ireland, drafted a collective speech for Lynch'.[57] Lynch delivered an emotional address, promising to immediately establish field hospitals close to the border.

While this announcement raised nationalist morale, Stormont re-acted with outrage. Ian Paisley, whose supporters had already played a central role in the Derry violence, immediately announced the mobilisation of his UPV and demanded an audience with Chichester-Clark, calling for more action from the Stormont government.

On 14 August, several hours before the deployment of the British Army, the Bogside defenders were forced to retreat to a second barricade because of the noxious atmosphere. 'The C.S. gas was landing round about the barricades by the new flats. It appears to me that in about a quarter of a second it affected you. The atmosphere was polluted. This is what struck me. You could see it landing and then the next minute you started crying.'[58] The RUC then advanced, occupying the first block of flats to allow them greater access to the whole of the complex; it was unknown to the Bogsiders at the time whether women and children still occupied the flats. From this elevated position, the RUC further saturated the Bogside with gas while continuing to throw petrol bombs both at the nine-storey block of flats and also down into the crowd. Bernadette Devlin told Scarman that when she shouted to an RUC man asking whether there were women and children in the flats, the reply came back, 'We'll burn the bastards out.' She claimed that the policeman taunted her and the crowd by shouting, 'When's the white flag coming out?'[59]

In the Bogside DCAC members Paddy Doherty and local GP Dr McDermott held a press conference to outline the fact that hundreds of marauding Paisleyites, openly supported by the police, had wrecked and burned premises and blanketed the area in a dense fog of CS gas. Nationalists across Northern Ireland watched in horror and indignation; unsurprisingly, fierce rioting erupted in Belfast, Coalisland, Dungannon, Dungiven, Enniskillen, Lurgan, Omagh and Strabane.

In their endeavour to crush the residents of Bogside, the RUC abandoned their responsibility to protect the public, becoming instead an armed sectarian mob. Their subsequent actions allowed a situation to develop where hundreds of 'heavily armed' loyalists, or 'Paisleyites', occupied Derry's city centre and adjoining thoroughfares.[60] One reporter identified the crowd through their Paisleyite 'rosettes' and noted how some 'were armed with cudgels, some had makeshift shields on which the Red Hand of Ulster had been painted, and others wore protective clothing such as crash helmets'.[61] This crowd attempted to burn St Columb's Hall, in the predominantly Protestant Waterside, and the Catholic-owned City Hotel in Shipquay Street, in the process assaulting members of the international media based there.[62] They then began dumping cars displaying southern registrations into the Foyle river and bombarding a local convent with missiles. The mob also attacked the offices of the *Derry Journal* while en route to the edge of the Bogside, where its members acted as reinforcements for the RUC. One RUC head constable recounted how a 200-strong 'Paisleyite' mob 'with their red, white and blue tam o'shanters' marched into Little James Street and threw stones over the heads of the RUC into the Bogside. They 'brushed [the RUC] aside' and 'engaged in stone throwing'.[63] There does not seem to have been any attempt to restrain this mob and, tellingly, the large stocks of CS gas available nearby went unused.

Police officers recorded how 300 gathered 'at the bottom of Great James Street ... chanting Paisleyite slogans, while equipped with helmets, shields and sticks. Their presence caused consternation among the growing numbers of Catholics at the top of the street, who feared an attack on their cathedral, St. Eugene's'.[64] When nationalists gathered at the top of the street, RUC reservists launched a baton charge with assistance from the loyalists massed to their rear. Without warning, the RUC men then fired live rounds into the nationalist crowd, hitting a number of people – including Gerald McDaid, William Joyce and Jack Doherty. John Porter watched an 'RUC man fire up Great James Street' while 'other policemen' started 'pulling out guns and doing the same thing'.[65]

Dr McClean recounted that 'Jack Docherty [*sic*] was brought in [to the hospital], having been shot in the knee ... Another young lad called McDaid [had] been shot in the chest ... many Bogsiders refused to go to the hospital for fear of arrest, but these gun-shot casualties had not been rioting and were happy to go to hospital.'[66] William Joyce, who was shot in the skull, 'saw four police on the left-hand side firing their guns. I saw the flash of the guns from the left-hand side of the footpath where there were four police firing at the crowd.'[67] Despite police denials, Scarman concluded that the injuries had been inflicted by 'bullets of the type issued to police armed with revolvers, [and] that some policemen did fire in the direction of the crowd hostile to them'.[68]

In a separate incident during the early hours of 14 August in Sackville Street, an ITN team filmed an RUC man indiscriminately firing ten to twenty shots at a person who looked out of the window of a building, towards 'where this face was seen'. The reporter claimed that three other RUC men admitted firing shots. He then picked up six spent .38 cartridges and later submitted them to Scarman.[69] However, Head Constable Campbell denied that his men had fired their weapons, despite forensic evidence that three of the shells had 'been fired from the same .38 revolver, which was proved to have been on issue to a policeman on duty in the street at the time. The policeman, having since died, was not available to give evidence.' The cover-up continued. 'Because of this allegation and others there was subsequently a check on police ammunition: no deficiency was found. And no policeman reported that he had fired his weapon – which was his duty to do, if he had.'[70] But even the limited documentary record available through Scarman shows clear evidence of criminality rife in the RUC, and this is confirmed by many independent witnesses – mainly journalists from the south of Ireland, from Britain and beyond.

From its inception, nationalists had viewed the RUC as the armed wing of the Stormont regime, but the events in Derry marked the first time in which nationalist residents had come together in such unanimity to repel the police by force. Normally compelled by the balance of forces to submit, Derry's nationalists bonded together as never before to hold back the forces that were determined to invade the Bogside. They experienced a fleeting euphoria in their rare and unprecedented triumph defending the Bogside, and their sense of having bested their oppressors provoked bitter anger and desperation in the ranks of the RUC, the reserves and the restive, now outraged, loyalist mob.

Aidan McKinney, an eyewitness in Derry, related that loyalists dressed in the unofficial uniform of shield, baton and motor-cycle helmet mixed freely with police 'at the junction of Great James Street and Princes Street. At one time there was a group of individuals going up the street and saying; "That is a Fenian house", and "That is a Fenian house" and somebody right below me was saying "Burn the Fenian bastards out." That was right below this window.'[71] McKinney told the Tribunal how he watched from within clear view as an RUC armoured vehicle reversed into Great James Street and armed the Paisleyites with 'hardboard shields with cords through them and large sticks out of the back of the police personnel carrier'.[72] *Irish Times* journalist Denis Coghlan described an atmosphere marked by intense sectarian hatred as police stood by in the early hours of 14 August watching loyalists looting in Little James Street:

> As we stood there we saw two policemen coming down towards the mouth of the street with a man between them, carrying a man, or dragging him ... the police used their shields to hit him on the head ... there was a civilian ... running alongside the police, and he had a club and I saw him strike the civilian ... As he fell to the ground ... I saw him being kicked by a policeman [and] dragged through the crowd in a semi-conscious condition. There was shouts from the crowd of 'lynch him'... there was a very ugly mood.[73]

On 14 August RUC headquarters called out the B-Specials, 'a move calculated both to enrage and to terrify the Catholic population', as well as police reinforcements and replenishments of CS gas for the next assault on the Bogside.[74] Out of a total of almost 9,000, the USC had 582 men on standby in the surrounding district. Before the general call-up many had already been in action in and around the Fountain area, and had formed part of the loyalist mob, or had at least taken part in the Apprentice Boys' march.[75] This was also the day the decision was made to deploy British troops in Derry after pressure was applied by the Stormont government on Westminster for support.

The general mobilisation of the B-Specials was the last desperate measure of a bankrupt regime. The RUC command structure realised after almost forty-eight hours of extreme violent action that its force was desperately overstretched and unable to prevail against the resistance of the Bogside residents, and that it faced a wider challenge in the form of fierce nationalist protests which had by then erupted across Northern Ireland. Nationalists knew well the violent sectarian history of the B-Specials. At Dungannon, just hours before the general call-up, members of the Kilnaslee USC platoon had fired indiscriminately into a nationalist crowd, wounding two men and a girl.[76] Their deployment onto the streets in a situation of near total collapse of Stormont's authority suggested that there would be no hesitation in deploying lethal force, and nationalists were understandably convinced that they were facing into the abyss.

B-Special adjutant for Derry city, Edward O'Neill, revealed that out of sixty-two B-Specials sent out from their Whitehall Headquarters on the afternoon of 14 August, fifty were armed with batons. 'The remaining twelve had no batons. On the way down to Waterloo Place I understand one of the District Commandants, S.D.C. Norris, called into a certain hardware shop and procured some pick helves …'[77] The Specials' mission was clear and specific: to 'hold the line' between loyalists and nationalists. However, the RUC command's decision to augment its regular forces by positioning the Specials – a force with a well-earned sectarian reputation – in the Fountain area directly bordering the Bogside only compounded the problem: in practice it meant that the loyalist mob was reinforced by a detachment from the B-Specials, and predictably this resulted in fierce attacks on nationalist homes and businesses.

At approximately 4.30 p.m., a sudden attack on nationalist homes and businesses was launched in Bishop Street. A detachment of RUC men from Larne, detailed to 'hold the line', instead allowed invading loyalists to flood the area; the mob was joined by the cohort of B-Specials. One RUC man told the Scarman Tribunal that there was no loyalist crowd at the time – only women, children and a number of youths.[78] But at around the same time *Irish Times* photographer Dermot O'Shea photographed 100 loyalists and a number of B-Specials attacking the nearby Long Tower Road.[79] The mob set fire to homes before petrol-bombing Catholic-owned businesses in adjoining Bishop Street.[80] William Hippesley recounted that he fled his home and business under a hail of bricks before the premises and the adjoining Barr's pawnshop, Heggerty's Drapers and McConnelly's, were petrol-bombed.[81] Police supported by an armoured vehicle then gassed a nationalist crowd that had assembled a short distance away.[82] Despite the official attempts to deny culpability, the evidence that a loyalist attack was carried out in collusion with RUC members seems irrefutable, with ample photographic evidence and numerous eyewitness accounts to support this finding. Nevertheless, Scarman concluded that the 'course of events in Bishop Street is not absolutely clear. During the afternoon some five buildings, all owned or occupied by Roman Catholics, were set on fire ...'[83]

The British Army arrived at the Bogside around 5 p.m. and determined to establish a peace line between the Fountain and Bogside. When this happened the RUC requested reinforcements of local B-Specials to occupy the Fountain area. One B-Special sergeant – who had himself taken part in the Apprentice Boys' mobilisation two days earlier – openly acknowledged the overlap between B-men and the loyalists, claiming that it was understood that 'as we men know the people who were gathered on Fountain Street we were to try and contain them'.[84] It was completely predictable that, far from containing them, USC men ended up mingling with their loyalist neighbours in the mob: this particular sergeant was photographed among the loyalist crowd talking to fellow residents of Eglinton. He later acknowledged that the Specials made no arrests in the Fountain, as 'we would have been attacked, this crowd would have turned hostile to us'.[85] Photographic and other evidence suggests another explanation: the B-Specials united with the loyalist mob to stage attacks, including the destruction of McMulligan's furniture business on Carlisle Road opposite Lower Fountain.

After the arrival of the British Army, the violence largely subsided, although crowds on both sides remained to observe the military deployment. However, a platoon of B-Specials under the command of an RUC head constable marched from Waterloo Place to the city walls overlooking (nationalist) Fahan Street. An *Irish Times* reporter, Tim Jones, witnessed members of the 'Ulster Special Constabulary throwing stones ... I did not see anything to justify the throwing of stones ... I was walking down Fahan St ... and saw members or some members of the platoon throwing stones into the Bogside.'[86]

Over the forty-eight hours from 12 to 14 August, the nationalist side suffered numerous casualties. Many feared arrest if they presented themselves at Altnagelvin Hospital in Derry and so were transported across the border to Letterkenny Hospital in Donegal. The RUC consequently established roadblocks manned by B-Specials on several arterial routes out of Derry. A twelve-man unit armed with ten .303 rifles and two Sterling sub-machine guns manned a checkpoint at Nixon's Corner on the Letterkenny road, for example. Serious injuries were narrowly avoided there late in the night after the sergeant fired a single warning shot for failure to stop, followed by at least twenty rounds fired indiscriminately from a Sterling sub-machine gun held by another Special on the scene.[87] It later transpired that the car fired upon was carrying medical supplies to Derry. Despite their antics here and in the city itself, Scarman remarked that 'by and large, the USC behaved in a disciplined way.

They certainly helped to restrain the Fountain Street crowd for a time, though in the end a serious riot did develop in Bishop Street.' This language was typical of Scarman: at every juncture he came down on the side of established authority and seemed fixated on rescuing the reputation of the now discredited police. He accepted that the USC were unarmed, claiming 'only their NCOs and officers carried firearms', despite clear photographic evidence showing B-Special constables armed with assault weapons.[88] Clive Limpkin noted this discrepancy, recalling how the B-Specials' arrival brought 'curious looks from the British troops as they march into Strand Road with rifles and sten guns, despite the Scarman's report's assertion that they carried no weapons'.[89]

The Bogside area of Derry consisted of approximately 900 acres, comprising slums and tenements housing a population of approximately 25,000 Catholic/nationalists – about half the total population of the city. A common feature in both the Bogside and another strongly nationalist area, Creggan, was high levels of unemployment, especially among the male population: an RUC inspector reported 'about 4,300 unemployed out of an employable population of about 24,000,' with 'a lot of juvenile unemployment, school leavers particularly'.[90] Over the long period of Stormont rule frustration and bitterness had mounted in Derry, and from the mid-1960s onward it was especially palpable among the nationalist youth of the city. The Cameron Commission concluded:

The weight and extent of the evidence which was presented to us concerned with social and economic grievance or abuses of political power was such that we are compelled to conclude that they had substantial foundation in fact and were in a very real sense an immediate and operative cause of the demonstrations and consequent disorders after 5th October 1968.[91]

Against the backdrop of growing disaffection among nationalists in Derry towards the uniformed defenders of the Northern Ireland state, the rupture that followed 12 August seems almost inevitable. After repeated attempts by police, assisted by loyalist mobs, to take the Bogside, the teeming discontent among alienated young people in the Bogside and Creggan spilled over: they joined with residents to defend their areas, erecting barricades and conducting a fierce defence, animated by the not unreasonable assumption that they were facing an attempt at a pogrom.

Typical of this transformation among young people is the attitude shown by Creggan teenager Philomena Harkin. She had joined the Bogside resistance during the early evening of 12 August, though the dramatic change in her own perspective had been set off some fifteen months earlier. From the first attack on the civil rights demonstrators on 5 October 1968, Harkin's attitude towards the RUC had been transformed. She became increasingly alarmed as she watched residents subjected to invasions and RUC brutality, and was especially moved by the murder of Samuel Devenney. During the defence of the Bogside in August, Harkin joined with men, women and children in manufacturing petrol bombs. With others, she collected money for petrol bought from the nearest filling station, transported crates across the Bogside and assisted in defending the barricades against the combined RUC/loyalist onslaught.[92] When challenged about her conduct by RUC counsel before the Scarman Tribunal, Harkin brushed off the attempt to tag her and her comrades as the instigators of the violence that ensued. 'They had the guns,' she explained, matter-of-factly. 'We had the petrol bombs.'[93]

In *The RUC: a Force under Fire*, Chris Ryder regurgitates the stock narrative on the 'Battle of the Bogside', employing Deputy Inspector General Shillington's evidence to Scarman to exonerate the RUC. 'Shillington was only concerned with holding the interfaces adjoining the city centre businesses and shopping area in case it was petrol-bombed, looted or even burned to the ground.'[94] Ryder ignores the loyalist takeover of Derry city centre and the subsequent looting and violence, and his argument is directly contradicted by testimony from a British intelligence officer called Robbin, who insisted that the Bogsiders showed no inclination towards invading the commercial centre, but throughout the confrontation were reacting to police violence. '[W]hen the armoured vehicle moved forward it was met with a volley of petrol bombs and a volley of stones was thrown at the police and then the crowd moved back. When they saw the police trying to demolish the barricade they tended to regroup ...'[95]

The official version of events ignores the RUC's previous incursions into Bogside, which are crucial to understanding the tenacity of nationalist resistance: the evidence is clear that nationalist barricades were erected to prevent RUC incursions and the violence and destruction such assaults had brought in their train during earlier clashes. Eddie McAteer, the nationalist leader at Stormont, claimed that 'there was almost a fear of extermination, a fear of very great trouble and that the Catholic people of this city would be subject to a lot of violence. I am trying to describe the general state of fear.'[96] Commanding Officer of the 1st Battalion of the Prince of Wales's Own Regiment of Yorkshire, Lieutenant Colonel Todd, was stationed at 'Sea Eagle' in Derry and had observed the violence in the city during July and August. He confirmed to Scarman that, 'Yes, there was this fear, very definitely.'[97] Nationalist violence in Derry was largely reactive, generated out of quite rational and reasonable concerns for self-defence.

Shillington's response to charges of RUC and loyalist collaboration is remarkable and breathtaking in its arrogance where he defends collaboration between members of his force and loyalists. 'Even in this country,' he told Scarman, 'I suppose one finds some civilians who are public-spirited enough to want to help the police.'[98] His statement to Scarman on 2 October 1969 amounts to an artful attempt to dodge the fact, by then almost universally accepted among journalists and other observers from outside Northern Ireland, that the police and loyalists had operated hand-in-glove in violence directed against nationalist communities in Belfast and Derry. Police officers watched as busloads of Paisleyites and SDA members entered Derry days after the latter had led a murderous assault on the isolated Catholic community in Unity Walk, Belfast. Despite the fact that the RUC in Belfast had faced loyalist attack by blast and petrol bombs, the use of CS gas or live rounds in that context was unthinkable. Instead, the RUC surrendered the Shankill to John McKeague and his SDA.

For two days in Derry, loyalists attacked journalists and civilians at will, and burned Catholic homes and businesses. Not only were they unhindered by police, but in many instances it is clear that the RUC helped arm them. Indeed, the RUCR disobeyed direct orders, attacking the residents of Bogside while a loyalist mob egged them on from the rear. RUC and B-Specials opened fire indiscriminately, injuring numerous innocent civilians, employed noxious gas as artillery and subjected the nationalist population to a torrent of vicious sectarian verbal and physical abuse. Nonetheless, safely back in Belfast, Shillington considered the resort to CS gas 'the most humane thing to do'. In direct contradiction to the findings of the October 1969 Report of the Advisory Committee on Police in Northern Ireland, a committee led by Baron Hunt, Shillington eulogised the men under his command:

> In my opinion having seen them on the ground, both their courage and their discipline was of the very highest standard throughout ... If I may say so, I found my few days in Derry in many ways a most exhilarating experience.[99]

In reality – and as is well-known – only the arrival of the British Army brought a temporary end to the reign of terror against the

Bogside residents, perhaps preventing more lethal incursions being contemplated by a police force now seething with frustration at the inability of their firepower to get them into the Bogside. Lieutenant Colonel Todd told Scarman, 'the Bogsiders were very welcoming', and that the 'Army's arrival signalled the cessation of RUC terror.'[100]

Although it constitutes the largest collection of evidence available on these events, we need to approach Scarman's analysis of events with a considerable degree of scepticism. Two things are clear in reading through all the testimony placed before him: first, that senior police were engaged throughout the Tribunal in a cover-up of the failings of the men under their control; and second, that Scarman appeared willing, even eager at times, to indulge them. RUC members closed ranks during the investigation of the shootings; none were ever charged. Incredibly, the RUC armourers' report claimed that not a single .38 police issue round had been spent in Derry.

Yet despite his failure to hold the RUC to account, Scarman was in little doubt as to the event that precipitated the so-called 'Battle of the Bogside': 'The smashing of the barricade, the entry of the armoured cars and foot police, closely followed by Protestant civilians throwing stones, appeared to many as the physical embodiment of their worst fears.'[101]

The RUC and B-Specials connived with the SDA, Paisleyites and other loyalists from the first stone thrown at Guildhall Square on the afternoon of 12 August to the introduction of the British Army on 14 August. Yet, in spite of the world's media witnessing a rampaging sectarian force in Derry over a forty-eight-hour period, the unionist media remained loyal to its force: 'Salute the members of the Royal Ulster Constabulary. For after the way they have handled themselves in Londonderry over the past two days they must be rated the most self-controlled force in the world.'[102]

For the northern nationalist population, by midday on 14 August the RUC could no longer claim to fulfil the role of a civil police force. Its forty-eight-hour siege of the Bogside effectively removed any remaining credibility it might have enjoyed amongst nationalists. On the other side, police of all ranks felt demoralised by the British Army's deployment in Derry, a feeling exacerbated by the Bogsiders' apparent celebrations. As British troops flooded the streets bordering what became known as Free Derry, the reserve force, already en route to Belfast, plotted retribution against that city's nationalists.

4

ASHES TO ASHES: POGROM ON THE FALLS

The Battle of the Bogside exposed the RUC as little more than a uniformed sectarian mob. Over the following seventy-two hours, as a reaction to this, state forces and loyalist extremists wrought death and destruction in Belfast on a scale not witnessed since the pogrom of the early 1920s.

Between eleven o'clock on the night of 14 August 1969 and six the following morning, loyalist mobs attacked and burned nationalist residents from their homes at two separate interfaces between the Shankill and Falls roads, launching fierce incursions into nationalist areas around Divis and Conway streets. As Scarman later concluded, 'during this phase – and indeed at all other times in this area on the night of 14/15 – the Catholic crowd never left their own territory, which [was] "invaded" by Protestants'.[1] Scarman unequivocally identified the loyalist mobs as the aggressors, but his report fell short in its treatment of the security forces, often ignoring direct testimony implicating the supposed forces of law and order in these events.

Through a combination of contemporary eyewitness reports, RUC forensics, radio communications and direct testimony from victims and perpetrators, this chapter offers a close reconstruction of the sequence of events on the first night of the pogrom. On the basis of this large volume of evidence, Scarman's persistent refusal to accept that there was widespread police collusion with loyalists, and also the use of indiscriminate violence, fundamentally undermines his findings. In effect, the RUC and USC facilitated the loyalist pogrom through a wholly disproportionate use of deadly force against the nationalist population of the Lower Falls – a key feature buried in Scarman's findings.

The summer-long campaign of expulsions orchestrated in Belfast by John McKeague and the SDA acted as the essential prelude to the explosion of violence in mid-August. Two days before the Apprentice Boys' march in Derry, the Dean of Belfast, C. J. Peacock, had stated that 'in Ulster, people had not been good neighbours with those who they had disagreed with. They might plead that they had been brought up in that way, that history was behind them, but surely their eyes were open to where such un-Christian-like behaviour led them.'[2] Elsewhere, Methodist Minister Rev. John Turner warned the congregation of Carlisle Memorial church – not far from the scene of other recent expulsions – that 'this is not the time for big parades and demonstrations of political creeds. Instead, it is a time honestly to examine our own hearts and ask: Have I contributed in any way to this situation?'[3] These appeals represented attempts to assuage tensions caused by the near-continuous pattern of sectarian evictions in Belfast that summer. However, they fell on deaf ears as loyalists answered with the catch-cry, 'We have to show them who's master.'[4]

On 12 August, loyalists attacked three Catholic-owned public houses in the Crumlin Road area, setting fire to Gorman's and provoking a riot between themselves and nationalist youths. RUC records indicate that at 2 a.m. on 14 August loyalists launched an attack on the tiny nationalist community of Short Strand in East Belfast.[5] In West Belfast, Fr Patrick Egan received threatening calls at Clonard Monastery as he dealt with petitions coming to him from families throughout Belfast expelled before, during and after the Apprentice Boys' march in Derry:

Cases in point were Argyle Street, Ashmore Street and Wilton Street [a warren of streets now on the Shankill side of the peace wall]. It had been said that there were Catholics – who did not live there in big numbers – [who] had left their homes because of threats. Also, there were other areas, of course, in Ardoyne. I have personal knowledge of Dover Street [linking Falls and Shankill]. I think there were three [families] called at the Monastery at an unearthly hour in the morning looking for bed clothing.[6]

Yet despite spiralling violence and intimidation from loyalists, the RUC focused their attention on policing the nationalist community. On the evening of 13 August, the night before the outbreak of serious trouble, approximately 100 nationalist protestors left Divis Street and marched up to Springfield Road Barracks, several plain-clothes police in their midst.[7] Once there, Sergeant Devine refused to accept their petition criticising RUC behaviour in the Bogside and posted heavily armed men at the windows of the barracks, with another on the roof armed with a Sterling sub-machine gun. As the protestors moved off back towards Hastings Street, they met RUC Commer armoured personnel carriers designed for border patrols rather than urban street disturbances. These were accompanied by riot police on foot. A senior police officer ordered the crowd's dispersal and arrest of the 'ringleaders'. Commer trucks then apparently 'drove wildly' into Mary Street, Peel Street and Lemon Street off the Lower Falls, followed by baton-wielding policemen smashing windows in the tiny kitchen houses as they went.[8]

At 10.30 p.m. that night, an armoured vehicle entered Leeson Street off the Lower Falls. A head constable ordered his men to baton charge the gathering crowd, with the vehicle in support. During the charge, someone threw an explosive device and fired several shots at the armoured vehicle. The RUC radioed through to operational HQ in Hastings Street Barracks that they were under IRA attack. In response, Belfast Police Commissioner Harold Wolseley ordered their immediate withdrawal. 'That was the turning point in the whole set-up,' he remarked, 'this was no normal situation and very near a rebellion, a major insurrection.'[9]

The RUC then 'decided to cease police patrols in Land Rovers and re-deploy all forces in [Shorland] armoured vehicles'.[10] This extreme reaction sharply contrasts with the RUC's agreement with John McKeague just two weeks earlier when, after dozens of officers suffered injury from blast and petrol bombs during two days of concerted violence, the police withdrew from the Shankill to be replaced by B-Specials.

In response to the police baton charge, nationalist youths gathered outside Springfield Road Barracks and Sergeant Devine ordered the ten police constables on hand that if 'anyone succeeded in getting over the hoarding intending to invade the station they were to fire for effect'.[11] While stones and petrol bombs were thrown, two policemen claimed to hear shots and then fired eleven rounds, wounding two local young men, Smyth and Carberry. Carberry received a bullet in the neck while crossing Colligan Street [facing Springfield Road Barracks between McQuillan Street and Springfield Road]. Smyth received a gunshot wound in the right hip, which ballistic experts established came from a police revolver.[12] The remaining crowd dispersed under fire from a Sterling sub-machine gun on the barracks roof. Extreme as this police behaviour seemed, it served merely as a warm-up to the main event the following night.

Meanwhile, in the greater Shankill area, McKeague mobilised the SDA, which placed sandbags at the corners of the Crumlin Road opposite Ardoyne. Rather than defensive installations, these positions operated as staging posts for the dreadful attacks that followed over two hot summer nights. The security forces, in the guise of the B-Specials, at best ignored these preparations, but more frequently facilitated them. McKeague boasted:

The men who had said they would come with their legal guns were brought into the area ... these were set up at certain points. Sandbags were set up at Disraeli Street [which had recently witnessed expulsions] about fifty yards on each side down the street. Sandbag emplacements were put up. A mineral lorry was thrown across the road, and crates and things were built up so that they would stop any incursion into the area ... There would be roughly, in all, about six shotguns placed behind these sandbag emplacements with the order to shoot if there was an attack with guns into that street ... There was a quantity of stones, etc., ready behind these barricades, and also a first-aid post had been set up in a house for any casualties ... I had already issued the orders that that area would be defended with whatever we had, and if any incursion into that particular area took place, they were to meet it with everything that they had.[13]

McKeague also had armed loyalists on the streets, primed to shoot nationalists: 'Well, in my estimation, one shotgun in a Protestant's hands is worth anything when the rebels see them.'[14]

The presence of the media clearly undermined McKeague's narrative about loyalist 'defence'. As one *News Letter* journalist, John McRitchie, related: 'My experience ... was you could almost nearly have set up a typewriter and written your story in the middle of the Falls Road, they would not have minded, but let a notebook be seen on the Shankill and you were in trouble.'[15] McKeague's men constituted the backbone of the very loyalist mob that would later invade nationalist districts, in unison with the police, thereby instigating the pogrom.

In addition to the SDA, B-Specials flooded into the Shankill area. 'I was stopped on the Shankill many times that night,' McRitchie recalled. 'Anyone who drove a car up the Shankill that night could expect to be stopped, seven, eight, maybe nine times. There was a road block every quarter of a mile.'[16] The B-Specials' commander in Belfast, Commissioner Wolseley, claimed that 'we put USC out on the Shankill Road at every intersection from Dover Street to Tennent Street to keep the peace on the Shankill Road because we simply had not the [RUC] manpower to do it.'[17] Elsewhere, loyalists continued to threaten and evict: Mr Savage of Mill Road in Whitehouse, just north of the Belfast city boundary, was threatened to either leave his home or be burnt out.[18]

Tellingly, the RUC made no attempt to disrupt loyalist preparations, leaving McKeague in virtual control of large areas. A barricade established in North Howard Street (leading from the Shankill to the Falls) was not removed. 'DI Cushley ... was unwilling to open up another front' and 'regarded [loyalist] activities as defensive and perhaps legitimate'.[19] Nevertheless, an entry in the police log shows that (Catholic-owned) Finnegan's pub at the junction of Cupar and Argyle streets was looted (presumably by loyalists) – hardly a defensive act.[20] In reality, McKeague and the police shared a similar objective – to punish the nationalist community for the audacity shown by their Derry counterparts.

During the early hours of 14 August, McKeague called his men to arms to confront an apparent IRA 'rebellion'. Some hours later, Paisley led a delegation to meet with Prime Minister Chichester-Clark, demanding the mobilisation of the entire B-Special force and the establishment of a Protestant 'People's Militia'. Chichester-Clark replied encouragingly that 'It might come to that.'[21] As Boulton points out: 'Nobody seems to have thought it strange that, despite the gravity of the situation, the prime minister was prepared to sit through the small hours in conference on security matters with a clerical oddity who was the self-appointed leader of a private army of Protestant Volunteers.' But the co-ordination of policing strategy between state officials and loyalist paramilitaries reached back to the very origins of the state. Indeed 'Chichester-Clark had had similar sessions' just a few days earlier, first with Paisley's close associate Major Bunting and then with McKeague.[22]

Paisley's threat to mobilise a Protestant 'People's Militia' clearly influenced the prime minister. On the morning of Thursday 14 August, Chichester-Clark and his minister of home affairs, Robert Porter, together with senior RUC officers, decided to deploy 8,481 B-Specials across the North. RUC Inspector General Anthony Peacock ordered their general mobilisation for 3.50 p.m. This force, bolstering the ranks of the paramilitary RUC and often in combination with legally and illegally armed loyalist mobs, was directed solely against the 'disloyal' community. 'It was as if the Government had declared a kind of fearsome Open Season on Catholics,' as one eyewitness observed.[23]

On the Falls Road rumours abounded as direct threats against nationalist residents intensified. In Conway Street Eileen McGonigle recalled hearing of imminent loyalist attacks from her father, who worked for Wordies Haulage Company in Divis Street and travelled extensively throughout Belfast. Protestant schoolteacher James Sloan, who lived in Fifth Street (close to the Shankill Road) observed that on the evening of 13 August he 'came up the Falls Road and up Conway Street ... and noticed that they [nationalists] were evacuating their houses. The length of Conway Street they were moving out, taking stuff with them and barricading their windows I suppose against attack.'[24] Resident Owen McDonald of David Street, fifty yards from the Falls Road and linking Conway and Cupar streets, recalls that:

> On 13 August, people knew that there was going to be trouble so I shifted my family over to my mother-in-law's in Panton Street [across the Falls Road]. I brought the furniture out. Then shortly afterwards the house was burned. There were three houses in David Street: Mrs Tierney lived in the first house, we were the second house, and Mrs Hughes was on the other side. This was the second time that both these families were burned out; they were burned out in the 1930s.[25]

On the morning of 14 August corporation binmen threatened Catholics living in Conway Street. 'When the bin-men came to take the bins out at the top of the street, they told the people, put your bins out this morning and we are coming to get youse out tonight.'[26] As fear and panic set in, nationalists began to move their families out of the surrounding streets, including twelve families from Eastland Street.

By mid-afternoon on Thursday tension had reached fever pitch. Throughout the afternoon, Clonard Monastery, a Catholic church situated on the interface at Cupar Street, received a steady stream of threatening phone calls. In the early evening a Protestant from the Shankill visited his Catholic friend, Joe McCann, superintendent of the Falls Road Baths at North Howard Street, to warn that loyalists were manufacturing and storing petrol bombs in Third Street and other streets just a couple of hundred yards away. McCann, who had experienced a previous pogrom in his youth, contacted his supervisors seeking boarding material for his home, and moved his family to Garnet Street for safety. Shortly afterwards, a passing taxi driver informed Detective Sergeant Cardwell 'that there was a large quantity of petrol bombs at the junctions of North Howard Street and Fifth, Sixth and Seventh Streets'.[27]

At approximately 5 p.m., Catholic residents of Conway, Cupar, Norfolk and David streets left their boarded homes behind as rumours of an imminent attack spread like wildfire. Other nationalists with nowhere to flee boarded windows, barricaded doors and prayed the storm would pass. In the early evening, twelve-year-old James Steenson watched his father board up their Norfolk Street home and then run a hosepipe from the scullery in case of firebomb attack. Other Norfolk Street residents used scaffolding poles from a nearby construction site as barricades while loyalist crowds gathered on the Shankill end of Conway and Cupar streets, attacking and looting Finnegan's public house. 'My father came in and stood in the hallway,' Steenson recalled. 'He said, "Sarah take the kids down to their Aunt Bridget's" [in Abercorn Street North].'[28] A short distance away, loyalists attacked nationalists' homes in Argyle and Cupar streets, engaging in hand-to-hand fighting with residents. The loyalists then withdrew, warning that they would be back.

THE ATTACK ON DIVIS STREET

As darkness fell on 14 August, Commissioner Wolseley ordered the deployment of hundreds of B-Specials onto the Shankill Road. Loyalists mixed freely with B-men, many of whom were local men permitted to keep their service firearms and ammunition at home. Wolseley had effectively bolstered the ranks of McKeague's army. Paddy Devlin claimed that 'Crowds were organised early in the night and arms were brought in from rural areas in cars and given out to some of the men. Local people who knew the streets daubed white-wash marks on the doors or windows of Catholic homes.'[29]

Actively supported by the B-Specials, the SDA launched its campaign of terror at the junction of the Shankill Road and Percy and Dover streets, leading to Divis Street. They began with the few remaining Catholic-owned homes, many now daubed with white paint and already earmarked to be handed over to new, Protestant residents. They then searched Forsythe, Cargill and Upper Cargill streets before entering Boundary, Louden, Duffy, Townsend, Melbourne and Sackville streets. When they reached Percy Street, some left the main body, searching Westmoreland, Cumberland, Wigton, Crosby, Penrith and Lorton streets, clearing them of Catholic families as they encroached on the Falls Road. The mob then firebombed nationalists' homes on Beverley Street, physically attacking residents in Carlow, Morpeth and Warkworth streets, before reassembling in Percy and Dover streets just yards from Ardmoulin Avenue to await the signal for the main assault. On the Falls Road there were minor skirmishes between nationalist youths and a line of RUC in front of Hastings Street Barracks.

Having overseen earlier attacks on Catholic-owned businesses on the Crumlin Road, McKeague now entered Percy Street to direct SDA operations. Scarman later concluded that McKeague 'played an active role in the fighting in Percy Street. Wearing a crash helmet and carrying a stick, he arrived there with two fellow members of the Shankill Defence Association.'[30] McKeague boasted that 'we had sent for some people to be brought from other areas and with them also the local residents of the streets near to the Shankill Road. When they heard the attack was on, they immediately came down, they did not have to be asked.'[31] His supporters were identifiable by their distinctive armbands, crash helmets, staves studded with nails, batons and dustbin lids.

Only yards away in Dover Street, John McQuade, a unionist politician, marshalled 'Protestant civilians armed with sticks and hatchets behind the USC in Dover Street'.[32] USC Sergeant Harpur had already formed a line of men armed with revolvers, steel helmets and batons across Dover Street, just a hundred yards from Divis Street. Harpur's B-Specials then baton charged a crowd of ten to twenty nationalist youths gathered at the junction of Dover Street and Divis Street.[33] McKeague seized the opportunity, and the USC was 'supported in the fighting in Dover Street by Protestant civilians'.[34] Moments later, USC reinforcements arrived from the Shankill. Behind the fighting, loyalists firebombed the home of a Catholic family at number 132 before attacking Sarsfield (Bingo) Hall. They then succeeded in firebombing the Arkle Inn at the corner of Dover and Divis streets. Following this the B-Specials and loyalists broke onto Divis Street where 'the B-Specials lost control: and they did so in the early stages of the riot. After they lost control, some actively participated in the Protestant charges that ultimately drove the Catholics back into Divis Street and brought the Protestants themselves in force into that street.'[35] Paddy Devlin, MP, claimed that 'police in uniform, covered in civilian coats, were recognised amongst loyalist attackers in Dover Street'.[36]

Once on Divis Street, loyalists immediately attacked the Morning Star Hostel (a shelter to thirty homeless men) situated at the other corner of Dover Street. One of the residents, Brother Joe Acheson, recalled:

> I tried to organise the men in case they had to be evacuated, but the street outside became very dangerous as some petrol bombs were thrown and came through the windows of the hostel. Then I had to organise the men to fill the buckets with water and we managed to put out the fires. During the night, the Protestants started burning houses at the top of Dover Street near the Shankill end.[37]

The Livingstone family of Dover Street suffered a vicious attack as they tried to escape from their attackers via Divis Street:

> At teatime, crowds of loyalists gathered at the Shankill Road end of Dover Street and Percy Street … As we became aware of the violence on the street – some buildings were already burning – we were all moved to the back of the house. The late Johnny McQuade, a leading loyalist unionist firebrand politician, was directing the mob with shouts of 'work to rule boys' and 'kill the nits, they grow into lice'. Their first target was Sarsfields GAA club, which was a few doors down from us and was quickly set alight. A small loyalist who had once been a deliveryman and knew the street all too well identified the Catholic homes. Our mother had tentatively opened the door to the parlour in an attempt to see what was going on and the shaft of light drew attention to the house and a petrol bomb came through the window … loyalists began to kick in the front door [and] at this point our father and brother started to pile furniture against the

front door to hold back the baying mob. [Escaping out the back] we made our way across Divis Street. We were attacked with bricks and bottles by the RUC and B-Specials. My father stood with our baby sister in his arms shouting at them and telling them that they were just women and kids. The peelers just laughed and said 'F**k off you Fenian bastard'.[38]

In Percy Street, meanwhile, residents were resisting as McKeague's army firebombed their homes, while nationalist youths struggled to halt loyalists and the USC from entering Divis Street and the Falls Road beyond by stone-throwing from improvised shelters constructed from corrugated iron. Kevin Kennedy – then nineteen years of age – recalls that 'a group of us travelled through the district and came out onto the Falls Road at the corner of Albert Street. We had nothing to defend ourselves with except for stones. We dug up the square sets [bricks] from the streets to use; a few others arrived with petrol bombs. I witnessed the loyalist crowds coming down both Percy and Dover streets; the B-Specials led them in.'[39]

The violence escalated as an SDA member fired on the nationalist youths. '[A]s a result of the shooting,' Scarman found, 'the Catholic crowd retreated out of Percy Street onto Divis Street, allowing the Protestant crowd to capture their corrugated iron barricade.'[40] As Patrick McAteer from Turf Lodge attempted to escape towards the Falls Road, he was shot:

I was running up Percy Street, I heard a crack at a window then I felt my side. I was running towards the Falls; this was at the houses in Percy Street ... I heard a crack at this window edge. I remember my side, I found a pellet: somebody must have fired a shotgun from the Protestant side. There was a pellet the size of a pea and two small pellets. They were the first shots fired.[41]

Fearing arrest, McAteer did not go to hospital, instead removing the pellets himself. This evidence demonstrates that armed loyalists and the USC had seized control of both Percy and Dover streets, and were shooting at young nationalists attempting to defend the area. This combined action by the B-Specials and loyalists was the beginning of a pogrom in nationalist areas of Belfast, and thereby the start of the Troubles in Belfast.

One eyewitness recounted the trauma experienced by local residents:

> I remember men coming from the Shankill down Percy Street and Dover Street and I can remember them throwing what I thought at the time was torches into houses. What I quickly realised was they were petrol bombs, and they were thrown into the backs of houses, fronts of houses and over walls, hundreds of them. It was a continuous flow of petrol bombs that were thrown. The police and B-Specials were mingled among the Protestant crowd [and] firing on the youths at the top of Percy and Dover Streets trying to scatter them. When the bombing started, we saw men, women and children running for their lives. We were horrified as we watched people with their children in their arms; that to me was the worst part. The Catholics I saw running out of those houses were not prepared for what happened. Men were running with children on their backs. I remember a woman pushing and running down the road with two small children inside a Silver Cross pram and clothes stuffed inside and round the pram … the police and B-Specials were certainly not keeping the crowds back: they were part of them.[42]

Throughout the evening and night of 14 August the RUC oversaw this wanton destruction of nationalist lives and property. After a briefing held earlier at Hastings Street Barracks, headed by Head Constable Stinson, the RUC had placed two snipers on the roof, one constable and one RUC reservist, one armed with a 7.62mm self-loading rifle (SLR) and the other a .303 rifle.[43] The barracks was located at the junction of Hastings Street and Divis Street. A short distance away, four officers commanded by a constable positioned themselves on the roof of Millfield Technical College. Eyewitnesses also reported uniformed gunmen on the roof of the New Northern Mill. Together, all three positions overlooked the streets surrounding Divis Street and the Lower Falls Road. Furthermore, Commissioner Wolseley later admitted that plain-clothes RUC men 'were operating on the Falls Road on the evening and night of 14th August'.[44]

In addition, RUC heavy weaponry was concentrated near Divis Street. At 10.37 p.m. RUC Shorland armoured vehicles were ordered to the Falls Road to 'stand by at Milford/Divis Street'.[45] Twenty minutes later, several vehicles under Head Constable Gray moved up Divis Street towards the nationalist crowd. At about 11 p.m. a Humber and three Shorland armoured vehicles under Head Constable Stewart drove down Dover Street, smashing their way through hastily constructed corrugated iron defences, as loyalists ransacked homes and businesses in Divis Street, looting as they went.[46] A contingent of police under the command of Sergeant Stanford arrived there at 11.20 p.m.

Journalist Max Hastings succinctly summed up the different forces that were involved during the Divis Street action that night: 'There were on the streets of Belfast, four forces, closely engaged … First, the Catholics; then the B-Specials, all armed with revolvers, rifles or sub-machine guns; the RUC; and the Protestants from the Shankill, who began to mount heavy petrol bomb attacks on houses and factories on the fringes of the Falls Road area.'[47]

Several nationalists were struck by fire from sub-machine guns fired by B-Specials while standing in Divis Street. One young man claimed he was struck on the leg and, on his way to Sultan Street Hall (where a first-aid station had been established) for medical attention, was forced to take refuge in a house when the Shorland armoured cars opened fire.

On the opposite side of Divis Street, across the road from Percy and Dover streets, Mr McGarrigan, a resident of the flats, recounted how locals formed a human chain transporting stones and petrol bombs to the roofs of the Divis Street flats as the RUC vehicles, B-Specials and loyalist mob converged on Divis Street.[48] '[W]omen and children in the flats were terrified that the RUC would do to them what they had done in Derry: the men were, therefore, determined to keep them from entering the flats.'[49] Meanwhile, Max Hastings noted that 'Up the side streets, police and B-Specials were massing, with Protestants from the Shankill Road also clutching petrol bombs, dustbin lids and sticks, behind and beside them.'[50]

At one minute to midnight, two parties of RUC officers under the supervision of two sergeants converged and then collectively charged and 'pushed the Catholic crowd into the forecourt of Divis Flats'.[51] Sergeant McPhillips explained how he'd 'made up my mind after assessing the situation for about five minutes to do the baton charge down towards Divis Street and Divis Tower'.[52] Police also recklessly drove their Shorland armoured vehicles at the crowd, scattering the nationalist youths and residents protecting their homes, with many women and children in their night attire running for their lives.

At midnight, and on the back of RUC baton charges, McKeague, McQuade and other loyalists then charged onto Divis Street en masse from both Percy and Dover streets. One SDA man shouted, 'We have entered the Falls.' Sergeant McPhillips recalled that 'I could not honestly say whether it was Protestants who came out of Dover Street or Protestants who came out of Percy Street who attacked the Catholic property.'[53] The fact remains that, but for his actions, the mob would not have had the opportunity.

Watching from his home at 19E Divis Tower, Felix McCaughley had a panoramic view of events leading up to and during this attack:

I saw a crowd led by either police or B-Specials approach the Falls Road from both Percy Street and Dover Street and there were about twenty of these uniformed men in front of each crowd. From the height of my flat it was not possible to see whether they were regulars or 'B' men. They seemed to be in contact with each other since the movement down each street was very similar in speed. There were about 100 persons in each crowd as they came down the streets and amongst them I saw white armbands and white helmets. In the meantime, I saw that a crowd from our side of the road had gathered … and were facing the crowd as they came towards the Falls Road. I then saw petrol bombs and stones being thrown from one crowd to the other and this was sometime between eleven o'clock and midnight …. [I] then saw the armoured cars again come up from Hastings Street. They were firing their guns. I saw from the tracer bullets that they were firing above the heads of the people on the Falls Road and this caused them to scatter and leave the immediate area. The armoured cars then stopped at Percy Street and continued firing towards the one side of the road. I then saw the crowd with the accompanying policemen come out of Percy Street and Dover Street and firstly force the barriers off the windows of the shops. Having got the barriers off the windows they then smashed the windows and set fire to the band room in Dover Street.[54]

A member of the crowd who defended Divis claimed that:

It was dark at this time; the [nationalist] crowd was milling about St Comgall's School. The next thing there was a fuselage of shots came up from the direction of Ardmoulin Avenue and onto the Falls. There were people running about, there was complete panic. Nobody knew what was happening. There was [sic] people saying they were being put out of their houses, there were people burned out … In the midst of it all, a car pulled up and I heard people shouting 'Here's the IRA',

'Here's the IRA' and these two guys got out of the car with uniforms. They had khaki uniforms with belts and caps on, the women were shouting, 'Here's the IRA', and it turned out that they were either St John's Ambulance or Knights of Malta. One of them said to us 'It's even worse up the road [Cupar/Conway streets]', but then a couple of people were taken in his car, I think they were hurt or shot.[55]

At this point, a lone nationalist gunman positioned himself at the corner of Gilford and Divis Street, not far from the Divis flats. He fired a number of shots from a revolver, injuring three RUC men and Herbert Roy – part of the loyalist mob – who died afterwards from a chest injury caused by a single .38 round. 'Hearing the shots Sgt McPhillips drew his revolver and moved to the corner of Dover Street from where he fired three shots at a man in the mouth of Gilford Street …'[56] The RUC and B-Specials reacted to this fire with ferocity:

The next thing I heard was shooting and I saw either three or four armoured cars [Shorlands] come up Divis Street firing their guns. There were 'tracer' bullets being fired, so I could see the line of fire. As they came level with the flats, they fired towards ground level and then gradually elevated their line of fire right up to near the top floor of the building.[57]

Head Constable Gray arrived from Hastings Street with an additional party of men, equipped with Sterling sub-machine guns and revolvers, also pouring fire across Divis Street.[58]

Journalist Max Hastings witnessed the aggression and recklessness of the police reaction. He claimed that at around midnight, at the corner of Dover and Divis streets, he witnessed RUC officers armed with Sterling sub-machine guns and revolvers fire into the Divis flats: 'I watched this for forty minutes … officers could not tell me what they were firing at.'[59] This firing would continue well into the night. A while later he watched as one of the Shorlands suddenly screeched 'to a halt, and a long burst of fire from its heavy machine gun echoed the length of the street. Behind the corners half the way down the road lay police whose sub-machine guns and revolvers had been blazing intermittently for more than an hour.'[60]

Terrorised nationalists fled, many running into the flats complex of Divis attempting to hide from police fire. Seán McErlean, who lived at Albert Street and was studying at the time in Queen's University, had been watching events from the Divis/Albert Street junction. When the shooting began, he instinctively ran home attempting to gain access:

> I remember hammering at the door and they wouldn't open it because the shooting had already started and the streets were beginning to empty ... I must say it was the most frightening experience of my life because I had never heard gunfire of any sort before in my life. This was gunfire of huge proportions, machine-guns, small arms and shotguns. The other thing that impinged on my memory apart from the knock on the door and trying to find the safest place in the house was the gunfire from the Shorlands, tracer bullets that were bright red. I recognised them immediately, they seemed to be firing when I looked out the back window down towards Divis and St Peter's [the Catholic pro-cathedral], I could see these red tracers coming up at a thirty to forty-degree angle into the sky. They seemed to arch right round from St Peter's right up and down Divis Street.[61]

Night-shift worker John Toner watched from the premises of Andrews' Flour Mill on Percy Street as the Shorland armoured vehicles opened fire, seemingly not caring who they were firing at:

> The mobs came down Percy Street and started burning houses and the women came down with them and they were carrying milk crates

full of petrol bombs. They were handing them out to the men. The Shorland tanks were there too. And then the Shorlands ... opened fire with their machine guns, Brownings, and they splattered Divis Flats with them. The women came down carrying the milk crates all full of petrol bombs, and they just put them outside the gates of Andrews' Flour Mill ... Yankee Bill's was at the corner of Percy Street, it was a book shop and we were in the inside of Andrews' Flour Mill and we were able to get onto the granary roof and go and get them. They were [barricaded] in their outside toilet ... Everything was on fire, it was an old wooden toilet and they were elderly. John Finucane, myself and different other ones, funny enough he was a Protestant, Jackie Morrow, he went and got one or two out ... The people living in those homes would have burned to death without our help ... When the Shorlands came down and they were outside Andrews' Flour Mill, there was a guy from Andrews' Mill; he was on the roof and he was just watching. He was a Protestant (Stanley Kerr), and they opened up and the chunks out of the wall from the Browning ... they battered and battered away at it.[62]

Max Hastings, still at the corner of Dover Street, also observed the Shorlands firing wildly: 'But whereas most of the fire I may have seen from the police at the mouth of Dover Street was directed in the broad direction of Divis Tower, when I first saw these armoured cars they were firing up the street.'[63] Hastings recorded that the police embarked on a rampage of machine-gun fire that scattered every observer who witnessed it. An armoured vehicle sprayed the buildings with heavy machine-gun fire, sending chips flying off the concrete parapets, wreaking havoc within. Such was the ferocity that an RUC barracks some distance across the city mistakenly thought they were under attack.[64]

Senior police officers decided to increase their firepower in the area and additional Shorlands were quickly dispatched to Divis Street from Ardoyne, where a major loyalist assault on nationalists had been launched almost simultaneously to the attacks on Percy and Dover streets. Commanded by District Inspector Gilchrist, RUC Reserves and B-Specials manned these Shorlands, each equipped with self-loading rifles and Sterling sub-machine guns.[65] Browning machine guns mounted on these vehicles rained fire across Divis Tower and the flats. These guns could release 500–600 rounds per minute covering over 1,000 metres. They struck Divis Tower, penetrating the flats at '1B, 3D, 4C, 6D, 7D, 8D and 9D and the entrance hall of Divis Tower'.[66] The RUC and USC fired for effect, shooting into the homes of innocent citizens, causing death and multiple injuries.

Cleared of nationalist defenders, the shops in Divis Street between Percy and Dover streets were easy pickings for loyalists. 'The first shop they burned was McAlea's ... the next thing the rest of the shops went up. Silvestri's ice cream shop, the fruit shop, a holy shop and a clothes shop. There was a pub at the corner; it was also fired.'[67] It wasn't just the loyalists who were involved in this wanton destruction. Alice Bell, whose father had a business in Ardmoulin Avenue, claimed that 'the RUC used the machine guns on the Shorlands to shoot into my aunt's shop. They couldn't get out to put the petrol bombs out, because they were shooting in all the time.'[68] Mr Linton, a British soldier home on leave, also identified RUC men among the loyalist mob that attacked his home at 141 Divis Street.[69]

Divis Street resident Mr Shannon watched on as 'three armoured vehicles had come down Percy Street [and] about 200 Protestants emerged from Percy Street on to Divis Street. Some of them jumped on to the railings surrounding St Comgall's School and threw petrol bombs at the building ... Petrol bombs were then thrown at houses [on] Divis Street to either side of Percy Street'.[70] McKeague was commanding this assault and his men attacked St Comgall's school with petrol bombs, with others petrol-bombing homes and businesses at the corner of Gilford Street.

All the while, RUC officers looked on, as towering fires blazed on Divis Street and terrorised nationalists gathered their families and fled for their lives. Throughout the entire ordeal, those who did flee met with fire from the RUC snipers on the roof of Hastings Street Barracks, Millfield College and the New Northern Mill. Brendan Wilson recalled:

> When the Shorlands arrived, everyone scattered when they heard the machine-gun fire coming from them. That was not the only fire that was aimed at us. Firing was intensifying towards anyone showing any resistance. We believed there was rifle fire coming from the high point of the tech [Millfield Technical College, bottom of Divis Street]. So, we remained close to the walls for cover, bullets ricocheting off the walls. In the dark, we could see the tracers coming from the Shorlands.[71]

Any nationalists who were injured attended Sultan Street first-aid centre, fearing arrest if they presented at the nearby Royal Victoria Hospital.

As an inferno engulfed hundreds of homes and businesses, the SDA triumphantly planted a 'Union Flag in the middle of Divis Street'. McKeague, who directed operations at the scene until two in the morning, clearly revelled in his recollection of events: 'In that we reached the Falls Road or that particular area of Divis Street we had gained our own territory again and we were out on the road [Divis Street] and as far as we were concerned we had made our point.'[72]

For several hours during the burnings on Divis Street, the SDA also controlled the interlinking streets leading from the Shankill, which they used to transport petrol bombs and direct USC reinforcements. McKeague and McQuade were witnessed on an earlier occasion checking their barricade in Third Street [200–300 yards from the Shankill Road]. James Sloan claimed that when men needed to be moved to Percy Street, where violence was escalating, 'a shout went up the street [Third Street] that there was someone looking for a lift, the police or the USC were looking [for] transport. They were asking car owners in the street, knocking doors to see if they could get a lift [to] Percy Street on the Shankill Road.'[73]

Meanwhile, during the mayhem on Divis Street a number of loyalists and B-Specials attempted to invade the Falls Road by using other routes, including North Howard Street, situated between Northumberland and Conway streets. One nationalist eyewitness recalled, 'We made our way down the Falls Road until we reached North Howard Street, where we saw a loyalist mob coming down the street. There was B-Specials with the crowd. The crowd had bricks, stones and petrol bombs.'[74] As a result of this confrontation with nationalist youths, the loyalist crowd did not enter the Falls Road at North Howard Street.

Divis Street had become an open firing range: throughout the night, RUC men and B-Specials opened fire with Sterling submachine guns, SLRs and .45 Webley revolvers. The Shorlands continued to fire indiscriminately, striking at least nine storeys of Divis Tower, with shots entering living rooms, bedrooms, kitchens and bathrooms. Ballistics reports indicate that one Shorland positioned at 101 Divis Street fired upon homes at Nos 5 and 6 St Brendan's Path, and No. 10 St Brendan's Walk. The Browning rounds also struck an electricity transformer at the corner of Divis and Pound streets.[75] Hastings, an experienced war correspondent with military experience, concluded that the fusillade from police vehicles 'was rather higher than in South American riots I have seen. I would certainly say several thousand rounds of ammunition were fired.'[76]

Browning rounds ripped into the flats, slicing through the concrete and striking several residents in their homes. At close quarters, Hastings witnessed indiscriminate firing: 'Upstairs, a nine-year-old Catholic boy who had been sheltering in the back room of his family's flat, lay on a bed with half his head blown away by one of a burst of [four] heavy calibre bullets that smashed through the frail partition walls.'[77] Scarman concluded: '[H]aving considered all the evidence relating to the use of guns in Divis Street we have no doubt that at least one of the Shorlands opened fire on the flats, hitting St Brendan's block and the city face of the Tower block, and killing Patrick Rooney.'[78]

In addition, RUC snipers positioned on the roof of Hastings Street Barracks struck the bedroom, corridor and bathroom of 6D Divis Tower with several 7.62 rounds from a British military SLR. A second RUC sniper hit the floor above with his .303 Lee Enfield, before firing into the living room of 8D. Snipers then trained their weapons on residents of the Whitehall Row maisonettes, killing Trooper McCabe, a Queen's Royal Irish Hussar home on leave.[79] In the process of saving the lives of defenceless women, 'McCabe was shot by one of the police marksmen on the roof of the Hastings Street station'.[80]

At this stage nationalists may well have been wondering just where the IRA was, as they might rightly have expected it to come to their aid. The Dublin-based IRA Chief-of-Staff Cathal Goulding responded to news of the attacks in Divis Street by suggesting reasoning with the pogromists. 'Goulding had no understanding of the Belfast situation. The night the trouble broke out he phoned [Proinsias] MacAirt [a well-known Belfast republican] and asked him to go and talk to the Protestant mobs and reason with them. MacAirt tried it but we know what the result of that was.'[81] Goulding consistently failed to reconcile the formulaic Marxism that he and the Dublin-based republican leadership had embraced with the harsh reality of an ascendant and bellicose right-wing loyalism abetted by the state in launching vicious attacks on working-class nationalists.

John McKeague later provided a frank explanation for loyalist motivations on this night: 'We gave them a lesson they will never forget.' This sectarian rationale mirrored the profound racism that had been directed against the black civil rights movement in the American South, and fatally undermined official republican rhetoric about the workers' republic and the unification of the Catholic and Protestant working classes.

Max Hastings claimed that he did not see any guns in the Divis complex and identified 'a certain amount of ill-feeling against the IRA for not having produced any'.[82] There were a few efforts made, however. Some republican veterans did attempt to defend nationalists that night, but they had very little success. Billy McKee recalled: 'It finished up that we had to go and get a number of lads together of the pre-IRA crowd and some of us had to go onto the Falls and by God when we got onto the Falls ... they [loyalists] were coming down Percy Street and Dover Street and there was a gun battle.' McKee travelled down the Falls Road, but police sniper fire from the New Northern Mill stalled him at the crossroads formed by Northumberland, Divis and Albert streets and the Falls Road: 'I said get in and I pulled them back ... you had to get back because of the bullets.' McKee spotted a uniformed man on the roof of the mill: 'He was firing down and the bullets were hitting the ground all right and I seen them jumping. It was rough going.'[83] Senior police officers claimed that continuous incoming gunfire justified police conduct, but multiple accounts confirm that so far the fire from a solitary nationalist gunman constituted the only armed action from the nationalist side.

Approximately one hour after the shooting of Patrick Rooney and Trooper McCabe, at 2 a.m., six local men entered the grounds of St Comgall's school, opposite Dover Street, and fired on the loyalists. These men had a Thompson sub-machine gun with a single stick magazine, two rifles, a sten-gun and two or three handguns. Leading republican Brendan Hughes later recalled:

[W]hen the Loyalist mobs came down off the Shankill [they]

were attacking St Comgall's school with petrol bombs, stones and everything. I mean, they just wrecked the whole front of the school. I knew the school, I had gone there as a child and I showed [name omitted], the IRA guy who had the Thompson, how to go through the school, through the classrooms [and] up onto the roof. I remember that McKeague, I think it was McKeague … was leading [the crowds]. I was on top of the roof with [name omitted] [and the loyalists] were firing petrol bombs, a massive mob of people, right onto the Falls Road. I was trying to encourage [name omitted] to shoot into the crowd [but] he was under orders from Jimmy Sullivan, the O/C [of] the IRA at that time in the Falls area, not to shoot into the crowd, [but] to fire over their heads. So, he emptied a magazine over their heads, which did break the crowd up. They retreated back into the Shankill and we retreated off the roof.[84]

The defenders holed up in St Comgall's school expended their limited ammunition within minutes. RUC radio transcripts confirm the short duration of the shooting:

2.04 a.m. heavy shooting from Falls Road

2.06 a.m. [DI Cushley] heavy shooting from school [St Comgall's]

2:10 a.m. [DI Cushley] machine gun mounted in school grounds – more casualties.[85]

At that point the defensive actions ended.

At Leeson Street, several hundred yards from St Comgall's school, 'they had a couple of guns alright, but as far as I know they had no ammunition, because one of the wee lads that came up to Lucknow Street [Clonard area], he turned round and said that "I'm out". We checked the gun; it had no ammunition.'[86]

Unsurprisingly, at this point the school and surrounding area became the target for intense police and B-Special fire. Shorlands fired hundreds of rounds from their .30 Browning machine-guns, raking the entire school building. Police officers and B-Specials using rifles, Sterling sub-machine guns and revolvers poured rounds into homes and businesses alike, including 11 St Comgall's Walk, 16 and 17 St Comgall's Row, and into the entrance area of Divis Tower. An RUC man positioned at 129 Divis Street fired his Sterling sub-machine gun repeatedly, its rounds striking the St Comgall's Walk home of Mr Donnelly. Another RUC officer fired his Webley revolver from outside Grant's shop into Mrs McGee's home at 16 St Comgall's Row, at the same time striking 17 St Comgall's Row. The Whitehall Row maisonettes suffered similar damage when police officers and B-Specials fired from their position at Townsend Street, a short distance away from Hastings Street Barracks. Police sprayed indiscriminate fire into shops and homes from 140–150 Divis Street, wounding a young boy at Terrins butcher's shop.[87]

Throughout the night streams of terrified residents fled their burning homes in streets leading from the Shankill down to the Falls. Nationalists living on the St Comgall's school side of Divis Street opposite Percy and Dover streets attempted to help, but likely realised that they would share their neighbours' fate before long.

The unmistakable reality is that nationalist districts faced the August siege with no real armed defence. As the RUC itself admitted, in stark contrast to the situation on the Shankill, 'the number of fire-arms legally held in this [nationalist] area surrounded by Divis Street, Falls Road, Grosvenor Road and Durham Street would have been very small indeed.'[88]

The overwhelming weakness of the nationalist response did not deter the police from using the full arsenal at their disposal. '[D]uring the period that the three vehicles were in Divis Street, a considerable number of rounds of Browning (Shorland) ammunition were discharged in the direction of the flats on the south side of Divis Street.'[89]

Having left the devastated family of nine-year-old Patrick Rooney at No. 5 St Brendan's Path, Max Hastings had crossed Divis Street and entered Beverley, Dover and Percy streets, where loyalists and state forces drank tea against the backdrop of burning homes that had been hastily evacuated by nationalists. 'In Beverley Street [a] lot of [Protestant residents] were leaning out of their doors and various people were coming in and out carrying tea and this sort of thing; it was a sort of social centre.'[90] While the RUC fired randomly up Divis Street, Hastings witnessed one B-Special firing round a corner, while another 'emptied his revolver' into a street light.[91] An armoured personnel carrier then pulled up, 'stacked to the roof with cases of ammunition and assorted weaponry', with one policeman lamenting that 'Dr Paisley has been telling us this would happen these nine months, but none of us had the sense to listen'. For Hastings this was a telling remark 'that explained much [about] Catholic feelings towards the police'.[92] In Hastings' view the astonishingly nonchalant atmosphere in Beverley Street demonstrated that the IRA had not stationed any snipers, as 'had there been any marksmen of the remotest consequence operating that night they could have mown down half the RUC'.[93]

At 3.15 a.m., without any basis, a constable at Donegall Pass RUC Station radioed 'that streets off Falls Road have been [booby] trapped and the IRA have moved in. Strategic points have been marked for burning down before the weekend.'[94] This false information spurred further police violence. At the time, Shorlands continued up and down the Falls Road unobstructed, strafing homes, shops and businesses. Mr McCormick fled from a Shorland firing in Divis Street. Mr Linton witnessed Shorlands firing into Derby Street on four or five occasions as they passed Divis Street. Paddy Kennedy, MP (NI), testified that after a Shorland had fired on St Comgall's school it travelled up Divis Street, firing down Albert Street. At a first-aid station in Sultan Street, Dr McAllister heard Shorlands discharge their Brownings on three occasions down Sultan and Plevna streets.[95]

Two hundred yards up from Divis Street, along the Falls Road, mob attacks and indiscriminate police fire hemmed nationalist residents into their homes on Lemon, Peel, Mary, Colin, Alma, Omar, Balaclava, Patton and Raglan streets, which all faced towards the Shankill Road. Mary Street resident Lily Fitzsimmons described the scene around her:

I thought it would never end. I remember the B-Specials shooting. The houses across the Falls Road from us were all burned out by Protestant mobs. Everyone on our side of the Falls were [sic] running around, we didn't know what to do. All the streets around us, Colin Street, Raglan Street, we were only a stone's throw away from the 'Black Pad' [as an area of the Shankill was popularly known]. The rumours were rife and we were told that our houses were next and the mobs were coming back to burn our houses on our side of the road.

We were defenceless. We had watched as the RUC and B-Specials shot at us, and Protestants destroyed our houses. No one was there to protect us except for young lads throwing stones and bottles. Myself and my neighbours, Alice Barrett and Mary Hillis, went looking for empty milk bottles, sugar and old rags. Men were throwing nails and other things on the road, anything we could think of to try to protect ourselves against the loyalist mobs. People were grasping at straws; there were no firearms to protect us: this was desperation, we were frightened. There was no IRA – we were undefended. We witnessed the Shorland armoured cars shooting up the Falls Road and into the side streets. The loyalists and B-Specials had burnt down the houses on the other side of the road while the RUC either helped or stood by and did nothing. It is very difficult to explain how frightened we were. I will never forget it.[96]

On the Lower Falls, residents squatted in terror as the Shorlands fired at will. Hastings observed that 'the armoured cars began to career the length of the Falls Road emptying bolts of heavy calibre ammunition in the direction of any supposed threat.'[97] They continued to fire as they entered Balaclava and Derby streets. From the Grosvenor Road, another Shorland discharged its weapon into Leeson Street, then into Osman and Theodore streets.[98] Paddy Devlin, MP, witnessed the frantic firing from the Shorlands and, at approximately 3 a.m., vainly appealed to Commissioner Wolseley to bring an end to the police action, after eleven attempts to reach him by telephone:

> I told him that the armoured cars were going up and down the Falls firing on people who had been burned out of the other side of the Falls Road and asked him would he stop the armoured cars firing … I was very angry about it. I said to him did he think the old-age pensioners from Conway Street and the young children from Norfolk Street were firing on these barracks?[99]

The O'Rawe family from Peel Street lived only yards away from the Fitzsimmons. As improvised boards and barricades proved futile against the intense firebombing on the other side of the Falls Road, Mrs O'Rawe fled with her children to relatives in the Beechmount area of West Belfast. Richard O'Rawe (15), his father and grandfather remained behind to save their home when the shooting began. Years later O'Rawe recalled his grandfather saying, "'Wait till you see, the police will come now". And so, they did. Police came in armoured cars, careering through the narrow streets, firing first at random and then with deliberation at the street lighting.' The elder O'Rawe knew from experience what was about to happen. 'Unionist incendiaries would invade the area and systematically burn the houses.' Richard vividly described the scene. He could tell that the attack was not focused on any single point:

> It was as if the attackers were making a broad-fronted assault with the intention of penetrating wherever a weakness presented itself ... peering through the skylight [I] saw flames rising from neighbouring streets. A wall of flame and smoke separated the entire length of the Lower Falls from the Shankill.[100]

The residents of the Falls paid a heavy price for the Bogside resistance.

THE CONWAY STREET AREA

As one loyalist mob invaded Percy and Dover streets, further up the Shankill, at approximately 10.30 p.m. a second contingent invaded Conway and Cupar streets, employing the same search-and-destroy tactics against homes there. The mob seems to have advanced systematically through Tenth, Ninth, Eighth, Seventh, Sixth, Fifth, Fourth and Third streets, expelling the Catholic minority from their houses as they went. Other loyalists emerging from McKeague's headquarters entered Wilton streets, North and South, snaking their way into Northland, Midland, Southland, Crossland and through into Nixon streets. In complete control of the area, members of the SDA then entered Urney, Argyle and Ashmore streets. Loyalist spotters led the gangs, proudly carrying Union Jacks, into Canmore Street. They then firebombed a Catholic-owned home at 66 Sugarfield Street, proceeding through Bellevue, Westland and Eastland streets, pursuing and evicting nationalists from Ernie and First streets, before finally merging at Ashmore Street, where they quickly cleared the few remaining Catholic families.

Having consolidated these areas, McKeague's forces loitered off

Ashmore, Conway and First streets, awaiting the signal to attack the predominately nationalist Conway, Cupar, Norfolk and David streets, which ran directly onto the Falls Road. RUC Head Constable Owens and fourteen men watched around 200 loyalists with SDA armbands, many wearing crash helmets and armed with iron bars, sticks embedded with nails, bottles and petrol bombs, but did not intervene.

RUC radio calls indicate that at 10.30 p.m. loyalists from Argyle Street and the Shankill end of Cupar Street simultaneously launched petrol-bomb attacks on nationalist homes in Ashmore, Conway and Cupar streets. 'Eventually there were about ten people from the back of the [loyalist] crowd threw petrol bombs into those houses on Conway Street on the corner of Ashmore Street and set them on fire.'[101] Head Constable Owens observed that following this the mob 'ran completely amok'.[102] Resistance became impossible when armed loyalists fired into Conway Street, wounding two nationalists.

At 10.45 p.m. the mob swelled further on both Conway Street and Cupar Street, tearing protective boarding from windows and firebombing homes. In Cupar Street 'a petrol bomb was thrown into the upstairs window of a house [which] caught fire and more petrol bombs were thrown at other houses in the block from which the residents fled in their nightwear'.[103] John Nugent, his wife and two young daughters were forced to flee from their Cupar Street home. The mob also firebombed the Boomer family, an elderly couple and their daughter, on Conway Street, who fled from their home when it was engulfed in flames. Residents, some in their night attire and carrying children, ran screaming down the alleyway between Conway, Norfolk and Cupar streets. Mr McLaughlin suffered a similar experience; as petrol bombs crashed through his living-room window he ran into his backyard. Neighbours spotted him attempting to scramble over his back wall but he became stuck. They came to his aid, assisting him to escape down the alleyway. Meanwhile, the Maxwells, a mixed couple from 21 Conway Street, hid in their backyard as firebombs crashed through the front window, burning their home to a shell. Flames also engulfed the Doyle, Hennessey and McCarthy homes. Amid the mayhem, the RUC control room received desperate calls from residents of Elmfield and Cupar streets: 'People burning us out – police helping them'.[104]

At 11.30 p.m. Head Constable Rooney arrived with two Commer armoured vehicles: 'his first action [in common with Sergeant McPhillips in Dover Street] was to drive his vehicle between the crowds and baton charge the Catholic crowd' down Cupar Street and onto the Falls Road, thereby facilitating the loyalists.[105] The 'Catholic crowd' consisted of residents of Cupar Street and nationalists trying to stop the loyalist crowd. At the same time, another head constable led three separate baton charges, driving residents of Conway Street onto the Falls Road. Head Constable Rooney retrospectively claimed that he acted instinctively. It was 'not the Protestants', he noted, '[who] were throwing missiles at his men'.[106] To attack innocent and unarmed nationalists while loyalist mobs wreaked havoc, seemed the natural and instinctive reflex of RUC men deployed in the Lower Falls.

The loyalist mob overwhelmed hastily erected barricades on Norfolk Street before firebombing the Steenson, Cullen and Mooney homes. The police baton charge left loyalists unimpeded to burn out the rest of Norfolk Street. In David Street, at approximately 11.35 p.m., loyalists attacked Owen McDonald's home with petrol bombs, and the neighbouring Hughes and Tierney families were lucky to escape. As the three homes burned, the RUC mingled with loyalists and made no attempt to intervene. Head Constable Rooney claimed that in Ashmore and David streets he watched the mob 'dancing around burning houses'.[107] By this stage, the fire brigade noted, 'approximately twenty-five houses well alight'.[108]

A Protestant resident of Sugarfield Street, from which his

nationalist neighbours had already fled, stated that 'there was something outside working, and these people [the loyalist mob] had to just do what they were told ... I am convinced of that. I have nothing to say about the Roman Catholic families in our own area beside us.'[109]

One young Protestant – a future enlistee in McKeague's Red Hand Commandos – provided a loyalist perspective on the significance of these events:

Stones, then bricks and then petrol bombs flew in the air between the crowds. In a matter of minutes, I could see ferocious flames bursting out of homes in the lower Catholic end of Conway Street. People were running from their homes carrying their furniture while others stood and fought in the pitch [sic] battles. The violence spread to nearby Cupar Street and Norfolk Street, with pitch [sic] battles and petrol bombs again flying through the air as more homes caught fire. There were only a few policemen in the vicinity, who were helpless, and had given up once they had lost control of the streets. Law and order lay with the mobs. Homes and buildings were bursting into flames all over the place and families running for their lives, carrying whatever possessions they could with them. Then in the middle of this mayhem the first shots rang out and to me it was the point of no return. I knew even at that tender age that things would never be the same.[110]

Police claimed that during the charges they heard three single shots coming from the nationalist side. Head Constable Owen informed Scarman that he 'heard other shots and he and his men fired a volley of shots in the air ... The shooting from the Falls Road direction continued and [he] authorised his party to fire for effect. This time two short bursts were fired from a Sterling.'[111]

A nationalist resident from Leeson Street described 'chaos in these streets. I remember a small group of men, one had an old hand gun and he was firing at the loyalist mobs coming down the streets towards the Falls. But the Catholic crowds who were trying to hold back these mobs were being fired upon from the loyalist side. The man on the Catholic side was hit, and he was taken firstly to Greenan's Garage in Panton Street, and then to a first aid station in Sultan Street.'[112]

One resident of Conway Street provides a similar account:

When the lad came out of the crowd from the Falls, he started firing, while he fired and moved back into the crowd again, a number of policemen stepped out and they fired, you could see the uniform and you could see the flashes of the guns ... you could hear the [loyalist] crowds, it was black, all the lights were knocked out at the top of Conway Street, some of the lights had been knocked out on the Falls, but not all of them. All you could hear was the shouting and roaring and the singing of the Billy Boys.[113]

At 12.07 a.m., in the mistaken belief that he lacked the necessary firepower to police the nationalists who had gathered on the Falls – many of them driven from their now burning homes – a head constable called in 'heavy vehicles':

The vehicles moved off down Conway Street then turned two abreast with the third behind. At the end of Conway Street, they turned right into the Falls Road. As it turned one vehicle ... was illuminated by a petrol bomb thrown at it and a burst of Browning gunfire was discharged from it.[114]

This was the first shooting of the night by the Shorland-mounted Browning machine guns, before that on Divis Street where it would have fatal and devastating consequences.

On duty in Hastings Street, RUC District Inspector Frank Lagan monitored police radio as events unfolded:

> I got the impression that the large assemblies of people were on the Falls Road area and adjacent to the streets of Percy Street, Dover Street, Conway Street, and that there were also large crowds of people in these actual streets, and confrontation was taking place between them. It seemed that the orange/green line had been breached by the Protestant people and that they were down towards the Catholic end of the streets, and that burning of these houses was taking place.[115]

The RUC knew that the aggression had emanated from the loyalist side, yet rather than withdrawing the Shorlands, they were continually directed against the nationalists. Local man Brendan Wilson claimed that further up the Falls Road the Shorlands careered up and down the section of the road around Leeson Street, firing indiscriminately. 'While I was standing at the top of Leeson Street [thirty yards from the junction of Conway Street and the Falls Road] we saw a Shorland armoured car coming down the Falls heading towards the city. We stood in the doorways as it passed. It was lucky we did because the men inside opened up, shooting down Leeson Street: the bullets went ripping past us.'[116]

Nineteen-year-old Theresa Girvan, heavily pregnant, had been visiting her parents' home in Dunville Street. She described the alarming scene as she left and walked onto the Falls Road:

> Agnew's car showrooms were on fire. There was shouting and women in their bare feet and nightdresses carrying crying children ... The B-Specials were behind, shooting guns in the air around them. A sniper on the roof of the Silken Wren [fabric factory] fired and a bullet went so close it lifted the hair up over my head. Because I was

so heavily pregnant all the young people grabbed me and ran me up the street.[117]

As the loyalists continued to press their attacks, terrified residents ran from their homes. With momentum behind them and the police actions ensuring that they would face no resistance as they moved forward, the mob advanced, kicking in doors, lobbing petrol bombs and screaming obscenities. Here too, loyalist women carried crates full of petrol bombs past seemingly indifferent police officers, fuelling the inferno. Flames rapidly engulfed each small kitchen house, rushing up the walls and stairs and ripping through bedrooms, in the process destroying homes and breaking hearts. Some families, like the Cullens and O'Malleys, would never see their Norfolk Street homes again. James Steenson recalled:

> We spent that night with my aunt listening to the sounds of machine-gun fire and men and women screaming. Next morning about 7 a.m. my father James and my oldest brother John came walking and limping down Abercorn Street. Blood was running from dad's head and John had a twelve-inch gash in his leg. Mum was waiting and wanted to go back home, but my dad's words are still with me to this day: 'Go back inside Sarah and remember your house the way you saw it last night'.[118]

Just like the RUC snipers who held elevated positions in Divis and Lower Falls, loyalist snipers on top of the mills further up the Falls Road fired on fleeing victims in this area throughout the night of 14–15 August. This sniping forced several Catholic residents to take drastic action. 'I was on the Falls Road during the serious rioting just as they were burning Percy and Dover Streets. The shooting was getting heavier and people were shouting that there was a sniper on Grieve's Mill [at the corner of Conway Street and the Falls] firing down into

Panton Street. So a group of men went into the mill and emptied the slush oil made up with paraffin oil and that was set on fire.'[119]

One event early on the morning of 15 August demonstrated clearly the nature of police and loyalist violence. Around ten houses in the block between Ashmore and David streets had already been firebombed, as had several houses opposite, next to the, by now looted, Kilfeather's public house.[120] Relative calm had returned between 4.30 a.m. and 6 a.m., and nationalist residents of Conway and Cupar streets returned to salvage what they could from their burning homes. However, at approximately 6 a.m., loyalists gathered again for a final assault, burning Kilfeather's pub. Uniformed RUC looked on as loyalists then attacked the residents who were trying desperately to extinguish the flames and retrieve valued possessions from their homes. Nationalist MPs Paddy Devlin and Paddy Kennedy claimed that the RUC actually chased residents 'who were trying to prevent the destruction of the homes'.[121] Four families reported having to flee abruptly as a Shorland armoured vehicle suddenly arrived onto Conway Street from the Shankill and opened fire, even while loyalists set about burning the remainder of the street.

During the main assault, in the early hours of 15 August, the Butler family of Conway Street suffered a traumatic experience as Mr Butler, a disabled war veteran, panicked when his two sons struggled to remove him from his burning home. Paddy Devlin claimed:

I myself saw police armoured cars in Conway Street, standing by as the mobs broke the windows of hastily abandoned Catholic houses before pouring petrol in to burn them. In scenes that had not been paralleled for fifty years, I saw with my own eyes old people and former neighbours flocking out of Conway Street, where my grandparents had once lived at number 32 and my own mother and father at number 80.[122]

At approximately 7 a.m. a witness reported what he believed to be a Shorland firing shots while loyalists followed in its train, setting fire to more houses.[123] Another Conway Street resident claimed that:

> I saw the bullets coming out of the turrets. I seen [*sic*] them screeching, they came down Conway Street and turned right at the bottom of Conway Street facing up the Falls Road towards the library and Clonard Picture House, and while it was turning the turret was firing, the turret was actually spinning round firing. So that it wasn't firing at any one person or at any [specific] people: it was just firing, with the gun on a swivel and it didn't seem to be in control, it looked as if it was out of control, but maybe it wasn't; maybe that was the way it was built … but as it was spinning it was firing. So, inside the turret they must have been deliberately firing at anything, at everyone, because there was people all over, people had run into Bell's Cleaners at the bottom of Conway Street, people had run down Balaclava Street, people were running down Milligan Street, people were running up Norfolk Street, this was just firing, people were in a panic.[124]

One young man from further up the Falls Road walked into a veritable war zone on his way to work:

> Going to work … I walked down the Falls Road. When I got to Conway Street all I could see was mayhem, I could see people running about with bits of furniture and the smoke and the smell and the shouts, and as I came to Conway Street I looked up and I could see houses burning and people running into houses pulling furniture out. I could see a big crowd of loyalists – maybe 150 or so, and maybe approximately forty–fifty nationalists opposing them, fighting almost hand to hand. This would have been around numbers 2–26 [Conway Street]. The loyalists were in complete control of where that intersection was.[125]

Residents, objective eyewitnesses, journalists, historians and others who have paid careful attention to the documentary evidence conclude almost uniformly that the RUC were complicit in the devastating violence and destruction around the Lower Falls. Boulton notes in summary that 'in Conway Street, running south of the notional "Orange-Green" line between the Falls and the Shankill, sixty houses were burnt to the ground while RUC men, according to Scarman, stood by and took no restraining action'.[126] There can be no real doubt that the RUC and USC attacked the nationalist community with overwhelming firepower and that their actions facilitated loyalist attacks. Even to the dispassionate observer, this constituted an unjustifiable and disproportionate attack on defenceless civilians. As *Times* reporter Julian Mounter wrote:

> I saw the shooting last night. Today I saw the blood and the bullet holes and I will never believe that the police who engaged in a Falls Road battle behaved correctly. Why automatic weapons were used by the police in an area thick with homes and flats where women and children were exposed to bullets as plastic ducks in a shooting gallery … Patrick Rooney aged nine, was in a back room standing next to a wardrobe now splattered with blood … Why the Special Constables, so hated by the Roman Catholics in that area, were sent to the scene of the trouble or, if they were there already, why they were allowed to stay …
>
> Two vivid pictures will remain in my mind. One is of a sergeant of the Special Constabulary who spent the ten minutes I observed him dashing to-and-fro shooting indiscriminately at anyone who moved: 'Stop or I'll kill you. Stop or I'll shoot.' He looked totally unbalanced in the situation with which he was confronted … The other is of a policeman – I do not know whether he was a Special or a Regular – spraying bullets at the top of a building from where only two or three petrol bombs seemed to come from.

Evacuees from Clonard. *Courtesy of the Belfast Archive Project*

Clonard. *Courtesy of Gerry Collins*

Clonard. *Courtesy of Gerry Collins*

Clonard, Kashmir Road. *Courtesy of Gerry Collins*

Bombay Street. *Courtesy of the Belfast Archive Project*

Bombay Street. *Courtesy of the Belfast Archive Project*

Bombay Street. *Courtesy of the Belfast Archive Project*

Conway Street. *Courtesy of the Belfast Archive Project*

Percy Street, facing St Comgall's School. *Courtesy of Gerry Collins*

A street in Catholic Ardoyne. *Courtesy of Hugh McKeown*

Houses in Catholic Ardoyne. *Courtesy of Hugh McKeown*

Bus barricades in Brompton Park, Ardoyne. *Courtesy of Hugh McKeown*

Catholic homes on the Crumlin Road. *Courtesy of Hugh McKeown*

The Crumlin Road. *Courtesy of Hugh McKeown*

They might have had guns up there, but while I watched I saw no evidence of it.[127]

Billy Barrett from Mary Street had just finished a night shift at an American company based on the Castlereagh Road in East Belfast. He was dropped off by a work colleague at around 8 a.m. near the bottom of Castle Street, and walked up towards Divis Street:

> When I got to Divis Street I couldn't believe what I saw – utter destruction. Buildings and houses in flames, the smell was unforgettable … When I arrived at my own house the door was locked: nobody was in. I was worried about my mother and father, especially my father because he was ill. I walked back onto the Falls Road looking for my parents. As I approached Conway Street I couldn't believe my eyes – devastation. It was surreal: people were running into and out of burning houses grabbing their belongings before everything was lost. People were carrying bits of furniture and as they came away the flames were still engulfing entire blocks of houses. People were standing around; there was a feeling of helplessness, but there was also a palpable fear. The scene was really indescribable, and I will never forget what I saw that morning. To think that I had left the Falls Road several hours earlier to go to work and when I came back an entire district was obliterated.[128]

By daybreak, television crews captured newsreel images of burning homes in Conway Street, as pitiful residents carried away the charred remains of their modest lives. McKeague's pogromists had dispersed, as had their guard of Shorlands. Some slept off the alcohol looted from Catholic pubs, others headed back to SDA headquarters a short distance away at Wilton Street to revel in the intoxicating power unleashed by the pogrom. The Popeheads, Taigs and Fenians were firmly in their place – burned out; taught a lesson they would not soon forget. Their appetite for destruction not yet whetted, loyalists would return for more within hours – this time to Clonard and Ardoyne.

5

FROM EPICENTRE TO PERIPHERY: CLONARD AND ARDOYNE

As bleak as things appeared on Friday morning, the onslaught that Belfast's nationalists were confronted with had not yet reached its halfway mark. Hundreds of smouldering homes already lay burned and looted. While police returned to barracks, awaiting a supposedly imminent IRA attack, lines of nationalist refugees snaked up the Falls Roads, seeking shelter from the most destructive loyalist assault since the founding of the Northern Ireland state. For those who had lived through the sectarian rioting of the 1930s – and some who lost their homes in the Lower Falls had been rehoused after being burnt out in that earlier purge – the worst nightmares of Belfast's deeply troubled past seemed to be coming back to haunt them.

Schools, community centres, cinemas and other assorted buildings operated as makeshift refugee centres, sparking for others scenes reminiscent of the Belfast Blitz when, in April 1941, locals had sought shelter from Hitler's Luftwaffe. Scarman noted that:

… the chief activity to be seen in Percy Street, Dover Street and Ardmoulin Avenue (as well as in Conway Street, Cupar Street and Norfolk Street) was the evacuation of Catholic families from their homes. Hand carts, cars and vans were used to carry away furniture and household effects. Lorries and other vehicles were hijacked for the same purpose … In Beverley Street Protestants were moving into houses which had been left empty by Catholics.[1]

As dawn broke on Friday 15 August, many residents returned to salvage what they could from the remnants of their homes in the Lower Falls. West Belfast man Joe Robinson witnessed the after-effects of the previous night as he made his way to a mid-morning doctor's appointment at Unity Walk:

> I remember ... walking down the Falls Road. The next thing I remember was a lorry loaded with people's furniture and belongings, people were sitting on top of it. There was a lot of shouting, a lot of noise, so I kept walking down the road. I got as far as Conway Street, and there was a lot of confusion [there]. But I didn't know what was going on, so I kept walking until I got to Dover Street. There were houses on fire in Dover Street, and people's belongings were sitting out on the footpath. I carried on, the lorries were coming up the road, [and] five or six lorries must have passed me heading up the road ... As I was walking home this was still going on, all the confusion and burning.[2]

Elsewhere, local man Brendan Wilson recounted how:

> ... a lorry arrived at the corner of the Falls and Cupar Street. The men in the lorry shouted that there was a family needing help up the street. The house was up past the clinic [Cupar Street] close to Ernie Street and Tully's Bar. I was on the back of the lorry when we arrived. There was an angry mob outside the Catholic home baying at them, and as soon as we got them out, the house was petrol-bombed.[3]

One of those assisting in the evacuation was Anthony Bell, whose bag-making company on Ardmoulin Avenue lay next to the burning homes. His traumatised young daughter later described the scene:

The next thing was I saw my dad's van coming up the Falls Road. I waved him to stop. I asked him, 'Where were you and where have you been?' He said, 'Alice, I'm busy; I'm getting people out.' I looked into the back of the van and it was absolutely horrendous. There was a woman and her children huddled in the back of the van with lots of furniture round them. My dad was actually moving them somewhere, I don't know where – up to Andersonstown for safety.[4]

Meanwhile on Balaclava Street, Brian Conlon also assisted in the frantic evacuations:

By [early morning on Friday 15 August] my father made the decision that we would go down and help [along] with my brothers and neighbours ... we were helping to bring down furniture. We were up all night and all morning. Somebody said about going up to St Peter's Secondary School, up in Briton's Parade. We must have hijacked a few lorries or were given the lorries, but there was furniture put on the lorries. I went up Cupar Street and put furniture onto a lorry. It was a big shock to everyone that this could happen, especially with the so-called protectors of law and order – the RUC ... I was speaking to a few guys who had been working in Lawther and Harveys [Cupar Street], about six months after: they were actually hemmed in; they couldn't get out to go home, they were on night shift. There were different floors and they were able to stand and watch. They saw RUC and B-Specials throwing petrol bombs along with the crowd. The RUC, the B-Specials and the people were all one in doing the depredation.[5]

This area bore the brunt of the ensuing violence, and evidence in Scarman hints at the loyalist rationale, for, while community relations had been generally good, some under the influence of figures like Paisley and McKeague clearly resented what they perceived as

Catholic encroachment on loyalist areas. A Cupar Street resident, the wife of one of 'quite a number' of local B-Specials, told the Tribunal that while it was 'no reflection on [the] Roman Catholic population … it is not very long ago [that] Cupar Street was entirely Protestant, but as houses went empty Catholics moved in'.[6]

Astonishingly, given the scale of destruction on 14 August, RUC District Inspector Cushley 'interpreted the Catholic exodus from border areas [on the edges of the nationalist districts] as clearing the decks for further trouble that evening'.[7] Yet the large-scale movement out of vulnerable nationalist areas was not being carried out in order to facilitate the IRA offensive imagined by state forces; quite sensibly Catholics were seeking to avoid a repeat of the vicious loyalist attacks of the previous night. As things turned out, there was wisdom in their collective judgement.

Loyalist mobs carried out a new round of attacks on Friday 15 August with complete impunity. Their freedom to operate unimpeded derived in part from the close collaboration that loyalists naturally enjoyed from elements in the RUC and the B-Specials, but more fundamentally from the deliberately false premise upon which the entire police intervention was based: that the main feature of Thursday's and Friday's violence was actually the confirmation it provided of plans for a large-scale nationalist rebellion. Not only did Belfast's Police Commissioner Harold Wolseley mischaracterise events in hindsight when testifying before Scarman, but his assessment excused civilian fatalities – even that of nine-year-old Patrick Rooney:

> You see, this was akin to almost a rebellion in our opinion. There were areas into which we could not go without fighting our way in – I presume – at that stage. This was not a normal riot by any standards. The whole thing was a pretty – akin to a civil war … I mean you do not go shooting women and children, but if they happen to be there

and get hit, it is a terrible thing, but these things will happen under those circumstances.[8]

While he ignored loyalist violence, Wolseley insisted that the (near-defunct) IRA represented the real threat, admitting under testimony that loyalist violence 'was one of the sort of blind spots that [the RUC] have', given that 'the training of the Force from its inception had always been against what we called the subversive elements, the IRA and so on'.[9]

In time-honoured fashion, Chichester-Clark's government responded to events by invoking the Special Powers Act – not in an effort to curtail loyalists or apprehend ringleaders like McKeague, but, astonishingly, to arrest nationalists and republicans, and in the process concoct a dubious legitimacy for police actions the previous night. While nationalist homes burned in Conway and surrounding streets, yards away in Kane Street (Clonard), the RUC raided the home of veteran republican Proinsias MacAirt, arresting him. At 4.30 a.m. on 15 August, 'Mr Wolseley, in consultation with his deputy, Mr Bradley, made two decisions. The first was to order the arrest, with a view to detention under (Special Powers) Act of a number of suspected members of the IRA. This was done [because] Bradley [and] the Commissioner were "satisfied that the night's events had been the work of the IRA". During the morning ... six men in Belfast were detained under the Act.'[10]

In the immediate aftermath, Chichester-Clark reinforced the point that subversive elements 'were to the fore in the events of last evening' and that 'well-disciplined and ruthless men working to an evident plan attacked the police at a number of points in the city'. He quoted an unverified 'reliable' source, claiming that the IRA was planning cross-border raids.[11] This was little more than propaganda, contrived to excuse unionist violence and mollify the international news media and the British government.

CLONARD

Loyalist attacks resumed as early as midday on 15 August. In one instance, while Charles Hemsworth and other locals helped evacuees on Cupar Street, loyalist petrol bombers attacked their lorry as it turned onto Kashmir Road, with the furniture then strewn onto the street.[12] Clonard's terrified nationalists knew well that, as they had watched their neighbours' homes burn the previous night, unless they were checked, the loyalist firebombers would return to finish the job.

On witnessing the scene on Conway, Cupar and Norfolk streets on his way to work at the Falls Road Baths, Noel Devine (whose grandfather had been killed in the 1920s pogrom) decided to evacuate his parents to Turf Lodge:

> The tension was so strong that after work I got into my car and drove to my father and mother's house in 31 Bombay Street. They were both pensioners. I didn't want to worry them, but I asked them to come to my house and stay the night. My father didn't want to leave, but he decided to go. Some hours after we got to my house we heard the Clonard Monastery bells, so we knew it was trouble, and we knew it was Clonard.[13]

Built in 1911, Clonard Monastery's location on the semi-official frontier between the Shankill and the Falls left it 'very vulnerable to attack'.[14] In 1921 loyalists had shot a Redemptory lay-brother dead on its premises. Bordering Cupar Street, Deputy Commissioner Bradley identified the monastery as the specific target of the second night's violence.[15] This assessment was confirmed by a colleague, who told Scarman that the monastery and its church 'would certainly be regarded as one of the main targets if an invasion took place'.[16] Before the attacks in the vicinity of Conway Street, the monastery had received numerous threats over the telephone. When Fr McLaughlin,

resident priest, had made the RUC aware of this in the early afternoon of 14 August, they assured him the police would 'take necessary
action to secure and protect his property'.[17] By late that evening the
monastery was operating as a refugee centre for hundreds of families, many still in their night attire. Again clergy contacted the barracks and, once again, the RUC assured him that protection would
be forthcoming, if necessary. In the end the only police in Clonard on
the night formed part of an attacking loyalist mob.

Early on the afternoon of 15 August, McLaughlin contacted a
neighbouring Protestant minister, Rev. Beattie, to organise a 'peace
corps' in an attempt to prevent violence breaking out in the Clonard
and Cupar Street areas, but this initiative was too late. Mobs gathered
from Cupar Street to the entrance of Kashmir Road, leading into
Clonard, as both nationalists and loyalists hijacked lorries to
barricade their respective areas. By 2 p.m. loyalists had once again
raided Finnegan's pub, looting the remaining contents before razing
the building. One hour later, the Catholic-owned Kilfeather's pub
on the corner of Ashmore Street suffered a further attack, and its
contents were looted and the premises torched.

At approximately 3 p.m., in a courageous attempt to prevent a
new round of carnage, Beattie called for a meeting of the Protestant
residents of Ashmore, Cranmore and Cupar streets, but his efforts
would be in vain. Nearby he witnessed the mob manufacturing
petrol bombs as they polished off the contents of Finnegan's pub.[18]
Charles Hemsworth claimed that 'the minister said that he had never
seen so much free drink being consumed as in Cupar Street that
day, even by the youngest persons'.[19] Before the meeting even began,
John McQuade, MP (NI), scuppered the peacemaking efforts of Rev.
Beattie and Fr McLaughlin. He later informed Scarman:

[Beattie] informed me that he was with a Roman Catholic priest
and a Republican had a peace pact. I informed the people that there

was no need for any peace pact; if people would obey the law of the land and recognise the constitution there was no other need. I then warned the women and children to go to their homes, and keep off the streets. I told the men they would have to be prepared to defend themselves.[20]

Meanwhile, fuelled by a heady cocktail of incendiary rhetoric and looted alcohol, loyalist mobs proceeded to attack Kashmir Road and Bombay Street before spreading through the Clonard area as a whole. The mob had apparently returned to finish their work from the previous night.

Clonard resident Mrs Barbour recalled that people in her area had begun to remove their furniture and some had advised her to board up her windows:

I picked up a piece of plywood which I thought would cover the leaded lights [stained glass] on the door, and while I was hammerin' it on, the shooting started down at the end of the Kashmir Road. And I was busy hammering the thing on, and nobody would help me because everybody was flying and nobody would stand and tell you what was going to happen or what.[21]

The loyalist attack appeared to have been co-ordinated to ensure that Protestant workmen had time to return and participate, and to prevent their being stranded amongst the nationalists. The largest employer in the area, James Mackie and Sons, was situated a short distance away from Clonard. Despite its location in a predominantly Catholic area, its workforce was almost exclusively Protestant. Mackie's closed early that afternoon, in time for some of its employees to join the attack on Bombay Street. One Protestant employee confirmed to the Scarman Tribunal that when leaving work he had armed himself with an iron bar. 'Some of the hundreds of fellow employees who went with him into Cupar Street on their way home may also have had similar weapons.'[22]

Patrick McParland, a Catholic resident in the area, claimed that the new round of trouble commenced as soon as the Mackie's workers were safely back in loyalist territory:

> The Catholic district began to be showered with hundreds, perhaps thousands of petrol bombs. They must have been up all Thursday night preparing that amount of petrol bombs. This was not a spontaneous riot. The RUC had guaranteed Clonard Monastery's occupants that they would defend the area against any sectarian attack. The RUC lied, they did nothing.[23]

The loyalist mob was soon swelled with reinforcements from streets further afield, a substantial number of them armed. Loyalists from Foreman, Malvern, Snugville, James, Berlin and Keswick streets attacked and burned Catholic homes and a hairdresser's at the corner of Kane Street as they advanced into Clonard. A hail of petrol bombs thrown from Cupar Street then rained down on Bombay Street, setting fire to two residences.[24] The mob also set fire to Victor's shoemaker's shop at 72 Kashmir Road at the junction with Bombay Street.

Fr McLaughlin again appealed to the police, but to no avail. Bombay Street resident Rita Canavan claimed that '[o]utside a shoe shop on Cupar Street, members of the RUC and B-Specials were standing with a crowd of loyalists. We thought the RUC were there to stop the loyalists invading the area … We were wrong, they gave us no protection at all.'[25] Rita and her neighbour, Mrs McCarthy, fled in terror, quickly followed by other women and their children.

Loyalists rushed into the small streets, firing weapons and petrol-bombing homes as they went. With many adult males still at work, the daytime defence of Clonard relied on approximately twenty nationalist youths. At 3.45 p.m., Fr Egan heard shots and rushed to Waterville Street, where fifteen-year-old Gerard McAuley lay dying from a 'medium or high velocity bullet fired at close range which entered the chest and heart, passing right through his body'.[26] Minutes after he administered the last rites to Gerard McAuley, Fr Egan anointed a further five people, claiming that loyalists had shot up to twenty people in rapid succession.[27] In desperation Fr McLaughlin again telephoned the police:

> I was terribly agitated and worked up and terribly afraid there was going to be a holocaust and that the whole area was going to be wiped out, I was absolutely convinced that this was an attempt not merely to wipe out the Monastery but the whole area. I was really in desperation for help and I said to the man whoever answered the phone: 'Why are you not coming up to help us?'[28]

Loyalist gunfire brought an abrupt halt to the fire brigade's attempts to quell the petrol-bomb induced inferno now engulfing Bombay Street. As the firemen fled, local residents courageously took control of the abandoned equipment, but the intense gunfire forced them, too, to retreat and relinquish their homes to the flames.

At approximately 5 p.m., frantic residents urged Fr Hanley from Clonard Monastery to ring the church bell to summon help. Instead, the 'decision was taken out of his hands when a young boy in a hysterical condition ("really he was mad, his eyes were bulging and he had lost all self-control") rushed into the bell-tower and rang the bell'.[29] Fr Egan recalled to the Tribunal how traumatised local residents had clung to him in the streets, crying, 'What are we going to do? This is the end.'

The few priests left in the monastery believed that their building would be the next target. Egan telephoned British Army headquarters in Lisburn, who informed him that the army was on its way. 'This did not satisfy me ... because I saw people being gunned down and the houses were blazing at the time.'[30] Interestingly, subsequent loyalist accounts corroborate Egan's graphic testimony. One participant, who subsequently joined the Ulster Defence Association (UDA) claimed:

> Suddenly flames appeared from behind the 'enemy' lines and Big Thompson shouted in awe: 'The bastards are fleeing their homes'... It was the signal for attack. The rest of the night was spent burning rows of terraced houses in Cupar Street, Bombay Street and surrounding areas. The police were powerless to prevent the raging mass's rampage of burning and destruction. I saw one young fellow smash the front windows of a tiny kitchen-house with a flagpole and light the billowing curtains. Soon the place was ablaze.[31]

Amidst the mayhem, two local former IRA men attempted to defend their homes and families. One approached republicans in surrounding areas in search of weapons, but was told they had none. I secured the testimony of both men, who are described as witness A and B in the following extended account of the violence. The essential context for the reader is this: there was no official IRA presence in the area and although local residents did fire on the mob, this represented an improvised defence of homes mounted by local residents in reaction to violence initiated against them. The testimony points to the absurdity of the broader claim by the police and unionist government that an intended IRA offensive provoked police and loyalist violence:

> *Witness A:* I arrived back to my parent's house in Clonard with nothing. I met Seamus Simpson who had been connected to Tom Williams. Simpson gave me his licensed shotgun and five rounds of buckshot. I then met [name omitted] in Clonard. I was delighted to see him because up to now I was on my own. [He] had acquired a Beretta 380 with nine rounds of ammunition. So at least ... together

we could do something. We were there around an hour when people in the area began running and shouting, claiming that houses were being burned in Bombay Street by a loyalist crowd. Tommy [last name omitted] and I went to Bombay Street; hostile loyalists who had begun burning the houses confronted us. They were throwing petrol bombs into the houses. What happened then, Clonard's population cleared, it became a ghost town, the place cleared. Many people went to stay in the monastery … During this period sporadic attacks were coming from Cupar Street corner, at Vera McNeill's shop, and Kashmir Road hill and Kane Street. They were attacking from different places, and we were running from street to street trying to keep them back.

Witness B: I fired three rounds at them, and then our crowd shouted, 'Let's get them we have guns.'

Witness A: I then fired five rounds into the loyalist crowd. It became hand-to-hand fighting, I was standing with a brother of Tommy's, [name omitted], holding the shotgun by the barrel and lashing out trying to move them back. This fighting lasted a long time … Some of the local people saw [name omitted] and me with firearms and they realised that we were members of the IRA.

Witness B: We were ex-members at this stage.

Witness A: We then asked people round us if there were any legally held weapons within the area, was there anything at all?

Witness B: [name omitted] came out with his Bruno .22 rifle.

Witness A: We were told there was a house in Clonard Gardens; the family were away on holidays, and there was a .22 rifle and a shotgun. We forced our way in and we found them in a wardrobe along with a couple of boxes of ammunition … In total we had a number of hunting weapons which were useless compared to what we were up against. The loyalists, who were B-Specials and police trained in the use of firearms, had .303 rifles, Sterlings, Bren-guns and Webley revolvers. I could clearly see them … I knew many of them: some lived in the next street to me; many went in and out of Davy's the bookies in Lucknow Street and them going to work in Mackie's foundry. I spotted the two ... father and son, the son in particular with the two Enfield revolvers shooting them up the Kashmir hill. I saw Blackie [last name omitted] with a white shirt on, with his Sterling sub-machine gun at the corner of Sugarfield Street.

Witness A: I remember Adam [last name omitted] and his brother together with a man who lived near Vera McDade's; they were in the crowd.

Witness B: Adam's brother was a senior member of the B-Specials; he was shouting out the orders and using a whistle. He was armed with a .303 rifle.

Witness A: The reason I knew these people was because they lived beside us.

Witness B: The Mackie's workers were released from work and this made things worse. At the time myself and [Witness A] were two individuals in Clonard. It was about five o'clock when Billy McKee, [three names omitted here] arrived ... We were standing beside the butchers. McKee came to us holding a large football sock. McKee asked, 'Who's in charge here?' My reply was, 'You are,' because he was a '40s man and we looked up to him. He swore me into the movement when I was seventeen. When I seen [*sic*] him I was delighted, because I knew we were not on our own. He gave us the sock, it was full of ammunition, there were a lot of .22 and .45 bullets. They also brought a .45 Webley, a 22 automatic, a Smith & Wesson 45, and another revolver I didn't recognise.[32]

At 5 p.m. loyalists invaded Lawther and Harvey Haulage Company, Cupar Street, removing a number of vehicles and setting fire to the premises. Sometime before 6 p.m. Mr Beattie heard shooting as he drove towards Ashmore Street. 'Turning into Cupar Street he saw a man firing a gun (probably a shotgun) towards the Catholic crowd in Kashmir Road. Mr Beattie telephoned the police and reported what he had seen.'[33] Around the same time, a local nationalist recounted how they had positioned a flatbed lorry across the opening to Bombay Street to prevent the loyalist advance. As flames engulfed the first homes on the street, he spotted a man with a rifle standing menacingly over an injured resident:

> I threw a few petrol bombs, and when I seen [*sic*] the man on the other side I got a petrol bomb, I never lit it, I went out of the wee entry, I shouted at your man, leave him alone you so-and-so, and your man, who I know now was Alex Robinson, was shouting, 'Help me, help me!' I was about to throw the petrol bomb over towards the lorry or your man whoever he was, who I thought was going to shoot him again, [when] I got shot in the hand, I had a petrol bomb in my hand, lucky enough I hadn't lit it, because if I had I would have been snookered … The blood was running out of my hand and my groin.[34]

Another nationalist carried Alex Robinson from Bombay Street to Clonard Gardens to receive medical assistance. He also went to Andersonstown, returning with a shotgun and fourteen cartridges: 'A lorry was burning across the opening of Kane Street, Cupar Street. I looked through the cab. Two men with one rifle were close together. I took aim, pulled the trigger, nothing happened. It had an automatic safety catch; by this time my nerves had gone. I blasted both of them.'[35]

A handful of shotguns, however, stood little chance against the pile of advanced weaponry now in the hands of the loyalists and B-Specials. The Tribunal heard evidence that the pogromists fired high velocity weapons for several hours, including .303 rifles and .445 Webley revolvers (B-Special issue) against nationalist residents in Kashmir Road, Clonard Gardens, Bombay Street and Kane Street. The head of ballistics found spent rounds in front doors, halls and stairs, living rooms, bedrooms and windows, along with numerous shotgun pellets embedded in walls in each of the streets.[36] Despite multiple urgent warnings, the RUC had allowed a co-ordinated and bloody sectarian assault on Clonard to be carried out unimpeded. Uniformed officers fraternised with loyalists and apparently engaged in throwing petrol bombs, while members of the B-Specials, armed with high velocity weapons, formed the backbone and leadership of the mob itself. This was a pogrom.

Meanwhile, further down the Falls Road, another gang of loyalists attempted to burn those nationalist homes that remained standing in Percy Street, Dover Street, Beverley Street and Ardmoulin Avenue. Nationalists attempted to block off the Falls Road by driving a bus along Ardmoulin Avenue and across into Percy Street adjacent to the gates of Andrews' Flour Mill. Loyalists, however, burned this bus along with homes on the east side of Percy Street. An Ardmoulin Avenue resident claimed before Scarman that he'd 'observed a crowd of ten to twenty [loyalists] at the Percy Street end of Ardmoulin Avenue kicking open doors and throwing petrol bombs into the houses, by this stage the other residents of the street had fled'. The witness had 'telephoned both the police and the fire service but neither came'.[37]

The introduction of the British Army onto the streets of West Belfast now appeared inevitable. The cabinet office in London received a stream of frantic calls from leading nationalist representatives, including Paddy Devlin, Paddy Kennedy and Gerry Fitt.[38] British Home Secretary James Callaghan claimed Gerry Fitt telephoned him a number of times stating that 'only British troops could restore calm in Belfast ... only British troops could save them from the wrath of the Protestants and he urged that they should be brought in at once'.[39]

Conversely, the RUC were also requesting army assistance. Inspector General Peacock's request was dispatched to the British Army General Officer Commanding Northern Ireland at 11.30 a.m.

on 15 August 1969, informing him that the RUC could not control the situation in Belfast and that his men 'had to fall back to defend his police stations'. However, this request was made for the explicit purpose of suppressing an IRA uprising; little concern was shown over the pogrom underway in the city. This is a significant point: while it has become one of the unquestioned cornerstones of the history of the recent conflict that British troops were brought in to 'keep the peace', or even to 'protect the Catholics', RUC motivations point in a very different direction. Peacock claimed that:

> Information is to hand from a reliable source that an infiltration of members of the Irish Republican Army is about to commence from Éire into Northern Ireland. It is the intention to escalate the degree of control over inward-bound traffic, and to this end assistance in the form of patrol by armoured cars is also requested. The information indicates that the infiltrators will be armed, and the support of mobile armoured units, which I cannot supply, would be of material assistance in countering these subversive activities against the Government and people of Northern Ireland.[40]

The statement, later regurgitated by Stormont ministers, merely served to excuse the murderous activities of both state forces and loyalists. There is no doubt that the RUC were fully aware that loyalists intended to use lethal force against Belfast's Catholics. Indeed, the police repeatedly ignored clear evidence that armed loyalists were proceeding from the Shankill to nationalist areas. The control room at RUC commissioner's headquarters, Belfast, received two telephone calls during Friday's attacks on Clonard and Percy Street – the first at 15.46 p.m.; another at 15.57 p.m. – to that effect.[41]

By the time the army arrived, dozens of homes were ablaze and hundreds of families had fled, with residents suffering a substantial number of injuries. Some of the taller buildings on the Falls Road had actually been set on fire by the nationalists themselves to prevent loyalist snipers from firing on fleeing residents from a height. The towers formed a fiery backdrop as the British Army cautiously approached from several directions.

Before deploying, British Army officers met with the RUC command, who claimed that the IRA lay behind the violence and that soldiers faced potential ambush on the Falls Road. One senior police officer described 'armed bands roaming the grounds of the [nearby] Royal Victoria Hospital', who had 'also taken over the operating theatre', while 'the premises on the north side of the Falls Road and Divis Street were occupied by armed men with snipers on many rooftops'.[42] Once on the ground, however, the army quickly realised that the frightened and fatigued Falls residents posed little threat, while in contrast they encountered violence from loyalists, who viewed their presence as a barrier to further attacks on nationalists.

Lieutenant Colonel Fletcher (2nd Battalion Queen's Regiment) advanced his troops through the side streets from the Shankill towards the Falls Road, passing the charred hulks of nationalist homes en route. On police advice, battle-ready British soldiers wore steel helmets, while most carried SLRs replete with fixed bayonets, and others Sterling sub-machine guns or General Purpose Machine Guns (GPMG). By 6.30 p.m. the British Army had established itself on the Falls Road. The soldiers quickly positioned themselves at street corners along the road, placing barbed-wire entanglements and aiming their GPMGs in the direction of the non-existent IRA menace. One eyewitness claimed:

They were marching up the road from the town centre direction. They were taking up positions at the corners of streets. The man in charge was shouting for them to keep their backs against the wall. The soldiers were young and afraid. Their commanding officer was squealing at them to back their backs against the wall.[43]

At the same time 250 soldiers from the 1st Royal Regiment of Wales set up a command post at Springfield Road Barracks just a few hundred yards from Clonard Monastery.

Despite their incongruous positioning, desperate nationalist residents welcomed troops with open arms. Loyalists initially watched in disbelief as soldiers marched past on their way to the Falls Road, but once they realised that the army might frustrate their pogromist designs, the mob launched a co-ordinated petrol-bomb (and later gun) attack on British soldiers positioned at Northumberland Street.[44] In spite of the army's presence a short distance away, loyalists maintained their attacks on Percy, Dover and Beverley streets. One senior police officer noted – without taking any preventative action – that 'some of them were well under the influence of drink and my assessment of the thing was that between drink and hatred they were practically insane, some of them'.[45] A short time later, loyalists petrol-bombed Colonel Fletcher's men in Dover Street.

Loyalist snipers ensconced on the roof of Andrews' Flour Mill, Percy Street, overlooking the Falls Road, directed fire on local nationalists engaged in conversation with the army:

> I was very scared, I was so scared that I decided that I was going to go up to St Comgall's school, and I ran up the street and into St Comgall's. My father was really angry with me … So then I was in the middle of St Comgall's school with him and the British Army and I remember then [that] in the middle of talking loyalist snipers opened up and we all had to lay down on the ground. The loyalist snipers were shooting and I was laying and so was my dad.[46]

A young nationalist named Patrick McAteer had been among a crowd watching loyalists attempt to push through the burnt barricades in Percy Street when loyalist snipers targeted the assembled crowd. At 7 p.m. McAteer identified sniper fire from a church spire close to Percy Street and the Shankill Road. 'One of the lads was standing at the corner of Percy Street. They fired, striking a wall: I think they were firing from the church ... I heard [the lad] say "That just missed me, they shot at me."' McAteer and others ran across Divis Street, taking cover at the bottom of the maisonettes. On a balcony above them, British soldiers asked one another where the shot came from, confirming McAteer's view that the fire originated from the church spire. McAteer claims that a soldier then fired a couple of rounds, which only temporarily silenced the sniper, who resumed firing a 'couple of minutes later'.[47]

Despite urgent calls for help, the army remained on the Falls Road and the loyalist assault on Clonard continued unabated. 'Fr McLaughlin decided, given the gravity of the situation, to go directly to Springfield Road Barracks. As he entered, he observed police officers sitting around drinking tea, but was informed that they were under orders not to leave their barracks, fearing an imminent IRA attack.'[48] Fr Egan then went onto the Falls Road, 100 yards from Clonard, seeking help from the military, but to no avail. The RUC had imposed its own contrived parameters on military activity; the army abided by them.

At 7.40 p.m. Egan telephoned British Army Headquarters in Lisburn directly to plead for help. Thirty minutes later, 2nd Lieutenant Adams and a platoon of men entered Cupar Street to ascertain the border between nationalists and loyalists. They faced immediate attack from loyalists in neighbouring Argyle Street, which forced their hasty retreat.

A second platoon of soldiers eventually arrived at Clonard at approximately 9.30 p.m. Fr Egan brought the officer to the upper floors of the monastery, where they watched as Clonard burned. Egan suggested Cupar Street as the obvious location for troops.[49] Five minutes later the platoon was redeployed to Waterville Street to prevent the burning of St Gall's primary school. As they entered

Bombay Street, the houses on both sides blazed. When their commander, Lieutenant Adams, dispatched one of the men under his lead, Private Tyler, in the direction of a smouldering shoemaker's shop, the private was shot twice by a loyalist carrying a .303 rifle. One soldier fired a warning shot as they dragged Tyler to safety, while another directed fire at the alleged shooter. These were the only two shots fired by the British Army in Clonard that night.[50] It should be noted that this first British soldier to be injured during the Troubles was shot by loyalists.

Despite the British Army's presence, the attack underway on Bombay and Kane streets still raged. After a series of warnings, Adams ordered his men to fire fifty cartridges of CS gas; loyalists responded with a hail of petrol bombs.

At 11 p.m. Fr Egan spotted a group of loyalists from Cupar Street lurking in houses:

> I saw them distinctly throwing petrol bombs into [St Gall's] school from the corner of Waterville Street. I saw these doors being kicked in. There are six houses in a block. You will notice there are nine houses in that little block between the school and the Kashmir Road ... I saw the doors being kicked in, windows being broken, and petrol bombs being thrown into some of those houses. I saw the school attacked on three separate occasions; the first attempt was approximately 5 p.m.

British soldiers offered Clonard residents cover so that they might enter Bombay Street with abandoned fire brigade equipment to extinguish the fires, but loyalist gunfire forced them back. Egan recounted how 'as the night [of the fifteenth] wore on it got worse, and I could see petrol bombs being thrown into houses that I thought were already burning. There were quite a lot of petrol bombs thrown from an alleyway alongside the monastery, one landed in the back-yard, yards from the kitchen door.'[51] Egan suggested that the British military actually sanctioned defensive efforts by local residents:

> From the monastery I could see people coming up along an alleyway which leads from Cupar Street along the back of the school ... This is a very vulnerable point all during the night because there were no soldiers there at all and we were relying entirely on local men to protect us at that point, it was a most dangerous point. I drew the attention of soldiers to that point but they said something to the effect that they had not sufficient men and I told them that we had men there doing their best. They said: 'That's fine. Try to protect it as best you can.' There were quite a number of petrol bombs thrown up along that lane-way ... There was shouting and calling names, very uncomplimentary, directed against the British soldiers and ourselves. This went on all night. I got the impression that quite a lot of these people were drunk from the way they [were] behaving.[52]

A resident of Cupar Street recollected his own precarious position:

> We lived on the corner of Cupar Street and Sugarville Street; we were the only Catholics on that part. If the loyalists wanted to burn our house the rest of the street would have caught fire, so that didn't happen because Protestants lived in the rest. On Friday night crowds gathered on both sides of Cupar Street and Kashmir Road. The houses of Cupar Street backed onto the houses of Bombay Street, and what was happening was the Protestant mob entered the houses of Cupar Street and then threw petrol bombs into the backs of the houses in Bombay Street ... They were attempting to burn not only the houses in Clonard, but the school and Clonard Chapel. If I looked up Cupar Street, there was Belleview [sic] Street and Lawnbrook Avenue: any of the garden houses were Protestant and all the houses in Cupar Street on one side up to Kane Street were Protestant. One man who

lived in those houses was a B-Special. The loyalist crowd wrecked the houses from Lanark Street into Cupar Street. Any Catholic living in that immediate area was chased. It was well organised.

The further you went up Cupar Street the less Catholics living along there became [sic]. After Wilton Street there were very few Catholics. When these Catholic families were moving out they were abused while objects were thrown at them … The circumstances of us having to leave our home were that Protestant people living a few doors down came to our door and told us for our own safety to get out. These were good people and they did not want anything to happen to us. They had heard from their own community that something bad was going to happen and we should get out right away.[53]

Undoubtedly, the deployment of the army contained what was already an advanced and substantial pogrom. By contrast, independent eyewitness evidence suggests that the police facilitated rather than checked loyalist violence – even after British troops had been deployed. By midnight on 15/16 August, for example, loyalists had erected barricades at every entrance to the Shankill Road. In Lawnbrook Avenue, police armoured cars arrived as officers mingled with the mob. The sight of the armoured cars provoked panic among nationalist residents, who assumed it portended a new round of impending attacks. Max Hastings heard nationalist residents, who were 'very afraid of the police', plead with the army to keep the armoured cars out of the [Clonard] area.[54] Loyalists then attacked Hastings and other reporters as they accompanied Lieutenant Adams and his men into Bellevue Street. When a number of police officers and loyalists asked the army lieutenant for protection from the Catholics, Hastings recalled that 'at the time it seemed a sort of mildly sick joke'.[55]

During the early hours of 16 August gunfire and petrol-bombing became more sporadic. When relative calm was eventually restored, a Cupar Street resident recalls how:

When the army moved in and things were quiet I walked down towards my house. A soldier was sitting at the corner of Kashmir Road opposite my house. When I approached him, he shouted 'Halt!' I explained to him and pointed out that I lived in the house at the corner and I wanted to gain access. I told him that we had personal belongings and needed in. He permitted me to enter the house. I was shocked at the destruction: the first thing I noticed was the gas meter was broken open and emptied. The people who did this were clever enough to turn the gas off at the mains, because if they hadn't the rest of the houses in the row would have exploded. The soldiers saw a lot of looting but their orders were not to get involved. We left with nothing; all our belongings were left behind. My brother was in the auxiliary fire service and his uniform was destroyed. My father was an air-raid warden during the Second World War and we had kept his belongings, but they were also destroyed. Our house was not burned: it was wrecked and destroyed. They smashed the stairs to bits.[56]

The rays of summer morning sunlight revealed a scene of wanton destruction:

> To capture the atmosphere, you must remember that on that particular evening of the 15th [nationalists] felt completely abandoned; they felt that nobody cared … their homes were burned and the people were being shot down in the street, so they were very embittered at that stage.[57]

Rita Canavan claimed that the following morning a priest told all the families to return home, except for those from Bombay Street. 'We thought the house had been looted, we never imagined the whole street had been burned to the ground. There was nothing to salvage. All we had were the clothes we stood up in.'[58] Another female resident of Clonard recalls:

I was met with a street in ruins; it was like something from a war film. People described it as something reminiscent of the Blitz and it took me back to that as a child, to the fear and terror, the panic, the noise, the smells, the unknown … When I first set eyes on Bombay Street that day, I was shocked, it took a minute for what I was witnessing to sink in. The street was destroyed.[59]

ARDOYNE: 14/15 AUGUST

While the inferno on Bombay Street has become an iconic image of the Troubles, the two nights of sustained violence in Ardoyne hardly registered in the public consciousness. Yet, the campaign of sectarian attacks throughout the summer portended that this small but densely packed nationalist enclave in North Belfast could hardly avoid its own brush with loyalist extremists. In fact, the area bore the brunt of a co-ordinated police and loyalist assault. It also suffered a double indignity when the Scarman Report partially absolved completely disproportionate state violence on the spurious grounds that nationalists fired first – an allegation without a shred of ballistic evidence, and one flatly contradicted by scores of eyewitness accounts. In the end, Scarman chose to lend credence to an absurd version of events concocted by state forces, even despite the weight of evidence discrediting them.

Ardoyne was always likely to feel the loyalist backlash. McKeague's gangs had been active in driving out vulnerable Catholics along the Crumlin Road interface since May. A barrage of taunts and intimidation throughout the summer of 1969, but building in intensity through early August, increased the sense of dreadful anticipation in the vulnerable area. In the days immediately preceding the pogrom, loyalists threatened the local Holy Cross church. Many alarmed residents and terrified families – mostly women and children

– had already moved to safer districts before the outbreak of violence. Those left behind desperately erected barricades at the Crumlin Road end of Hooker and Butler streets.

The nationalist district of Ardoyne was separated from the Falls, Divis and Clonard in the west by John McKeague's power base in the Shankill area. On 14 August, several days after the organised expulsion of Catholic families from the Protestant side of the Crumlin Road (including Leopold, Palmer, Oregon, Ottawa, Columbia and Chief streets), McKeague turned his sights on Ardoyne. While one SDA section pillaged the Divis and the Falls Road, the other attacked Ardoyne from the loyalist side of the Crumlin Road. Highly organised and equipped with guns, helmets, batons and shields, they massed behind sandbagged bunkers where they had already stockpiled crates of petrol bombs. In a by now familiar pattern, rather than obstruct the mob, police spearheaded the attack on nationalist homes in Hooker Street.

As evening fell, one man observed McKeague gathering a massive crowd in Ohio Street in the Shankill area. On the other side of the Crumlin Road James Murray, manager of the Edenderry Inn, closed his business early in fear of the mob. By 8 p.m. 'a big crowd had gathered in Disraeli Street and as far back in Disraeli as I could see,' Murray recalled, 'from wall to wall of each house, from one side of the street to the other, it was crowded with people as far back as I could see, and the people were coming out towards the Crumlin Road and waving a Union Jack'.[60] A short distance from the Crumlin Road, loyalists drove four Catholic families from their Bainsmore Drive homes in a macabre warm-up for what was to come.[61]

At approximately 10.30 p.m., while loyalists in the west attacked Divis, Conway and Cupar streets, a number of journalists arrived on the Crumlin Road. Dick Walsh of *The Irish Times* witnessed approximately 250 loyalists travelling up the road, and that number swelled to 3–4,000 as the crowd advanced, en route to attack Ardoyne.

This group then merged with that from Disraeli Street and another from Rosebank Street, marshalled by men wearing armbands. The throng then stopped, facing Hooker Street. A barked order of 'Ready lads' heralded a barrage of petrol bombs on the Edenderry Inn and Rosebank Inn, as well as a bookmakers and a fruit shop.

One hundred police officers then formed a line across the Crumlin Road, but not to impede the mob. Instead, an RUC Humber armoured personnel carrier smashed through the barricades at Hooker Street, followed by baton-wielding policemen. The mob then poured into the pathway that the police had just cleared.[62] Another large group of loyalists, some wearing industrial helmets and carrying petrol bombs, then ran out of Disraeli and Palmer streets. 'One of the men wearing an armband said, "Now, lads, in" and the crowd ran into Hooker Street', while another fifty loyalists rushed into the adjacent Herbert Street.[63] Scarman stated that:

> Some of these armbands were white, improvised from a handkerchief; others were red, white and blue and seemed to have been specially made. Wearers of armbands were among the most active combatants from the Disraeli Street side and some of them (e.g. Mr Elwood) crossed into Hooker Street behind the police. By his own account Mr McKeague was present when the Protestant people crossed the Crumlin Road and entered Hooker Street and dealt with the people concerned 'giving them a lesson which I do not think they will forget'. But he did not himself enter Hooker Street.[64]

Local loyalist William Elwood claimed that the 'police asked for our assistance', and that they gathered bin lids to use as shields and rushed into Hooker Street behind their police escort.[65] In Hooker Street, 'they were smashing windows, setting some houses on fire, the majority of them ran right through and had gone into the street on the left-hand side leading off Hooker Street, into Butler Street.'[66]

Three police sergeants then led their men in two further charges into Chatham Street, as petrol-bombing loyalists followed in their wake.[67] Some Chatham Street residents vainly threw milk bottles at the invaders, but a mob of approximately forty loyalists beat them back. Sections of the mob then ran into a small street off Herbert Street, which intersects Chatham Street, and attacked a house with petrol bombs, trapping an old woman in her home – 'an invalid' who 'had no means of escape whatsoever'.[68] One Ardoyne resident, Robert McCargo, recounted how:

> I was standing in Herbert Street two police jeeps proceeded by a crowd of policemen, Specials and civilians into Herbert Street area [*sic*], who started to throw petrol bombs at the houses that were situated there ... There were civilians wearing armbands; some of them wearing helmets ... On each side of the street petrol bombs were thrown but fortunately they did not take effect on the left-hand side but they set the houses afire on the right ... I was shocked; I could not believe civilised people could come in and start firing petrol bombs without reasonable provocation.[69]

As uniformed police moved down Herbert Street, loyalists reassembled on the Crumlin Road, their first cache of petrol bombs spent. McCargo explained how 'I and the people I was standing with organised a chain of buckets of water from a house some twenty yards away, because the rest of the people closed their doors, they got frightened.'[70] Kathleen O'Kane recounted how:

> I remember the night of the 14/15 August very well. The Paisleyites came in, smashed all the windows and threw in petrol bombs. I was stuck in the house with two kids. My son Owen had just been born on 7 June that year. I was literally petrified. At one point I was sitting behind the door trying to keep the mob out. Then I

remember running down the street with my two kids in my arms, screaming. I ended up in a neighbour's house, Jean Cooney's, and she put mattresses down on the floor for us. I was just sitting there with two kids and I didn't have a bottle for the child. The Paisleyites were looking to burn us all out. I couldn't believe it. I was so angry and at the same time I literally couldn't speak.[71]

Nationalist resistance seemed futile against such overwhelming numbers and firepower.

Conditions further deteriorated when a large police contingent arrived from Tennent Street Barracks, entering Hooker Street and joining other police aggressors. According to one officer, loyalists once again moved in behind the police charge, firebombing nationalist homes. Police 'intermingled' with the mob as they exited Hooker Street, yet 'no arrests were made'.[72] A Protestant resident of Disraeli Street recounted how they joined in:

We moved from Hooker Street up to Herbert Street to give them a bit of a hand. There was a policeman, officer or a sergeant I do not know which ... We asked if he needed our assistance and he said, 'Yes, certainly', because in this case they were definitely getting a terrible hammering, so we had to give them a hand.[73]

The police apparently used alleged nationalist aggression from Hooker Street as the premise for a prearranged assault in co-ordination with loyalist vigilantes. The nationalists' resort to con-structing barricades – perfectly sensible given the recent history of SDA incursions into the area – appears to constitute the only evidence of nationalist 'offensive' activity. Yet Head Constable Seay told Scarman, 'I would say that so far as the police were concerned, it was completely impartial. No choice was left to us if we were to avoid being severely injured ourselves, first of all, and, secondly, to contain the crowd and keep them from coming out of Hooker Street across into Disraeli Street.'[74] The available evidence suggests that senior police officers directed armoured vehicles, 128 armed men, dozens of B-Specials and several hundred loyalists in a fearsome attack against the nationalist residents of Hooker Street.[75] Fr Ailbe Delaney told Scarman how a policeman assisted a loyalist bomber on the Crumlin Road: 'All I saw, he turned his back to me and to Butler Street and he appeared to get into a huddle with this young lad and the young lad emerged from the huddle with the petrol bomb in his hand … the loyalist youth subsequently threw the petrol bomb into Butler Street.'[76] In light of the overwhelming superiority in numbers and weaponry on the loyalist side, the predictable allegation that officers came under serious attack from Hooker Street appears dubious, to say the least.

At approximately 11.10 p.m. an RUC Humber carrying nine policemen, and armed with three Sterling sub-machine guns and three SLR rifles, led 'a heavily armed cavalcade' into Ardoyne.[77] Several armoured vehicles proceeded into Chatham Street and through into Herbert and Butler streets. Peter Toal of Butler Street heard shouts of 'They are coming up Hooker Street.' From the top of Hooker Street, Toal watched as the armoured cars roared into the street, followed by armed riot police and loyalist mobs. Approximately eight male residents attempted to hold back the invaders by throwing stones and petrol bombs. The cavalcade proceeded to turn left into Butler Street on its second sortie, before petrol bombs struck the leading vehicle in Herbert Street, forcing the driver to stall his engine. Crucially, officers subsequently claimed that they then came under nationalist fire from Butler Street: 'There were not more than about twenty shots fired altogether. I do not know how many were fired, as I was moving up the vehicle. I saw three or four shots fired as I was leaving the vehicle. And as I viewed it over the heads of the men I saw three or four shots fired then.'[78]

Toal, however, insisted the Humber smashed through barricades in Butler Street and was then hit by petrol bombs that set fire to its roof, whereupon the vehicle stopped, but that the police had met no gunfire. 'Immediately the doors were opened,' he recalled, and 'a burst of fire came from the rear of the vehicle. I could actually see the fellow staggering from the back of the vehicle ... whether it was a policeman or a B-Special I could not say ... I saw the figure silhouetted with the flames of the burning vehicle, the door of the vehicle opened and immediately it was opened this figure came out and the shots were fired by this figure.' Another three or four officers then exited the rear doors and helped the driver out of the vehicle. The policemen took cover before spraying surrounding homes with gunfire. Toal remained adamant that there 'were no shots fired [on police] even then'.[79]

Another witness, a young Brookfield Street resident, confirmed that no gun attack had been launched on the police, who fired indiscriminately. 'We were up lying behind a wall in Herbert Street at Butler Street, and several fellows ran down with petrol bombs, but before they got throwing the petrol bombs a big steel truck drove up and the doors opened and about seven men jumped out. They had some rifles and revolvers and just started shooting in every direction.'[80] Yet Scarman's findings on the Ardoyne attack hinged on his acceptance of police testimony that they were fired on and his rejection of consistent local eyewitness accounts.

The Tribunal established that the police occupants of the Humber fired twenty rounds of .38-revolver ammunition and thirteen rounds of 9mm Sterling ammunition, thirty-three rounds in total.[81] No officer received gunshot injuries and the ballistic report noted that no bullets from a nationalist gunman had been retrieved, which supports the eyewitness refutation of police testimony.

From their vantage point on the Crumlin Road, Ardoyne resident Thomas McMullan and Holy Cross priest Fr Marcellus watched the police/loyalist invasion of Hooker Street. The shooting began fifteen minutes later. Both men travelled to Chatham Street, where they 'saw a group of police, ten to twelve, at the corner of Chatham/Butler Street'; McMullan claimed that the firing came 'from that corner. It could have been either to the right or the left of that group of police'. Minutes later, he and Fr Marcellus together carried a nationalist who'd been shot in the head to the gates of Holy Cross church, and on to the Mater Hospital. McMullan subsequently transported over a dozen Ardoyne residents to hospital, all but one suffering from gunshot wounds.[82] Other wounded nationalists sought treatment elsewhere for fear of arrest in hospital.

Having arrived from Old Park Barracks, Sergeant St John and five officers joined the attack on Herbert Street, where 'we sort of intermingled [with loyalists] … I heard about the police being in front of the civilians but this crowd was fairly mixed. There were some civilians up at the front. I would say that the police were all at the front but there were some civilians amongst them.'[83] St John heard police fire from Butler Street: 'I drew the pistol … just about the same time it must have been the driver of the Humber had his arm out of the window with a pistol and he fired about four shots. He seemed to be taking fairly good aim, he was slow about it, and I thought, "He has them", so I put the pistol back.'[84]

One nationalist man claimed:

A line of police was drawn across Butler Street … I moved back down the road towards where the police were. As I passed Kerrera Street I could see two youths lurking in the shadow of the gable. One of them addressed me by name. I moved back across to speak to them. They said there had been considerable shooting in the Butler Street area and complained that there had been no guns on the Catholic side … Then I heard a heavy clatter of running feet and when I looked around the two youths I had been speaking to were running towards the armoured car and suddenly let go with a live petrol bomb. It splattered all over the car and flared briefly before going out. Immediately a fusillade of shots came from the car [Shorland]. They were tracer bullets – red slivers of light, which seemed to fly over my shoulder and then soar off into the night.[85]

Apparently, RUC officers fired into nationalist streets in panicked response to shots fired from other members of the same force. St John recounted how 'at some stage or other there was a policeman at the corner of Butler Street and the Crumlin Road and one at the corner of Herbert Street and the Crumlin Road with Sterling sub-machine guns ... They were firing down the street.'[86] One police officer emptied his .30 Browning machine gun into Butler Street from the back of a Shorland.[87] Head Constable Kyle stated that 'the next thing I heard was two very heavy shots from the Shorland armoured car, from that direction. I gathered they were two shots from the Browning machine gun.'[88] St John partially corroborated this claim, telling Scarman that:

I remember the two policemen being at the corners with Sterling guns. The next thing I have a picture of is two armoured vehicles, Shorlands, one at each of these junctions ... I am positive that I heard heavy machine-gun fire which must have come from these vehicles but which one it was I do not know.[89]

On the nationalist side, twenty-seven-year-old Sammy McLarnon of 37 Herbert Street was helping extinguish the flames engulfing three neighbouring houses and an adjoining shop when police fired at them from the Crumlin Road. McLarnon immediately returned home to evacuate his wife and two children. His wife, Ann, described what followed:

There was just this bright light coming from outside the house. We
saw these two fellas kneeling down in the street. Then the RUC went
over and talked to them. I thought at the time that it was our ones
and the RUC was going to arrest them. But it wasn't. The RUC said
something to them and then the two fellas and the RUC went away.
The 'B' Specials, loyalists and the RUC were together on the Crumlin
Road that night. Then I walked away to go into the working kitchen.
I came back into the living room again and then the shots came
through the window. There were three bullets, very close together.
The RUC tried to say at the inquest that they were ricochets but
they were at head height. They were obviously intended to kill. He
[Sammy, the witness's husband] was shot through the window. He
was pulling down the blind because he must have seen something.
The glass actually hit me in the face.[90]

Scarman concluded that McLarnon died from a gunshot wound
to the head from 'a 9 mm copper jacketed pistol bullet of the type
fired by a Sterling or Sten-gun or a Luger pistol'. Although 'police
shooting in the street was for a time heavy', Scarman added (without
any ballistic evidence, but only based on RUC testimony) that
the 'police were fired on first'.[91] Ardoyne residents maintain that
nationalists did not fire on police, but that the RUC and/or Specials
fired indiscriminately into homes adjacent to McLarnon's, including
35, 39 and 41 Herbert Street and No. 8 Butler Street.[92]

The gunfire from the Crumlin Road continued throughout the
night.[93] Robert McCargo witnessed a policeman firing single shots
from the Crumlin Road into Butler Street, while his civilian com-
panion screamed, 'There'll be hundreds of you dead before the
weekend.'[94] The police then shot Michael Lynch of Butler Street.
Local resident Leo Morris recounted how as police and loyalists
were 'smashing windows and throwing petrol bombs right on down
Butler Street', residents and local youths responded with stones and

petrol bombs. When a shot rang out from the Crumlin Road, Morris, Lynch and others took cover in the doorway of Mrs Reid's shop at the corner of Elmfield and Butler Street:

> As soon as me and Michael Lynch seen [*sic*] it was quiet for a moment and there was a crowd of people from Ardoyne, they were in Lower Elmfield Street, [we] ran out to try and get to the corner and as we did so Michael Lynch fell in the middle of Elmfield Street ... As he fell, he fell in front of me, and I jumped over him, and he was putting his hand up at the time and I tried to grab him and to run on, but when I grabbed him he was on his knees and he was getting up. There were that many that fell at that time, they were shot all round, and I did not know where all the shooting was coming from ... It was some time after that again I saw Michael Lynch and he was sitting in a car and I think there were another two in the car there and he was spewing up blood.[95]

Scarman concluded that it 'is impossible on the evidence to establish who fired the bullet which killed Mr Lynch, although in all probability it was the policeman who fired the Sterling into Butler Street'. Yet, again, Scarman claimed that 'though there were fatal consequences for a bystander, the police were in fact returning fire'.[96]

According to Michael McKeown:

> Next day I learned that two men – Samuel McLarnon and Michael Lynch had been shot dead by the police in Ardoyne. Several others had also been killed in Divis Street. Three years later I was astounded to read in the report of the Scarman Tribunal that there was no evidence of tracer bullets having been fired that night ... I know I saw them. And I attested to that fact in the written evidence I had submitted to the Tribunal.[97]

Scarman uncritically accepted police accounts, despite the ballistic evidence and eyewitness accounts from nationalist residents that no shots came from the Ardoyne side on 14 August and in spite of the fact that, as he noted himself, the police did not record all shootings in the 'schedule of discharges of firearms by the RUC' submitted to the Tribunal.

The Tribunal uncovered strong evidence that the 'nationalist' gunfire the police were reacting to actually came from their colleagues. Having been alerted by a priest, police discovered loyalists petrol-bombing the already burning Holy Cross Catholic girls' primary school in Chief Street. When one policeman fired two warning shots in the air, his colleagues, apparently assuming they had been attacked, proceeded to fire at the nearby Holy Cross church, just yards from homes in Ardoyne.[98] Sergeant St John stated:

Constable Rollason from Tennent Street, and I think it was about two or three other men were detailed to go into the church grounds and afford protection to them. While we were sitting, there was the sound of gunfire from the church … There was some near me who pulled their guns. The ones near me did not shoot but there were police that shot up towards the chapel grounds and I was roaring and shouting trying to get them to stop. 'There's policemen up there, there's policemen up there.'[99]

Evidence submitted by Hugh Megarry further undermines police accounts of nationalist gunfire. Megarry and a few women from Montreal, Ohio and Disraeli streets supplied refreshments through-out the night to police, B-Specials and loyalists on the Crumlin Road. Megarry stated that 'there were women making tea down in Ohio Street, and the streets off that, Montreal Street … I took tea up to the Crumlin Road myself [in] a kettle … up as far as Herbert Street. I was pouring the tea out'.[100] Apparently police and loyalists drank tea on the Crumlin Road while *under alleged nationalist gun attack.*

Megarry did claim that he heard gunfire when he brought tea to Chief Street, close to the burning Holy Cross girls' school, but this was undoubtedly the police gunfire identified by Sergeant St John. Moreover, no forensic evidence of bullet holes was discovered in any property opposite Ardoyne from where the alleged attack originated. In addition, 'all those who sustained gunshot injuries during the period 11 p.m. 14 August to 1 a.m. 15 August, were Catholic.'[101]

On reading the RUC's own accounts of this night, it is clear that they fired indiscriminately on unarmed bystanders while claiming to be *defending themselves from nationalist gunfire.* This supposed gunfire formed the premise for their armed incursions into nationalist streets, where, conveniently, hundreds of armed loyalists happened to be on hand to assist officers in their 'defensive' operation, which incidentally involved burning numerous homes. The alternative explanation suggests that police concocted the nationalist gun attack, for which no forensic evidence exists, to excuse a prearranged loyalist pogrom in Ardoyne, with a *modus operandi* that eerily mirrored similar co-operation between police and loyalists on the western side of the Shankill area that very same night.

Yet Scarman accepted the false RUC claim of an armed uprising, while largely ignoring the instrumentalist role of McKeague's armed SDA and the clear circumstantial evidence of police and loyalist co-ordination. Scarman concluded that '[b]y the morning [15 August], if not earlier, police action had been reduced to the patrol of the Crumlin Road with the limited objective of containing an armed uprising. Police officers were thinking of the situation in terms of rebellion: and the rebels, in their view, were to be found (and, if possible, held) in Ardoyne.'[102]

On Friday morning Ardoyne woke from a restless night to scenes of utter carnage and destruction. Police officers, many in armoured vehicles, had fired indiscriminately, killing two innocent residents – one in his living room – and wounding countless others. The charred remains of former homes bore testimony to the destructive intent of loyalist arsonists who had followed in their wake. Nevertheless, in an echo of the situation in the west, tensions on the Crumlin Road only increased that morning as massed loyalists patrolled the area. The manager of the Edenderry Inn was forced to flee the mob while attempting to salvage something from the smouldering remains of his business, leaving the remaining cellar contents to fuel the pogrom.

By early afternoon, desperate residents had hijacked Belfast Corporation buses as barricades on streets leading into Ardoyne. At approximately 4.30 p.m., as more residents risked attack from the mob to hijack buses on the Crumlin Road, a loyalist gunman emerged: 'a small man with a leather jacket wearing a helmet and tight trousers [came] out of Palmer Street with a gun and [fired the] gun'.[103] One witness said, 'he fired straight into a crowd who were trying to park the bus in a right place', wounding three people.[104] Another armed loyalist fired four shots into Harvey's fruit shop on Hooker Street. Peter Toal described how people in his shop ran outside and saw 'a mob entering Hooker Street from Disraeli Street with shotguns. I immediately closed the shop up and headed down home. On passing Hooker Street I saw one chap with his face buried in his hands and blood pouring out of them; another chap passed me going out of Hooker Street in the direction of Herbert Street with blood on his face.'[105] By this stage, Ardoyne residents had managed to locate two shotguns, and now directed defensive fire across the Crumlin Road, killing David Linton on Palmer Street and blinding another man.

Before the hijacking of the buses on the Crumlin Road, Belfast's police commissioner had ordered his Shorlands and armoured vehicles to the Falls/Divis/Clonard districts. By this stage, many old and infirm residents who could not leave Ardoyne had hunkered down in their homes, while those able-bodied men who stayed formed improvised community defence groups. Many of the women and children evacuated to the Holy Cross boys' primary school in Herbert Street. Hooker Street and Brookfield Street were practically empty. The majority of the people had moved out of the district altogether … The majority of all the other streets were pretty much the same, there were very few people left except the men with their houses.'[106]

Police dispatched a Humber to the local bus depot shortly after 6 p.m. to prevent further hijacking. Its occupants fired on 'the tyres of each bus at the front and at the rear of each line'.[107] The gunfire not only provoked fear and panic among Ardoyne residents, but prompted loyalist gunfire across the Crumlin Road. The gunfire also provoked the dispatch of two B-Specials, both armed with .303 sniper rifles, to the junction of the Crumlin Road and Tennent Street.[108] The Humber then proceeded down the Crumlin Road, joining a Shorland in Antigua Street. Having claimed to come under sniper fire from Ewart's Mill, opposite Cambrai Street, the Shorland's Browning machine gun opened fire, raking the building. Some rounds missed their target and flew past Holy Cross church and into Twaddell Avenue. When police also mistakenly sprayed the neighbouring Brookfield Mill, Protestant residents of Glencairn Estate mistakenly reported incoming gunfire from Ardoyne. Scarman surmised that the police 'went to the Glencairn Estate' to investigate 'the destination of [their] own fire from Antigua Street'.[109] There, police gathered their own spent rounds from Nos 189, 191 and a Post Office in Ballygomartin Road.[110] While travelling to Glencairn, police – again claiming to be under attack – directed fire into Hooker Street.[111]

Meanwhile, at 7.30 p.m. in Ardoyne, while women and children sheltered in the school, the remaining male residents met to discuss the area's defence. Their meagre, newly acquired arsenal amounted to two shotguns and a defective .303 rifle; the ensuing contest would be an unequal one.

At 8.44 p.m. loyalist snipers from Brookfield Mill fired on a young couple in Brookfield Street. As they dove for cover, a Shorland armoured car fired on them from the top of the street:

> I turned round and saw a police armoured car on the Crumlin Road at the mouth of Brookfield Street. It opened fire and I got hit on the legs … shots were coming from the armoured car … I fell to the ground. I was on the ground … and I got up to try and get away. My granny only lives about three doors down from where I got shot and I tried to make it down there but I could not and fell again. My Uncle Joe came and carried me into the house.[112]

A short time later Edward Campbell was shot by police in Brookfield Street. The Shorland gunner, identified only as 'Mr Y', discharged a total of forty-five rounds into Brookfield Street. A ballistics expert discovered bullet damage to the front of six houses in Brookfield Street, suggesting automatic fire from a point on the Crumlin Road, apparently from 'Mr Y's' Shorland.[113] The residents of 39, 41, 45, 49, 53 and 57 Brookfield Street had lucky escapes, perhaps because a concrete lamp standard outside number 61 caught much of the fire.[114]

Police communications proved pivotal in the escalation of violence. At 9.09 p.m. B-Specials detailed to guard the perimeter of Tennent Street Barracks opened fire on a passing car, requesting police assistance twice within a minute: 'Red 10 – Tennent St Station being attacked both front and rear … Red 10 – Tennent St Station is being attacked'. One hour later, the deputy inspector general ordered that 'all mobiles are to be armed with automatic weapons (at least one weapon). If shortage of Arms contact Headquarters.'[115] In fact, the B-Specials had fired on a German television crew, who police released after questioning.

While many officers merely panicked, others became trigger-happy. From the roof of Tennent Street Barracks, Head Constable Owens watched the unfolding events. 'I heard gunfire throughout the night in different directions, some from the Falls Road direction looking from the station, some from the Ardoyne direction as one looks from Tennent Street, some from the Oldpark direction as one looks from the station ... I heard at least one burst of heavy automatic fire ... Possibly something like a Browning.'[116]

The SDA's co-ordinated attacks on businesses began again at 10 p.m. Not far from Ardoyne, loyalists attacked, looted and burned nine public houses in North Belfast, including the Bowling Green, the Alderman, the Admiral and Bush Bars.[117] Head Constable Kyle doubted that the attacks were organised, but struggled to explain how so many businesses suffered the same fate between 10 p.m. and 3 a.m. He admitted, 'As far as I know they were all Catholic owned. The only one that I did not visit was the one at the Wheatfield. I had spoken to Mr O'Hara on the morning of the fifteenth, when he had remained with his premises right up to half past six and the place was well secured, and then the next night it was set on fire.'[118]

Meanwhile, large loyalist crowds, clearly swelled with Dutch courage, once again congregated on the Crumlin Road under *de facto* police protection. SDA member and Rosebank Street resident William Elwood was again involved, and he petrol-bombed the improvised nationalist barricades: 'There was a bus had been erected, put across the street at Hooker Street, and the crowds were standing behind it. We were trying to throw them [petrol bombs] over the bus, but unfortunately they never really reached that stage, we were only able to throw them down the street.'[119]

At approximately 11 p.m., police officers reported fire from Hooker Street. Shorland gunners then fired four or five bursts totalling 100 rounds from Browning guns.[120] Peter Toal described increasingly heavy bursts of tracer bullets from machine guns from the

Crumlin Road into Hooker Street, Brookfield Street and Herbert Street. In an act of wanton terrorism, Shorland gunners mercilessly sprayed Butler Street, where the Holy Cross boys' primary school is situated, with their Browning machine guns, firing the 'whole nine yards' from their canvas-fed belts containing .30 ammunition. Firing several rounds per second at speeds of 2400/2800 feet per second, the bullets burst through a transformer box in front of the school.[121] Families who had taken refuge there screamed in terror. Individual police officers also targeted the school with military issue weapons, their rounds penetrating classrooms 7, 10, 16 and 18.[122]

The evidence suggests, therefore, that on the night of 15 August the RUC directed indiscriminate machine-gun and revolver fire against an improvised refugee centre containing innocent women and children. Scarman would later comment, uncharacteristically, that while 'It would not be right to condemn the police in their vehicles for opening fire when they were fired upon … the Tribunal has no doubt that these incidents provide an illustration of the unsuitability of the Browning for riot control. It was a merciful chance that there were no fatal casualties from Browning fire this evening in the Ardoyne.'[123] Elsewhere, he rather meekly confirmed that the 'police no longer felt inhibited about using the heavy Browning machine gun fitted on the Shorlands'.[124]

This was not the only example of buildings housing innocents being fired upon. On Fairfield Street a policeman fired his Webley revolver into John Rice's home, while other officers fired through the letterbox of 28 Brompton Park. Mrs Rafferty of 58 Butler Street discovered a 7.62 bullet fired from an SLR, which had passed through her house and lodged in the kitchen door. Police rounds also damaged bathrooms and bedrooms at 2 and 2a Oakfield Street, while the RUC fired three low-velocity rounds through the front door of 65 Chatham Street.[125]

While police, B-Specials and loyalists laid siege to Ardoyne, their radio calls indicated that anarchy prevailed elsewhere. The SDA ran rampant in McKeague's heartland, shooting, looting and petrol-bombing the few remaining families. Police received calls about armed loyalists in Wesley, Disraeli and Bray streets and the Crumlin Road, while the mob erected armed roadblocks on the approaches to Ardoyne. Loyalists proceeded to loot a petrol station on the Crumlin Road and targeted pubs and off-licences. On Agnes Street, while publican Mr Mallon and his family lay trapped inside his burning pub, loyalists baying for blood and alcohol rampaged outside. A call made from the premises stated, 'We are in the burnt bar at the corner of Agnes Street, hostile crowd threatening to kill us if we don't give out whiskey.' Another call at 2.51 a.m. asked police, 'What is being done about these houses on fire in Crumlin Road, Hooker Street and Herbert Streets?'[126]

Yet there was more to come. Loyalists had stored more crates of petrol bombs in Ohio and Bray streets, behind police lines on the Crumlin Road, in readiness for the next assault on Ardoyne. At approximately 2 a.m., and under covering fire from a Shorland, the mob crossed the Crumlin Road from Rosebank Street and entered Brookfield Street. Around the same time, Mrs O'Rafferty from Jamaica Street in Ardoyne called the BBC 'to say that [B] Specials were shooting indiscriminately from rooftops in the area. She appealed passionately for military intervention.'[127]

The mob systematically looted and burned twenty Catholic homes on Brookfield Street:

I saw them breaking windows and kicking the doors down with their feet and going into the houses ... They were carrying whatever they could carry out of the houses to the opposite side of the road ... [and] set [houses] on fire after they were looted ... I think twenty houses were burnt, straight from the end of Brookfield Street, Crumlin Road end, down to the bus ... I then went to Brookfield Street, and there was a police armoured vehicle sitting at Herbert Street with its guns pointed down Herbert Street, and a few yards, twenty–thirty yards on down the street, these people were carrying whatever they could across the street.[128]

This crescendo of loyalist fury marked the culmination of two days of sustained and co-ordinated police and mob violence. Yet the official inquiry stretched the very limits of credulity to excuse this conduct. A loyalist participant told the Tribunal that there was a smell of gas and the houses 'just sort of blew up, they did not go on fire'. He then admitted that loyalists had set fire to the houses, but claimed this was because of an IRA sniper in the end house in the street.[129] Astonishingly, Scarman concluded that 'no police evidence of the burning of Brookfield Street was available'.[130]

While Brookfield Street burned, a young pregnant woman sheltering in the school went into labour. She was rushed to Peter Toal's at 68 Butler Street, where a fellow refugee and nurse came to her aid. Toal recounted how he 'had at one time to dodge round the corner into Brookfield Street to avoid machine-gun bullets that were striking the roadway ... Machine-gun bullets coming up Brookfield Street ... on Saturday morning I carried the stretcher out of my house of the young woman that was after having a baby. The ambulance could not even get in ... I carried the stretcher out onto the Crumlin Road at the top of Butler Street. There were three armoured cars sitting there at the top of Butler Street.'[131]

All the available evidence suggests that, rather than participants in a pre-planned republican insurrection, the innocent residents of Ardoyne suffered an unprovoked and co-ordinated onslaught from police and loyalists. A seasoned solicitor who knew Belfast well recalled that his 'ever-lasting memory from the statements given by the residents of Ardoyne was that when the attacks began on Ardoyne by loyalist gangs, many people in Ardoyne had the same story: that they were watching *Gideon's Way* [then a popular television programme]. The attacks were unprovoked.'[132]

The sickening scenes in Ardoyne over two nights in August, their horror compounded by Scarman's later endorsement of the basic rationale for joint police/loyalist incursions into the area, changed that community's history forever. An age of innocence had passed. Peter Toal summed it up for Scarman:

On the Thursday night and Friday night, and days as well, never mind nights, people were in a terrible state. They expected to be annihilated. An attack was made. I myself saw the burning and saw the terror that night. I have never experienced anything like that, and I have been in the army and the war. I have seen the air raids everywhere and it had no comparison.[133]

6

PICKING UP THE PIECES

As dawn broke on Sunday 17 August 1969, vast sections of nationalist Belfast lay in ashes. Paisley's decade of vitriolic incitement had erupted into deadly sectarian fury as McKeague's SDA, the UPV and the UVF wrought an orgy of arson and murder on their working-class, nationalist neighbours. While Bombay and numerous other streets burned, the unionist establishment fiddled, blaming the violence on a non-existent IRA plot.

On that day Stormont's ministers held a news conference to account for the previous three days of carnage. International, national and local journalists – many of them witnesses to the events – listened in disbelief as the official representatives of the Stormont regime attempted to exonerate their own forces and pin the blame for the dreadful carnage of the previous days and nights on its main victims (some of whom, officials insisted, had burned their own homes), while conjuring the outlandish spectre of a fictional IRA conspiracy.

On Tuesday 19 August the nationalist *Irish News* described the hostile consensus among journalists regarding Sunday's press conference: 'The whole repertoire of Unionist apologetics was paraded in an attempt to explain the latest excuses of Government duplicity, [with] evasion and invention the orders of the day – but this time to no avail.' The report noted how some journalists grew visibly angry when confronted with official deflection and lies. Ministers pointedly failed to criticise the SDA or other loyalist organisations, or to offer a word of comfort for their victims. The B-Specials were stoutly defended, with any questions about their possible disbandment dismissed out of hand. The reporter rightly pointed out that police had failed to arrest a single Protestant extremist throughout the entire duration of the violence. As the press conference ended, many journalists raged against the government's flagrantly inaccurate account of events; events that many had witnessed at first hand. 'Little wonder that the correspondent of *The Times* should end his report with the comment of a foreign journalist as he left the room: "I have never been to a crucifixion before".'[1]

The newspaper reporters were not the only sceptics. Harold Wilson's government clearly did not accept the police's explanation that they had been confronted with an IRA invasion. As British troops arrived on the Crumlin Road in Belfast on Saturday afternoon to end the siege of nationalist Ardoyne, the unionist regime had urgently requested that Royal Engineers be dispatched to the border to blow up minor crossings to prevent cross-border raids. Home Secretary James Callaghan denied the request, claiming that it would worsen conditions in Belfast and Derry and damage British relations with the Irish Republic.[2]

A report in *The Times* on 18 August forcefully condemned the 'abysmal' performance of the four Stormont ministers who orchestrated the news conference. Chichester-Clark had argued that 'the whole thing started in the Bogside area, and then escalated from there', without mentioning the conduct of loyalists and police in the Maiden City. He then regurgitated the stock argument concerning the 'activities of extreme Republican elements and others determined to overthrow our state'. When one reporter pointed out to the Education Minister, Captain Long, that 'Protestants had gone into one area and burnt sixty-seven houses' and that his 'own investigation' suggested that 200 Catholic houses had been burned, Long breathtakingly replied that 'a tremendous amount of those fires have been started within those areas which were sealed off by the Catholic population themselves'. Chichester-Clark evaded questions about the B-Specials' direct participation in house-burning. When asked by a journalist to whom information for a potential inquiry should be given, the Minister of Home Affairs, Robert Porter, replied: 'to the police', at which point 'almost the entire hall burst into laughter'.[3] *The Observer* concluded unambiguously that 'Catholics had reason not to trust their new Premier. Twice this week he has seemed to be partial. He allowed the Apprentice Boys to shout their message of hate through the streets of Londonderry. And he armed and deployed the Ulster Special Constabulary, a sectarian militia.'[4]

Not all the media outlets dissented from the official message. Unsurprisingly, the unionist *News Letter* peddled the regime's line regarding a republican uprising. Initially it was asserted that the RUC had discovered an IRA radio transmitter together with code books in a derelict house in Conway Street, though the story was retracted when the transmitter's owner, Joseph Doyle, demanded an apology from both police and the press. In reality, Doyle, a Belfast City Corporation employee and radio enthusiast, had been forced to flee his burning home – elderly parents in tow – to evade the loyalist attack, a detail missing from the *News Letter's* otherwise lurid account. While oblivious to the plight of thousands of nationalist families, the paper's coverage featured a moving story about a Protestant pensioner who refused to move from his Argyle Street home of seventy-one years.[5] In addition, the *News Letter* also printed an interview with John McQuade – who had been active in loyalist ranks throughout disturbances in the west of the city. Predictably, the future MP for Woodvale reiterated the official position that the IRA was to blame.[6]

Not to be outdone by government ministers, Ian Paisley told his congregation that nationalist accounts represented anti-Protestant propaganda, 'as he had evidence that the Falls Road Catholics had set fire to their own homes ... all the Catholic homes were stocked with petrol bombs so when one was set on fire by Catholics, they all went up in flames'.[7] A few days later Paisley informed a press conference at the UCDC's headquarters in Shaftesbury Square that he wanted recruits for his 'new army', and appealed to all right-thinking Protestants to join him and save 'Ulster'. Calling for a boycott of goods from the South, Paisley urged that 'we ought to retaliate and show how we treat the military exercises he [Lynch] is engaged in'. Jack Lynch had kept his promise to dispatch medical aid to both County Louth and County Donegal to assist the wounded and refugees, and these were accompanied by military units, but he had no intention of ordering the Irish Army to cross the border. Paisley declared that 'we will not surrender our heritage' and urged Protestants 'to deal with fires and to get them [Protestants] rehoused after they had been threatened by extreme Catholics'.[8]

Incidentally, one eyewitness account suggests that although he was fully prepared to incite violence, Paisley baulked at placing himself in the line of fire. On 15 August, a Shankill loyalist claimed that:

On the Friday night that the troops came in I saw Paisley at the top of Percy Street [Shankill Road end]. There was still fighting going on at the bottom of it [Falls Road end] around Andrews' flour mill. There was a bus across the street and people were ferrying in petrol bombs from both sides and flat-topped lorries were moving families out. Suddenly there was a flare up and people surged towards it. Paisley appeared standing at the corner of Northumberland Street and was surrounded by five or six old women who were holding on to him. 'I have to get down there to help my people', he was saying, but the women were holding on to him: 'You can't go down there Dr Paisley, it's dangerous'. There he was, a big hulk of a man, being held back by these old women: if he'd wanted to, he could have got free of them. It would have been like bursting out of a paper bag.[9]

Many within mainstream unionism parroted Paisley's ludicrous claim that nationalists had burned their own homes. Leading Orangeman, the Rev. Martin Smyth, insisted that '[t]he fact is that scores of Protestants helped Roman Catholics only to be whipped in return by malicious stories of evictions which were groundless. There have been threats. There have been evictions. But most Roman Catholics left at their own wishes. Some fired their own homes.'[10]

However, having witnessed news reports, Protestant clergymen south of the border failed to draw the same conclusion as their northern brethren. Church of Ireland Minister and Dean of Cork, the Very Rev. F. M. K. Johnston, declared in his Sunday sermon, 'Today one is ashamed to be termed a Protestant. We repudiate the so-called Protestant spirit that deliberately sets out to suppress and intimidate, that allows and encourages ghettoes within cities and victimisation of men and women because of their political convictions. We have known no such ghettoes in the South.'[11]

Similarly, elements of the southern political opposition supported the overt condemnation of events made by Jack Lynch's Fianna Fáil government. Having travelled to Belfast, Derry and Armagh to witness the destruction, Irish Labour Party TD Conor Cruise O'Brien travelled with several TDs to London to meet Lord Chalfont at the Foreign Office. O'Brien demanded the deployment of a United Nations force as nationalists lacked confidence in 'the Stormont constabulary'. Given his later political trajectory, the remarks made by O'Brien in the immediate aftermath of the attacks are striking for their clear denunciation of the unionist regime.[12] The British press reported that 'Nothing less than the end of Stormont rule in the Six Counties will satisfy him and his colleagues. Troops were welcome now, but they must not be used to shore up Stormont. That must be swept away and government from Westminster substituted.'[13]

Cornelius O'Leary, a politics lecturer at Queen's University who was originally from Limerick, stated unequivocally that:

[A]ll the evidence suggests that the numbers of dead, wounded and homeless are overwhelmingly Catholic. The consequences are that the Catholics no longer have any confidence in the ability of the Unionist Government to maintain law and order impartially, and this conviction is shared by many who openly supported the efforts of Captain O'Neill to improve relations between the two religious groups ... the position has now been reached where the constitutional settlement, which in practice has meant rule by the Orange Order through the medium of the Unionist Party, is no longer tolerable to the Catholic minority of thirty-five per cent.[14]

In the aftermath of the regime's shambolic news conference, NICRA established an independent service for visiting journalists to counter 'the misrepresentation of the Government news service'. It raised the question: if government assertions about an IRA uprising were valid, where was the evidence of police casualties, or of republican attacks on Protestant property and persons? NICRA aptly characterised the previous Thursday night and Friday afternoon as a 'Protestant insurrection with the complicity of the police and B-Specials', before dismissing Chichester-Clark's proposal for a peace conference as 'a fatuous and sham attempt at window dressing'.[15]

While we should hardly be surprised by NICRA's reaction, it corresponded with the independent consensus that extended far beyond the nationalist community – that is to say, the consensus on events broadly accepted by international journalists with no real motivation to accept one side's version of events over the other's – that no republican rising existed. Among the journalists who actually witnessed the violence, opinion appeared unanimous: there were no nationalist guns, never mind plans for insurrection; the police had facilitated and frequently participated in extreme loyalist violence; and the introduction of the British Army averted a sectarian bloodbath.

The allegation that nationalist residents had burned their own homes as part of a republican plot left many of the worst victims of the violence crestfallen. In the wake of the pogrom, C. J. Devine, a Bombay Street resident, penned a letter to *The Irish News*:

> I am writing on behalf of the people of the Clonard district, whose homes have been burned to the ground, and the only reason is that we are Catholics. I am an ex-Serviceman of World War I. My number in the Royal Flying Corps was 196717, having joined the medical section at 17. I came home to Belfast in 1920, and lost my father from the effects of a beating he received during the riots of the time. I also received in the last war the rank of senior Civil Defence Officer and later was a leading fireman in Belfast Fire Brigade. When the Belfast Ambulance Service was formed in 1941 I was retained as a senior ambulance officer. During my 35 years of service to the Belfast public I have done everything that was possible to ease suffering in a humane way. For my services to the Northern Ireland Government during the wartime raids and to the Belfast Ambulance Service I was awarded the British Empire Medal by the Queen. Now I have been left without a home, it having been burned down, and with it all I possessed including the medal I cherished most, the BEM, because to me it was a symbol of charity and love of people. I am sorry for having to write this, but I could not let this pass without showing these people how wrong they are.[16]

A succession of independent journalists came forward to establish that not only had there been no armed conspiracy, but arms of any description had been an extremely scarce commodity when they'd been needed most in the nationalist ghettoes. *Times* correspondent Julian Mounter published an article entitled 'Doubts on the Role of the IRA in Belfast Gun Battles' wherein he claimed to have met men who 'fought for the Falls Road Roman Catholics'. He related that they only considered the use of firearms after the deployment of B-Specials, when two men were dispatched throughout the city in search of guns:

> Everywhere the answer was the same – the arms had gone years before in repeated raids by the RUC. We got a few rounds of ammunition but it was painfully small. By Thursday night we had one sub-machine gun, a rifle, and two or three pistols. The sub-machine gun belongs to a man who lives in Belfast and who has connexions with the IRA, but he is not one now. I am sure of that. He claims that they stole a truck and drove it to Donegal, but to no avail. They appealed in the streets in Catholic areas, but all they received was 'a useless revolver and four shotguns'. They telephoned their contacts in Dublin and were told that dozens of arms and weapons were on their way. 'All they came up with were two men and one rifle, and they arrived after it was all over … You must realise – no one understands this – we were terrified. We knew the "Prods" had guns; some of the Bs [Specials] who had more than one weapon had given their pistols to relatives. If the British Army had not come in we would have all been massacred.'[17]

While it is impossible to establish whether a massacre would have engulfed the whole of the Falls if the army had not arrived, there is good evidence that soldiers undoubtedly prevented an extension of the pogrom into Albert Street. According to Fr Patrick Murphy of St Peter's, Albert Street, even after the soldiers deployed, loyalists continued to threaten and attack his church, his parishioners and the newly arrived troops. St Peter's church, situated 100 yards from the Falls Road/Divis/Albert Street junction, lies just 200 yards from Percy and Dover streets, where the loyalist attacks began. Murphy related how on the night of 15 August, despite the presence of the army, 'there was great fear, great unrest and the people in the streets were building barricades, not only at the ends of the streets, facing what you would call maybe danger areas, but even within the complex of streets, at the end of each street to prevent vehicles coming through'. People were in a state of panic because of the killings and the large number of casualties, and while many families had already moved out, 'quite a number of people were still wanting to move, and moving'. Murphy proceeded to the junction, which was still under loyalist sniper fire, when a mob suddenly rushed down Northumberland Street from the Shankill: 'I heard the military shouting "Halt or we Fire". I think they called two or three times, and then they did fire. I was relieved indeed when I discovered it was gas they fired ... the crowd that were coming down Northumberland Street shouted and screamed and retreated.'[18]

While British troops had a salutary effect on the Falls, there is substantial independent evidence that police were working hand-in-glove with loyalists on the Shankill. During the army's confrontation with loyalists in Northumberland Street, a short distance away on the Shankill, Arthur Helliwell, correspondent for *The People*, claimed that '[o]fficers of law and order [were] showing civilians how to hide their guns. It didn't make sense.' He recounted how he saw two men carrying shotguns on the Shankill Road: 'A few yards further on the men were stopped by two armed policemen and I watched with amazement as the constables, with broad grins, persuaded them to conceal their weapons under their coats. "Good night and take care," said the police officers as the two gunmen moved off in the direction of the barricaded streets where all the afternoon sniper fire had echoed over the rooftops.'[19] The stunned journalist's graphic testimony confirmed the nationalist community's worst suspicions about the complicity of the police in the horror they confronted.

As part of the Scarman Tribunal investigation, Drs Poole and Boal of Queen's University's Geography Department compiled a residential displacement report arising from the violence in the summer of 1969. Employing a range of mostly official sources, Poole's team divided the city into zones which defined the areas of investigation. Belfast in 1969 contained 29,000 Catholic and 88,000 non-Catholic households of which 1.6 per cent suffered displacement. The team calculated the displacement of 1,505 (82.7 per cent) Catholics as opposed to 315 (17.3 per cent) non-Catholic households between July and August, with the majority in the western and north-western sections of the city. Although Poole rejected the refugee centres' estimate of 3,570 homeless families, he argued that the official estimate of 1,820 only represented a minimum figure, as 'some people who were refugees, did not appear on one of those three official lists'. Poole also revealed to Scarman that of the later expulsions in September, most came from the Old Park area of North Belfast: 'A total of 144 moves came from zone 213 (Oldpark area) ... Of the 144 lying in zone 213 that I suspect are predominantly September moves, 143 of them are Catholic and one is non-Catholic.'[20]

These figures appear to omit McKeague's campaign of expulsion between April and July; nor do they encompass the significant attacks throughout the autumn and winter of 1969. John Darby's *Conflict in Northern Ireland* points out that '[i]n August and September [1969] more than 3,500 families were forced to leave their homes, 85% of them Catholic. Two years later, during three weeks in August 1971, a further 2,069 recorded families left their homes.' A further study by John Darby and Geoffrey Morris claimed that a subsequent two periods of heightened violence led to between 8,000 and 15,000 families in the Greater Belfast area alone fleeing their homes.[21]

In the immediate wake of the August pogrom, work to alleviate the plight of refugees began in church halls in the smouldering no man's land between the Shankill and Falls roads. Dedicated churchmen, both Catholic and Protestant, came together, including Presbyterian Minister Brian Muir of Albert Street church, Rev. Kenneth Ruddock, Church of Ireland Northumberland Street, Rev.

McCollum, Townsend Street church, and Fr Murphy from St Peter's Catholic church in Albert Street. Murphy claimed that these men built a close relationship. 'I kept asking them to try to set up some kind of equivalent group of peacemakers as we would have on our side, to try to get together and talk about goodwill, reconciliation and so on, to prevent the thing deteriorating any more.'[22] These gestures of Christian charity and tolerance appeared all the brighter against the black background of sectarian hatred that made any such arrangements impossible.

The trickle of homeless nationalist refugees in the early summer had, by mid-August, become a desperate torrent of the dispossessed flocking to improvised centres for shelter and safety. Fr Murphy described a destitute multitude with nothing but the clothes they stood in – the human flotsam and jetsam of the pogrom. 'There was quite an enormous amount of work, I doubt if I would be qualified to describe it all, but I do know that at some time we estimated we had 15,000 souls to cater for in that way.'[23] The majority of West Belfast schools, several church halls and a youth club were transformed into makeshift refugee centres. The British Army commandeered the Falls Baths as a temporary billet, while desperate people forced the doors of Broadway Cinema to accommodate the ever-increasing numbers of evacuees.

Some of the individual stories were particularly harrowing. On Friday 15 August, Crew B of St John's Ambulance took a call from the Heysham ferry, 'where a Mrs Marley was evacuating to England with her family of four young children ... but tragedy struck as one of the children fell down a gangway ladder and received severe head injuries. The crew evacuated the whole family to the Belfast City Hospital.'[24]

Despite the desolation, little sympathy existed for the refugees among extreme loyalists. Paisley's *Protestant Telegraph* claimed that 'the so-called Roman Catholic refugees left their homes in Belfast and many of the houses were wrecked by their occupants before they pulled out'.[25]

Families were required to register at refugee centres. It was reported that up to 4,000 couldn't or wouldn't live in their previous Belfast homes. One hundred and sixty firebombed homes were unliveable, 200 severely damaged and a further 1,000 in urgent need of repair. It was estimated that 750 people had fled to refugee centres, with 2,240 staying with relations or friends.[26]

The situation became increasingly critical as more families sought overstretched support. The Doyle and Donnelly families fled Conway Street, arriving in St Teresa's School, where 'there were hundreds of people there from elderly people to babes in arms'.[27] Mrs Marie Higgins and her nine children fled her Mountpottinger home in East Belfast, arriving at St Aidan's refugee centre with nothing but the clothes on their backs. She claimed that 'a friendly Protestant woman who had tipped them off earlier said on Friday night: "Tonight is the night to be on your guard."' Mrs Higgins told a reporter that she had left all her possessions behind and now relied on donations to feed her baby: 'As in war, money has become a secondary consideration to living.'[28]

Weeks after the onslaught, 3,000 refugees still remained homeless. St Joseph's Teacher Training Centre at Trench House in Andersonstown quickly became the co-ordinating facility for these people. Volunteer staff supported by social workers attempted to cope with the influx. Although 3,000 people registered with the centre, a spokesman described this as just the tip of the iceberg:

> We are now becoming aware of vast numbers of people who have gone to relatives or friends or who have left completely that we didn't know about. At the last count the office recorded 2,800 homeless people who are 'billeted' in flats and homes of ordinary citizens. In four of the resident centres there were about 160 people living full-

time. The rest of the 21 centres are used for giving out food and clothing to the several thousand who are 'billeted' and to giving free legal advice and organising supplementary benefits. Although originally there were about 800 people living in the centres and around 3,500 housed by volunteers, the Trench House staff does not believe the problem is easing. 'I know people are still leaving houses because of intimidation ... there is no mass movement as there was at the time of the riots, but it is still going on.'[29]

Countless others found refuge in shelters in the Republic, facilitated by the Irish Army in their camps at Gormanston, County Meath, Finner, County Donegal, and a government camp in Kildare.[30] Some moved as far as Cork and Limerick. One refugee living with his wife and baby son in Gormanston insisted he would 'never go back to Belfast, except to collect a few things before leaving forever'.[31] Another man, who had worked at Belfast's docks, said that he was leaving for Australia with his wife and children. Michael Devine, correspondent for the *Belfast Telegraph,* reported that most of his interviewees intended to leave Ireland, but also spoke with 'others still hopeful that some sort of normality would return, yet had no plans for going back to their homes in Derry, Belfast or Dungannon'.[32]

Countless families did not register with the authorities but instead found places of shelter themselves. The Livingstone family didn't register in a shelter. Having fled their Dover Street home on the night of 14 August, they were discovered a short distance away in Durham Street by a passing motorist, a Mr Mallon. Mallon brought the family to a bungalow which he owned several miles away in Carryduff. 'We had lost everything and in the days, weeks and months that followed our mother managed to get food and clothing from refugee centres in Belfast while travelling back to Carryduff on the bus with her goods stuffed in pillowcases. We stayed in that bungalow for three months until we were rehoused in the Divis Flats.'[33]

Others who asked for help, received none. Owen McDonald, from David Street, claimed that 'we received no financial benefits; I wrote away to the Bernadette Devlin fund but received nothing. I went to Mr Robert Young, Corporation Baths General Manager, seeking a week's leave, but his reply was that he could not pay me for a week off. I said that I did not come looking for money but for a week's leave.'[34]

The Refugee Relief Co-Ordination Centre at Trench House condemned the authorities' 'inadequate and tardy response' to the crisis. After three weeks and 500 families registered homeless, Belfast Corporation provided fifty-nine temporary units, consisting of fifty caravans at Beechmount and nine wooden huts on Cullingtree Road, off Albert Street. The O'Neills, Laverys, O'Hanlons and fifteen other families moved to the Beechmount site, spending a cold winter in squalid conditions. One couple from Norfolk Street, who had been separated from their three sons, recounted how 'we were left with just what we stood up in', while a visiting aunt from America flew home with only her handbag for luggage. The couple praised the kindness of Protestant neighbours and friends, before identifying the 'very poor' conditions in Beechmount.[35] The Northern Ireland Housing Trust promised to provide 114 temporary units in six weeks' time, an inadequate response given that an estimated 500 families remained homeless.[36] Paddy Stott, formerly of Cupar Street, gave some indication of the turmoil and disruption involved:

What happened to us I can't forget about. I have photos of my parents standing outside our door; a house I was born and grew up in was now destroyed. My mother, brother and his wife made homeless. My mother was living for a period in a caravan and then she was shifted into a wooden hut. It took a long time to get her settled into permanent accommodation.[37]

Transport proved vital in the mass evacuation, with countless lorries and vans hijacked, borrowed and loaned. The travelling community assisted greatly, conveying many families from the north of the city to the west. Patrick McAteer expressed 'great respect for Paddy Dundum in particular, who risked his own life ferrying Ardoyne families to refugee centres on the Falls'.[38] John McGreevy, a north Belfast docker, recalled how transport vehicles helped evacuate desperate families. Beginning in mid-August, this service actually lasted a number of years:

> In 1969 we formed a group. When people were getting burned out we would have got lorries and went up to help people get their belongings out. The phone rang in the office and someone would have said, John pick someone up at the gates. You never asked any questions, you picked them up, and went and done what had to be done. We used lorries at the docks to move people from their homes.[39]

John and his family had been forced to flee their own Torrens Crescent home and Alec Leebody, a Protestant work colleague, came to his aid. McGreevy explained how Leebody 'told me that a lorry would be up in fifteen minutes and a man would stay with you until you are ready to leave. I would have been out sooner but the man who lived next door when he was coming out of his house they [loyalists] fired on him. So the fellow who was driving me out stopped to give the other fellow a hand.'[40]

Paddy Carlin recalled helping two friends living in a street on the other side of Queen's Bridge, East Belfast in 1969. 'I think they were the only Catholics in the street. My brother and I got a lorry to help them move. When we arrived, I was very nervous because there was a large crowd of Protestants standing at one side of the street. There was a blacksmith, Jim Keys; a Protestant man who was a friend and a work colleague. He was there and he stopped any violence, he said to the crowd, "they're going, just let them go".' Carlin's future wife, Philomena Mooney, had lived in Norfolk Street: 'She told me they were lucky to get out, it was very lucky nobody was killed in the street ... They moved from there to a shelter on the Glen Road; they finally got a house up there.'[41]

On Monday 18 August thousands gathered in silence amongst the ruins, as the coffins of two children and Trooper John McCabe – the locally born soldier killed by police while home on leave – made their final journey up the Falls Road.[42] Paisley gratuitously claimed that police snipers had killed McCabe as he fired a machine gun from the Divis flats into the Shankill Road. McCabe, an ex-RAF man, had been standing beside his son on the balcony when he was shot, while a military spokesman confirmed that a 'soldier should not have gone on leave with any weapon and, from the information they had, he had not done so'.

With his Lower Falls constituency a charred ruin and hundreds of homeless families amongst the multitude, head bowed before two white coffins, an obviously emotional Paddy Kennedy, MP, echoed local opinion that 'Under no circumstances would police or B-Specials be allowed into the Falls Road.'[43] His colleague, Gerry Fitt, called on 'the support of the British people in [demanding] a full investigation into the present state of affairs in Northern Ireland. We call for the suspension of the present constitution and that Northern Ireland be ruled from Westminster.'[44]

On 19 August, the British Prime Minister Harold Wilson summoned James Chichester-Clark, Brian Faulkner and Robert Porter to London. Wilson baulked at shutting down Stormont and instead dictated a raft of reforms through the Downing Street Declaration. This joint government communiqué guaranteed every citizen of Northern Ireland ... the same equality of treatment and freedom from discrimination as obtains in the rest of the United Kingdom but copper-fastened the principle of consent: 'We attach very great importance to reaffirming the pledge about Northern Ireland not ceasing to be part of the UK without the consent of the people of Northern Ireland.' James Callaghan later commented, 'Northern Ireland was in fact acknowledging for the first time since 1922 that the UK Government's view on civil and other rights must be listened to.'[45] The reforms also included the creation of a housing executive, which removed the power to allocate housing from (typically unionist-dominated) local councils, and a range of measures was announced to tackle discrimination in public employment, as well as pushing for 'one person, one vote' for local elections and an end to gerrymandering. In the days and weeks that followed, a committee to investigate policing would be established under Lord Hunt, while Scarman would investigate the recent disturbances.

Wilson had conceded most of NICRA's demands concerning electoral discrimination in voting, electoral boundaries and housing allocation and employment, in substance if not in letter. Arguably, his failure to move Terence O'Neill the requisite distance in confronting unionist domination, at a meeting they had the previous November, demonstrated his reluctance to grasp the Northern Ireland nettle. Nevertheless, to unionists it appeared that a radical Labour government sympathetic to nationalist claims was now undermining the foundations of the Orange state. This suspicion received apparent validation with the publication of the Cameron and Hunt reports later that year, both of which incensed loyalism and led to an escalation in violence and expulsions.

Throughout August, ripples of loyalist violence persisted in the aftershock of the pogrom. While RUC officers remained in Protestant districts, observing rather than preventing violence, loyalists turned their ire against British soldiers erecting barbed-wire entanglements at every junction leading onto the Falls Road. The army understood little about the sectarian geography of the myriad side streets between the Shankill and the Falls, a situation not helped by their misleading initial briefing from senior police officers. As has been established, troops who arrived battle-ready to confront an imminent republican attack were welcomed with open arms by Falls Road residents, sure that their presence had prevented a massacre. Indeed, 'Ian Paisley, like a prophet of doom from the Old Testament, told a rally that the presence of the troops was the biggest confidence trick ever played on Ulster because the soldiers themselves had told him they were there to "keep the Catholics happy".'[46] Nevertheless, while Paisley continued to bellow against Rome and Dublin, his excuses could no longer conceal the ugly face of sectarian conflict.

Loyalists, assisted by state forces, had driven thousands of nationalists from their homes. However, from the loyalists' perspective the military's arrival disrupted an as-yet only partially completed campaign of sectarian cleansing: they lamented the failure to secure another two days. 'McKeague boasted of his role and revelled in the notoriety. "Forty-eight hours" became the slogan to be used either boastfully or wistfully in Shankill Road pubs to express loyalist confidence that, had the troops taken just forty-eight hours longer to get into position, the Catholics would have been burnt out of Belfast.'[47] Not confined to loyalist drinking dens on the Shankill Road, journalists overheard members of the unionist regime express similar sentiments. 'If only the bloody British Army hadn't come in,' a Unionist senator complained at large in the members' dining-room at Stormont, 'we'd have shot ten thousand of them by dawn.'[48] The period after August witnessed the continuation of the symbiotic relationship between Paisley's rabble-rousing and McKeague's brutal and calculated manipulation of the hatred stoked up by the clergyman's incendiary rhetoric.

As the embers of Ardoyne still glowed, Paisley gave an inflammatory Sunday sermon at the Ulster Hall. Apparently, the Catholic church in Ardoyne had acted as an arsenal as the priest handed out a steady stream of pistols, rifles and machine guns by motor car.

When the police arrived, the church lay empty, cleared in the ten minutes before their arrival.[49] In reality, the RUC had stood in the church grounds throughout the pogrom. Sarah Nelson offered some explanation for the failure of Paisley's followers to question even his wildest conspiracy theories like this one. His 'church won many adherents by conversion. People made a dramatic commitment which involved total trust, not just in God's truth, but in Paisley's version of it ... Paisley also attracted people who held most strongly the historic Protestant conviction that Catholic "rebels" were treacherous and devious people, with an undiminished desire to destroy Protestants physically.'[50]

There is evidence that Paisley's apocalyptic rhetoric encouraged Protestants to leave majority-Catholic areas. Baroness May Blood recalled how Paisley actually provoked the evacuation of Protestants who, up until that point, had experienced no violence:

> We had Mr Paisley arriving and coming to tell us they were coming to get us out. I had sisters living up the Springfield Road in a new housing estate called New Barnsley, which was mixed, and Mr Paisley went up and told them that they were coming up to put all the Protestants out of their houses, and that they should get out now and set fire to what was left.[51]

Paisley also stated publicly, and again inaccurately, that an eighth of the city lay in republican hands and that the IRA had established a machine-gun post in Devonshire Street, off Grosvenor Road, and had units as far afield as Seaforde Street, East Belfast. Prophesying Stormont's imminent suspension, Paisley claimed that Dublin sought to 'create an international situation by taking over a certain part of Newry ... Ulster loyalists need to prepare themselves for the worst'.[52]

Like Paisley's rhetoric, McKeague's campaign of expulsion continued unabated. The hammer fell hardest on vulnerable nationalists in North Belfast. Two days after events in Ardoyne, seven families fled their homes just yards from the Mater Hospital, with other homes attacked in nearby Fairview, Twickenham and Carlisle streets. Three Catholic families living in Ligoniel's Glenbank Place had received threats to 'leave your homes or be burned out' and took shelter in a nearby school. Also in North Belfast, loyalists attacked businesses in Manor Street, including Kearney's Bar, Byrne's Bar and an off-licence in Summer Street.[53]

Less than one week after the initial assault on the Falls and Ardoyne, dozens of nationalist families fled their homes at Carlisle flats, Crumlin Road. 'There was four blocks of flats and more than half are empty.' One woman returned to her home but was horrified by the destruction and theft. The *Belfast Telegraph* noted, 'They don't even have a teapot to make a cup of tea. Nearly all their belongings have gone and the only clothes they have are what they were wearing when they ran in fear …' The woman is reported as saying, 'Since we left on Friday we have slept somewhere different every night … And now that Paisley has started up again God knows what will happen. If they would just leave us alone to live our lives in peace it would be all right.'[54]

In such a heady atmosphere, loyalists again attacked, looted and finally gutted Gerard McKeown's pub on Snugville Street in North Belfast – the twelfth such attack since 1965.[55] On 21 August John McQuade again claimed that Catholics were not victims of loyalist attacks, but of an IRA clearance policy.[56]

After a meeting of bishops on 23 August 1969, the Catholic hierarchy expressed its horror at the violence, especially in Derry and Belfast, noting 'regret that the true picture of these events has been greatly obscured by official statements and by the character of the coverage given in certain influential news media'. The statement continued that over two nights police and loyalists attacked defenceless communities, concluding that 'we entirely reject the hypothesis that the origins of last week's tragedy were an armed insurrection'.[57] Paisley quickly branded the statement 'one deliberately designed to condone the violence of his [Cardinal Conway's] flock and encourage them in their dastardly campaign of murder, arson and riot' while warning Protestants 'not to be deceived by a peace operation launched by leading Romanists, Ecumenists, Communists and Anarchists. This is the devil's lullaby to chloroform Protestantism in order that the rebellion in our midst might have a better chance of success.'[58]

On the Shankill, McKeague 'bragged to the Press that his members have "literally hundreds of guns," and if they need more "we have rich friends"'.[59] The SDA also established pirate radio stations, including Radio Ulster and Radio Orange, which McKeague employed to co-ordinate further attacks on nationalist homes. Some Shankill unionists began, however, to express concern at the negative publicity drawn on their community: McKeague was denounced in some circles as a sexual predator and a sectarian rabble-rouser. Statements from the Shankill Unionist Association, Woodvale Unionist Association, and the Worshipful District Master, District No. 9 Loyal Orange Lodge, made it 'clear that the association has absolutely no connection with this so-called Shankill Defence Association ... and its chairman Mr John McKeague,' who do 'not represent the views or opinion of Shankill Unionist Association or Unionists in this area'. Ironically Paisley's UCDC joined the chorus of disapproval.[60] This marked a significant public breach, but a man with designs to harness the support of the working-class electorate could not easily ignore the voice of respectable loyalist opinion.

On the nationalist side, improvised defensive blockades mushroomed under the dark shadow of Paisley and McKeague's rhetoric. Paddy Devlin, MP, described how hundreds of nationalist families expelled from mixed housing estates flocked into the barricaded area for safety. Each night brought more refugees, carrying little but their horrifying stories from the east and south of the city: 'We got some schools open to shelter and feed them but there was terrible misery and poverty.'[61] Despite the presence of the British Army, residents gradually replaced the temporary vehicle barricades with impressive pavement block walls, often including wooden huts that allowed hastily formed defence groups to maintain a twenty-four-hour vigil. On Balaclava Street, where 'many were not working at the time', vigilantes 'were well fed, and people in our street brought you sandwiches and soup'. Interestingly, 'the army were our friends then, and they would come up behind the barricade and put their guns down, have a cup of tea and yarn and so forth'.[62] The sight of tea-drinking squaddies and nationalist vigilantes chatting on the barricades only fuelled loyalist resentment.

In late August John McQuade released a statement claiming that the 'Roman Catholic Hierarchy have the power to end fear'. He continued that:

> [T]hese people while demanding British rights shrink behind their barricades and away from British responsibilities. They must realise that by calling for an end to our democratically elected Government the vast majority of people can no longer give lip service to the Civil Rights Movement … Now the demands are for the disbanding of the USC, disarming the RUC and the suspension of the Stormont Government. These latest demands have exposed the true heart of the Civil Rights Movement and People's Democracy to be the black heart of Republicanism.[63]

Paisley addressed hundreds at a Stormont rally called to protest at the alarming threat to unionists of disarming the B-Specials, warning 'loyalists in Ulster to prepare for the worst'.[64] He called on loyalists to unite as they did in 1912 when they established the Ulster Volunteers to fight against Home Rule. Elsewhere, expressing concern at the Downing Street Declaration as a whole, Paisley once again exhorted 'Protestants to band together again as they had done in 1912'.[65]

On 26 August fourteen Catholic families were forced to flee their Highfield Drive homes after loyalists distributed dozens of letters warning them to 'Get out – You never know when you are going to get a petrol bomb thrown in to the house.'[66] Fr Murphy, who had arranged shelter for families from Percy, Boundary and Dover streets and Ardmoulin Avenue, now received groups from Duffy Street, who told him that they could not return as Protestant families had been moved into their homes and given their belongings. Similarly, eleven nationalist families were evacuated from Donegall Pass, and a number from the West Circular Road, including a priest.[67] Although in some instances threatening letters with live rounds had replaced petrol bombs, the end result was the same, except that the evacuees usually left a habitable, vacated house.

On 27 August British Home Secretary James Callaghan arrived for a three-day visit. In Belfast he witnessed hundreds of homes and businesses destroyed by fire, and heard repeated pleas from nationalist residents for social justice and protection from state forces and loyalists. When Callaghan declared his intention to meet all concerned, including Paisley, a new grouping, the New Ulster Movement (NUM) were 'astounded to learn that the Home Secretary is prepared to listen to the man who has probably done more than anyone else to bring Northern Ireland people into disrepute both at home and abroad. The moderate people of Northern Ireland whether Protestant or Catholic, regard Mr Paisley with utter contempt.'[68] Callaghan apparently told Paisley to stop giving 'inflammatory statements', the same advice that he himself subsequently received from Saffron Walden, part of a British Conservative fact-finding group.[69] Unsurprisingly Paisley did not relent, declaring that 'we are at war in this province with the hierarchy of the Roman Catholic church' which, in his imagination, headed a republican conspiracy to drive Protestants into a united Ireland.[70]

At the end of August, loyalists fired eight shots at three Ardoyne vigilantes in Etna Drive, while, in another loyalist attack, a Mr Boyle of Selby Street was forced to vacate his home.[71]

The start of September brought little respite to victims of intimidation. On 1 September the *Daily Mirror* blamed Paisley, 'the preposterous pastor from Ballymena, [who] continues to fight the bad fight against unity and progress in Northern Ireland. He is not only a burden to all men of goodwill who are trying to achieve reconciliation in Ulster ... He is a dangerous fanatic ... In knife-edge Ulster this demagogue of bigotry helps to perpetuate religious and political fears and hatreds. This is the tragedy.'[72] Two families fled their homes in Delaware and London streets, East Belfast, joining the many others in La Salle refugee centre. Also in East Belfast, loyalists attacked and burned two Catholic-owned pubs on Chadolly Street/Newtownards Road and Solway Street. In North Belfast, two nationalist families fled Carlisle Street for Unity Walk after being warned to 'be out by Sunday night or you'll be burnt out'.[73]

Also on 1 September the UVF released a statement that the organisation was battle-ready, with new battalions in the process of formation, and warning nationalists to remove their barricades. Loyalists subsequently hijacked ten vehicles and constructed barricades on the Grosvenor, Donegall and Ravenhill roads.[74] 'During a press interview across the barricades at the Donegall Road entrance one loyalist shouted "No Popery." Behind another loyalist barricade, a Catholic family was forced out of their home in Elm Street, Donegall Pass area.'[75] Catholic pubs still remained a favourite target, the victim this time situated on the Donegall Road. Journalists who arrived on the scene suffered attack, with several severely injured. Max Hastings, who had been present at the Divis flats attack, reported, 'One moment, there were two men yelling at me about the Pope-loving English press, the next moment there were sixty, pushing and shoving and shouting around me. I was more frightened than I had ever been in the worst of the riots and shooting battles.'[76]

On the more nationalist upper end of Donegall Road, Paisley stoked tensions by alleging that the Protestant community faced attack from their neighbours. Four churchmen from the area – two Protestants and two Catholics, representing Upper Broadway, Lower Broadway and Upper Donegall Road – strongly repudiated 'what the Rev. Ian Paisley said at his press conference … We stress that this is a mixed community and not as Mr Paisley insinuated a totally Roman Catholic area', where people 'have worked harmoniously together during this period of disturbances and succeeded in maintaining peace. We strongly resent Mr Paisley's remarks that this a hostile area in which children cannot go to school in safety.'[77] Ethna Byrne, a resident of Roden Street, which is off the Donegall Road, recounted the fear prevailing at the time:

> I remember August 1969 in Roden Street, there was murder on the other side of the road. The Catholics who had lived further up Roden Street towards the top of Donegall Road moved out and moved down towards the Grosvenor Road end for safety. Mrs Hughes, who lived next door to us, her son lived in the fourth house from the top of Roden Street and Donegall Road, moved out. Tommy Gorman lived off the Donegall Road, in a street that had a painting of King Billy on the gable wall. Kevin [Ethna's husband] and others helped to move Tommy out, I think they used Brendan McDowell's lorry. The dividing line came at the bridge on Roden Street; any Catholic above the bridge got out. Lots of Catholics moved out of that side of the Grosvenor Road, but many Catholics and Protestants who had lived together for years stayed. They stayed neighbours for a while until things got worse and then the peace walls started to go up.[78]

A short distance away in the Springfield Road, forty men, women and children left the Springfield/Clonard area and moved to Clonard Monastery for safety after threats from workers at Mackie's. Troops were brought in to safeguard the families. The following day, 3 September, loyalists strengthened their barricades on the Donegall, Newtownards and Shankill roads. On Broadway, loyalists invaded the mostly Catholic Iveagh Street, even using a car to ram into a nationalist crowd gathered there, one of whom died of a heart attack. Troops used fixed bayonets to force the loyalists back down the Donegall Road. In West Belfast loyalists again invaded Dover and Cupar streets, setting fire to vacated Catholic-owned houses. In East Belfast, loyalists surged out of Dee Street and Templemore Avenue, hijacking trucks and attacking yet another pub.

During the early hours of 4 September, loyalists threw three petrol bombs into the home of Alexander McKeating in Fortwilliam Parade, North Belfast. A horrified neighbour wondered 'why it should have happened here is beyond me ... Catholic and Protestants live here like happy families'.[79]

The NUM condemned the ongoing violence: 'The followers of Mr Paisley and the other rabid Protestant extremists are trying to get in on the act by erecting further barricades as a protest. In fact, it is nothing of the sort. It is a deliberate attempt to stir up sectarian trouble as has been recognised by a joint statement of clergy of all denominations.'[80] Paisley demonstrated his influence over the mob when he persuaded them to remove a barricade, receiving the thanks of British Army GOC Ian Freeland.[81] Following the violence around the Lower Donegall Road, nationalists vacated their homes in Monarch Parade, Rockland, Rockview, Tavanagh and Moltke streets.

In the early hours of 6 September, Mr O'Neill, Mrs McGee and Mrs Hawkins spotted loyalists entering Ardmoulin Avenue through burnt-out homes to evade detection by the army. On the previous night, the army had stopped a mob at bayonet point across Townsend Street and the Falls Road.[82] The residents had alerted troops to the mob. The army subsequently illuminated the area with their spotlights, whereupon the invaders fled. On 6 September the loyalists

returned and fixed a large Orange arch across Dover Street on the
derelict ruins of Catholic-owned homes. For weeks loyalists had been
taunting residents that the B-Specials would return and finish the
work of 14 August; many sang Orange songs or roared anti-Catholic
slogans. One resident claimed that of the forty Catholic families
once on the street, only fifteen remained. Another recounted that
residents stayed awake all night for fear of attack.

Most nationalists understood that the loyalist mobs were unrep-
resentative of Protestants in general, and the sectarianism on clear
display sickened many on the other side of the divide as well, as one
long-time Shankill resident explained:

> I'm torn apart now at what's happening to ordinary working-class
> people like ourselves. No matter what happens we'll still have to do the
> work, still have to pay the rent and the gas bill – same as the Catholics.
> The Protestants talk a lot about the Catholics 'being intimidated by
> the IRA'. Few of them seem to recognise the intimidation they are
> daily subjected to by their own so-called leaders.[83]

On the Shankill Road, McKeague had increased the number of barricades, boasting that 'we build better ones than the Papists, organise
vigilante groups, and supply them with anything from makeshift am-
bulances to sawn-off shotguns'.[84]

The attacks on nationalist areas continued. On 7 September, in
Percy Street, 'a crowd of about fifty who gathered on the Protestant
side jeered and shouted that they would help us out by burning us
out'.[85] McKeague's radio station then urged loyalists onto the streets
'to repel a rebel and Republican invasion'. Within minutes a mob of
2,000 had converged on Percy Street, where they attacked the army,
who had also heard McKeague's broadcast, with petrol bombs. The
troops fired CS gas, giving loyalists a taste of what they themselves
had called 'Londonderry Air' or 'Bogsiders' Delight' during the Battle

of the Bogside.[86] While many loyalists dispersed, 500 stood their ground. Following the confrontation between McKeague's loyalists and the British Army, eighty-seven-year-old Annie Keown – who a few weeks earlier had fled her home of fifty years just a few streets away – now evacuated nearby Dover Street, abandoning the idea of ever returning.[87]

Arriving from the Shankill Road end of Percy Street, RUC DI Frank Lagan judged that 'the use of gas against them [the loyalists] was an unfortunate mistake', and it was met at the time with shouts of 'British bastards'. General Ian Freeland concluded 'that there were too many people in position of influence still inflaming the population'.[88] Max Hastings perhaps filled in the blanks with the wry observation that it became for him 'impossible to regard the Protestants with anything resembling dispassion. I watched them hammering at the British Army, petrol-bombing Catholic houses. I heard Protestant "moderates" in the country areas expressing their fear and unconcealed dislike of the Catholics and their demands. I saw Chichester-Clark in the moments of crisis talking like an irritated schoolmaster at a cricket match.'[89]

In a separate but much more concerted confrontation, McKeague's appeal for assistance had prompted 3,000 loyalists to march on the Boyne Bridge, Sandy Row, heading for Divis Street and the Falls Road. The British Army positioned ten trucks across Durham Street and deployed hundreds of troops in full battle dress to prevent this loyalist invasion. The following morning, 8 September, the unionist *News Letter* reported: 'Orange mobs from Sandy Row try to invade Falls.' Three loyalist-run radio stations issued a call for 'all loyalist doctors' to report immediately to the Shankill Road.[90] Not all Protestants heeded the call. One man recalled that:

[T]here was a call to arms one time on Free [loyalist] Radio. There were lorries going up and down and we were living in Agnes Street at the time ... My Ma pushed me up the hall into the parlour and locked the door so they couldn't see me. They were recruiting [claiming] they were defending Dover Street and saying they are coming to get us.[91]

McKeague's tactics had changed little since his arrival on the Shankill Road in April 1969. While his potent and hateful ideology hypnotised many, his growing power over the mob alarmed many others on the Shankill and in the surrounding area. As Rosita Sweetman points out: 'In the short-term men like John McKeague appear to be in touch with the needs and fears of the working-class Protestants. In the long run all he wants is to ride to power on their backs.'[92]

As on the Shankill, in East Belfast loyalists had erected more barricades on the Newtownards Road and, after the by-now obligatory looting of Catholic-owned businesses, advanced on the nationalist enclave at Short Strand.[93] Elsewhere, in the east of the city, 100 Paisleyites forced Catholic workers to escape over the back fence of the Scottish and Newcastle Breweries, Church Street, where they met yet another Paisleyite crowd, screaming 'Get out Fenians'.[94] A correspondent from *The Times* gave some indication of the febrile atmosphere when he wrote that 'driving around east Belfast tonight I counted twenty-five hi-jacked buses jammed across the entrances to streets in the Catholic Markets area. In Woodstock Road a car overturned and set on fire to form a barricade. More barricades were going up and crowds of Protestants are milling in the streets.'[95]

Living in East Belfast had become hell for nationalists. Born into a mixed marriage, Joseph Fitzpatrick became accustomed to the term 'Fenian' and routine but sometimes brutal sectarian attacks. 'One distinct incident: I was getting off the bus at Clarwood, East Belfast, three guys, one on crutches ... approached me. I had my school uniform on and they asked me if I was a Fenian, then set upon me.' Shortly afterwards loyalist gangs attacked the family home on Sandhill Parade, despite an RUC sergeant living on one side and a B-Special living on the other. The Fitzpatricks were finally forced out when they found an unexploded bomb on their windowsill, compelling them to resettle in West Belfast.[96]

In North Belfast, 'Radio Orange' directed loyalists back to Disraeli Street and Ardoyne, while Catholic-owned pubs were attacked in Manor and Scrabo streets, and on the Albertbridge Road. The Admiral Bar at Oldpark was yet again burned. A short distance away in North Queen Street, North Belfast, the mob wrecked a Catholic-owned grocery shop for the second time in three weeks: 'The police advised me to leave yesterday evening for my own safety. Half an hour after I arrived home they phoned me to say that it had been wrecked again.'[97] Loyalists continued with their attacks over 5–8 September, and the over-stretched army prevented attacks on the Falls Road via Northumberland, Townsend and Percy streets.[98]

By now the nationalist barricades had become an affront to all shades of unionism. On 8 September, Chichester-Clark became embroiled in the controversy when loyalist riots swept Belfast attacking more nationalist-owned homes. He called the barricade building 'an act of deviance', and demanded from James Callaghan their immediate removal. On 10 September, Callaghan met members of the Central Citizens Defence Committee (CCDC) – consisting of nationalist representatives Gerry Fitt, Fr Patrick Murphy, Paddy Devlin and Paddy Kennedy – in London, and they agreed to remove barricades if Callaghan posted soldiers at the end of every street to prevent loyalist incursions. The barricades did come down on Wednesday 17 September, but, when 'three Catholic-owned houses were promptly burnt out by Protestants, the barricades went up again'.[99] Beyond the protection offered by the barricades, 150 people from Manor Street in North Belfast fled to St Clements' Retreat House on the Antrim Road, having been intimidated from their homes.

In Coates Street, yards from Hastings Street Barracks, army bulldozers pushed back loyalist barricades, while engineers erected barbed-wire fences, a process repeated in the Clonard area – in Clonard Gardens, Lucknow and Bombay streets and the Kashmir Road. The first 'peace lines' had appeared. A curfew on cars in certain areas between the hours of 9 p.m. and 6 a.m. then came into effect under the Special Powers Act. The imposition of an early closing time of 8.30 p.m. on Belfast's pubs provoked the rapid growth of illegal drinking clubs, or shebeens. Loyalist clubs soon emerged as makeshift bases from which the patrons could prosecute their reign of terror.

Loyalist rage reached new heights after the fatal shooting of a loyalist vigilante in Alloa Street, North Belfast on 8 September 1969. Nationalists living in both North and West Belfast had begun to arm themselves after the August pogrom. *The Irish News* reported that, on that night, Catholic and Protestant patrols had clashed at a flashpoint on Manor Street. A nationalist former resident described how loyalists came down Alloa Street: 'They were shouting "Come out you Fenian —." During the commotion I heard shots. It seemed like one shot, then two shots and then another two shots. I thought the two shots following the first one seemed to be in retaliation. As soon as the shots went off the flags (Union Jacks) went out.' When the UVF stationed a machine-gun in the middle of Avoca Street, the remaining nationalists relocated to refugee centres.[100]

Similarly, loyalists threatened the Lynches, a couple in a mixed marriage who lived off York Street, that their 'half-breed' children would be burned out and told them 'if you are so fond of Papists to go and live on the Falls Road'.[101] At the end of the month, Mrs Muldoon and her two children fled their Mayfair Street home: 'My best friends were Protestants. When these troubles began they were frightened to talk to me, they had been told they would be in trouble if they did.' The family moved to Brighton, England, where her case was raised at the [British] Labour Party conference.[102]

On the Shankill Road on 8 September more than 2,000 loyalists paraded for several hours with Orange bands and several Lambeg drums. The British Army were deployed to protect the Unity Walk flats. Another crowd attempted to invade the Falls from Argyle Street, while yet another headed for Ardoyne, again precipitating military intervention.[103] At the end of the month, many within the mob took part in the expulsion of fourteen Catholic families from nearby Highfield Estate. One resident said 'that community relations with his immediate neighbours had always been first-class. They have always been very helpful and we always got on well with them.'[104] With tensions at fever pitch, however, Protestant neighbours feared that if they protected Catholic residents they risked being targeted themselves.

On 12 September, the release of the Cameron Report provoked apoplectic rage amongst unionists. Paisley labelled it 'a document to be regarded with the utmost contempt ... I consider parts of it personal slander. I brand the three members of the Commission as liars.'[105] Loyalists responded with riots, including attacks on Catholic-owned businesses such as Roddy's Bar and Doran's butcher's shop.[106] Attacks also occurred in North Belfast's Shore Road and in East Belfast.[107] Angry loyalists petrol-bombed the Star of the Sea primary school on Hallidays Road.[108] On the eve of the commencement of the Scarman Inquiry, Paisley marshalled his thousand supporters against the Cameron Report's findings, ominously claiming that 'the fight is on'.[109] Nationalist politician Paddy O'Hanlon claimed at the same time to have evidence of twenty UVF training centres.[110]

Sectarian intimidation continued. The owners of the Cossack public house in Hillview Street received threats to 'Get out or we will burn you out'.[111] The following day, the Gibraltar Bar on Broughan Street was firebombed. Scarman noted the extensive damage to licensed premises. Not only did looted alcohol help fuel rage and lower inhibitions, but the licensed trade represented the biggest business interest among nationalists at the time. According to the Belfast and Ulster Licensed Vintners Association, 80 per cent of the 480 publicans in Belfast were Catholic. Their pubs had been targeted by loyalists in the pogroms of the 1920s and 1930s and they came under concerted attack again in 1969. In total, loyalists destroyed twenty-four public houses during the summer and early autumn of 1969, damaging a further thirty-six, with the destruction and damage of six and ten off-licences respectively. The Tribunal concluded that the damage, amounting to a quarter of a million pounds, represented 'the work of Protestant gangs'.[112]

RUC Commissioner Wolseley underplayed the significance of the attacks on public houses. 'From what I saw of them – and I saw several of these burning – it was just sheer hooliganism, nothing else.'[113] Other police officials contradicted this, noting that 'from the fact that many of them were burned at about the same time, [it was] assumed that the firing and looting of public houses was in some way planned or organised'.[114] The Tribunal concluded that 'the withdrawal of the police gave groups or gangs of angry or criminal Protestants an opportunity which they took. It was sufficient that a licensee should be a Catholic for his premises to be burned.'[115]

The McCambridge family lost everything when their premises were systematically attacked and looted:

[Our] off-License was the 'Oporta Wine Stores' in Agnes Street. He [Patrick McCambridge] was there up to the Troubles started until we were put out. The first thing that happened when the Troubles started, the first place they attacked or tried to get people to move were publicans or Catholic-owned businesses. It was too insecure to stay there, my father decided to clear the place out, because he knew if he didn't someone was going to be hurt or attacked in the place. So him and his brother and my two brothers decided they would go and start getting everything out of the off-license. When they were

ROYAL ULSTER CONSTABULARY

Police Report in Respect of Alleged Malicious Damage to Property

Name and Address of Applicant .... F. J. McCAMBRIDGE ....

Address of property alleged
to have been damaged .... 151 Agnes Street, Belfast. ....

Date and time when damage
is alleged to have been
caused .... Between 13th August, 1972 – 16th April, 1973 ....

City/~~County~~ of .... Belfast ....   Station .... Tennent Street ....

Division of .... 'C' ....   Date .... 12.6.73 ....

On receiving a report that the property of above-named had been maliciously damaged, I/ W. M. McCauley ....

.... visited the scene at 10a.m. on 16th April, **73** .

19 73 . The following facts were ascertained:

Applicant was forced to leave his off-licence premises during the month of August, 1969. His premises were closed and the keys were left with the Minister in charge of the Methodist Church, Agnes Street who used the applicant's premises to store emergency beds and beddings. These premises were taken over by members of the U.D.A. during the month of August, 1972, and used as drinking club. Several alterations were carried out to the premises. During the month of February, 1973, these premises were visited by members of the security forces who seized a quantity of drink. These premises were subsequently vacated by the U.D.A. during April, 1973, and when I visited the premises on 16.4.1973, I noted the following damage:

All windows on ground floor broken, counter destroyed, staircase pulled down.
Store – windows and doors destroyed, floor covered with broken bottles.
Upstairs drinking room – Stainless Steel sink unit pulled from wall, water
                        running down walls, ceilings and light fittings
                        damaged throughout building.

~~INSPECTOR/SERGT/~~ Const.

W. H. McCauley

The above report is forwarded for the information of (1) The Ministry of Home Affairs, Londonderry House, Chichester Street, Belfast (2) James F.Fitzpatrick & Co., Solicitor, 1 College
                                    Square North, Belfast, 1.

D. M. C. .... , Chief Superintendent
Assistant Chief Constable/Divisional Commander

Form 44/1

D478240.35m.10/70.0.gp.168
D488395.60m.6/71

PATRICK McCAMBRIDGE RUC REPORT
Courtesy of the McCambridge family

trying to clear stock out of the place they were attacked by a crowd when they were inside. So my father obviously phoned the police. The police came [from Tennent Street in a Land Rover]. The policeman, my father said, told anybody if they moved they would shoot them, that was the only way they would get out. I was at home with my mother and I remember my mother saying the rosary because my mother was so afraid that something was going to happen obviously to my father and two brothers. Most of the premises in Agnes Street at that time were Catholic owned; if they weren't Catholic owned, they certainly had Catholics working for them.[116]

The business was attacked on three separate occasions, the last one on 14 August 1969. The UDA later used it as a shebeen.

On 28 September, in a show of defiance to the British government, 100 B-Specials marched down the Shankill Road while loyalists once again petrol-bombed the Unity Walk flats complex and burned several nationalist homes on Coates Street. One terrified resident told a reporter that 'they came through from Sackville Street and Sackville Place, and there was absolutely no defence to their attack by the Protestants ... The police did little to control the Protestants.' A seventy-year-old widow stated that she 'couldn't stand it, I was frightened. I have lived with this situation for fifty years, but it had never been as bad as it had been tonight.' After the firing of CS gas, a 'large' army presence drove loyalists back 'from Coates Street into Sackville Street. A number of soldiers were injured.'[117] The CCDC identified policemen among the loyalist attackers.[118]

One *Guardian* journalist later gave his impression of Belfast at this time:

There was an indefinable feeling of being in a foreign country in Ireland, North or South – and, it must be admitted, there was some identification, some commonality between the ordinary

British squaddie on the street and the ordinary British reporter or
photography or television man who followed him around ... Like us,
he, the individual soldier, was no real part of the Trouble, like us, he
had been sent out from England to do a job.[119]

On 8 October, James Callaghan returned to Belfast in a follow-
up to his previous trip. Callaghan had already installed two of his
own senior civil servants there to secure reliable information. Two
days into his visit, the Hunt Report recommended the RUC's
disarmament, the replacement of the B-Specials with the UDR and
the establishment of a new police authority with representation from
the Catholic community. At the same time, Callaghan appointed
a new, English, chief constable, Sir Arthur Young. Paisley best
articulated unionist fury at all of this, condemning the Hunt Report
as a 'complete capitulation to the murderers and looters on the
street', while ordering B-Specials, 'Don't let anyone disarm you.'[120]
On the Shankill, McKeague issued a statement that 'the day is fast
approaching when responsible leaders and associations like ourselves
will no longer be able to restrain the backlash of outraged Loyalist
opinion'.[121]

On Saturday 11 October, 3,000 incensed loyalists, replete with
Lambeg drums and a sea of flags, decided to vent their anger against
the nationalists in Unity Walk. William 'Plum' Smith commented:
'The Shankill Road people massed in their thousands in protest at
what they saw as further appeasement to Republicans and a threat to
the whole principles of democracy and an end to the state of Northern Ireland'.[122] The new chief constable described how the mob:

... rose in their wrath to demonstrate against the vile things Hunt
had said about their wonderful police. They came in their thousands
down the Shankill Road, appearing like animals, as if by magic. Then
they marched to burn the Catholics out of the nearby flats. And as

they came down the street, they were halted by a cordon of exactly the police they were marching to defend.[123]

Yards from Unity Walk, the RUC formed a defensive line with the British Army behind, while extra troops marshalled the myriad side streets running into the Falls. As the strains of 'Billy Boys' and 'Derry's Walls' swirled ever upwards, and chants of 'We are the People' reverberated in the autumn air, 'Belfast was treated to the unfamiliar sight of Protestants waving Union Jacks while attacking the forces of the Crown, to the accompaniment of slogans such as "Englishmen go home, we want the B-Specials" and "Paisley is our leader".'[124] The loyalist horde roared into police lines like a tidal wave engulfing the bottom of the Shankill Road. A short time later, amid the squalid stench of alcohol and burnt petrol, loyalists brought their arsenal onto the streets:

> This man then walked boldly down the Shankill with an overcoat over his arm and I could see the end of a rifle protruding out from the overcoat. I watched in awe as he placed the overcoat on the top of a small telephone pill box[,] raised the rifle[,] cocked it with the bolt and took aim at the ranks of soldiers and police and fired … The rioting diminished, the gun battle had begun.[125]

Max Hastings described the loyalist attack on their former police allies. As police retreated to lines behind the British Army for protection, and without firing a shot in reply, loyalist rounds from rifles, machine guns and sub-machine guns hit twenty-two British soldiers, and killed one RUC constable, Victor Arbuckle, the first police fatality of the Troubles. The bitter fighting continued and by 1.45 a.m. the military was employing live rounds, challenging loyalism for the first time since the Belfast riots of the 1930s:

For weeks, they [the British Army] had stood by and watched while the Protestants abused them and fought around them with impunity. For weeks, they had stood in the streets for hours on end, unable to make a move ... Now, as a rain of rocks and missiles descended ... No one, English reporters, officers, onlookers, police, turned a hair as rioters were dragged down the street and thrown into wagons.[126]

A police surgeon at the time described the results as the worst riot injuries he had ever witnessed.[127] General Freeland later commented, 'We gave them a bloody nose.'

By the end of the fighting there had been 100 arrests, while two Protestants, Georgie Dickie and Herbie Hawe, lay dead. In addition, fifty civilians required hospital treatment, twenty with gunshot wounds.

As the Shankill raged, East Belfast loyalists attacked police with petrol bombs and directed sniper fire at the military. In North Belfast, the British Army moved in to prevent a loyalist mob from burning a Catholic church.

The following morning (Sunday) the British Army commenced searches on the Shankill Road, discovering numerous guns (a significant number legally held), an anti-tank pit and an illegal radio station. Richard Rose highlights that 'in 1969 there was one licensed gun for every fifth man between the age of 20 and 60 ... Without benefit of official licensing a variety of local groups in the Shankill and other troubled areas have quietly collected money and bought guns for use in troubled times.'[128]

Paisley quickly condemned the army for 'emulating the German SS'.[129] Yet, among more moderate unionists, the death of a policeman challenged some long-held prejudices. As Sarah Nelson rightly comments:

Many Protestants were ambivalent about the role of the security forces, but most felt it important to see themselves as law abiding, in contrast to the 'rebellious' Catholics. They found it hard to accept that they would initiate violence and only a minority would speak proudly of violent incidents. Most were disturbed and made strong efforts to rationalise these as defensive stands, or unfortunate lapses.[130]

The Shankill Road marked the third serious loyalist attack on the British Army since their arrival in mid-August. Loyalists described the army as a foreign force sent to appease the nationalists. In fact, the military and – for the first time, the police – had prevented the burning of Unity Walk and a potential bloodbath.

Two days later, James Callaghan returned to London apparently unperturbed by the furious reaction to his reforms, and to Hunt in particular. Callaghan then launched a scathing attack on Paisley in the House of Commons, accusing him of 'using the language of war cast in a biblical mould. I said that "Fight the Good Fight" sung in a peaceful English village church on a Sunday morning sounded very differently when it was sung in the Shankill Road after a night of rioting.'[131] Paisley retorted that he wanted 'to see the gun back on the belts of Ulster policemen and I want the Specials back on our streets. No more Republican enclaves! No more Republican pockets through the country! We're going to hold this province for our children and the Union Jack is going to fly through every part of it.'[132]

Several days after the Shankill riot, John McKeague attended a special UPV service in Paisley's church. On sight of McKeague in his church, Paisley demanded his removal, consummating their final split. A few days later, McKeague received three months in Crumlin Road Gaol for his role in the illegal march to Paisley's inaugural service on 5 October 1969.

7

ABSOLVING THE
ESTABLISHMENT

On 27 August 1969, thirteen days after the commencement of the pogrom, the British government commissioned a judicial inquiry to be led by English high court judge Leslie [later Baron] Scarman. After a long gestation, the Tribunal finally reported in April 1972, three months after Bloody Sunday (when British soldiers shot twenty-eight unarmed civilians in Derry) and not long after Ted Heath had suspended Stormont. While nationalists cried whitewash, unionists largely ignored the findings. The inquiry largely excused the RUC and the B-Specials, ignoring the murderous co-operation between state forces and loyalists, while validating some of the wider claims by unionist politicians and police:

> The Scarman Tribunal, set up … by the British government (supposedly to 'investigate' the upheavals of 1969) would politely chastise the RUC for permitting themselves to work in tandem with this loyalist mob. However, it stopped short of actually denouncing these actions. Indeed, Scarman placed responsibility for the wholesale destruction and violence that occurred that night upon the people of Ardoyne themselves.[1]

The inquiry did what British policy dictated in April 1972: it protected state interests. No charges were recommended even though state forces shot dead innocent citizens, including two children. Yet in the autumn of 1969 British policy had appeared to be far less favourable to Stormont and the RUC. On his arrival in Northern

Ireland James Callaghan had told Chichester-Clark that a Tribunal would inquire into the violence between March and August 1969. Callaghan then sidelined the RUC, surrounding himself with Scotland Yard security, with the British Army in close support. On 15 August he told Chichester-Clark that he had dispatched two senior English policemen, Robert Mark, Deputy Commissioner of the Metropolitan Police, and Douglas Osmond, Chief Constable of Hampshire, 'to act as observers and keep me informed'.[2] Four days later, on 19 August, Callaghan appointed GOC Lieutenant-General Ian Freeland as director of operations to ensure law and order in Northern Ireland.

Callaghan then instructed the Lord Chancellor, Lord Gardiner, to send for Scarman, who promptly arrived in Belfast. 'It was an indication to the public that things were moving and that we were getting the situation under control.'[3] Scarman's remit was clear: deal with events immediately following the Cameron Commission, which had only covered events in 1968 and the first part of 1969. The inquiry could compel witnesses to attend and, on occasion, grant immunity from prosecution. Responding to controversy over the Battle of the Bogside, Callaghan also established an inquiry under Harold Himsworth into the effects of CS gas. Apparently, the London government had decided to land another blow on the Orange State's already damaged reputation.

Clive Scoular noted that Scarman – the third such inquiry in several months – proved too much for some unionists:

> One committee investigation would have been difficult to bear, two would have been infinitely worse, but three became the final straw which was, in the long term, to break the Northern Ireland government's back. The timing of the setting up of these committees was nothing short of disastrous.[4]

INVESTIGATING THE RUC

Established in 1922 as a successor to the paramilitary RIC, the RUC's *raison d'être* was to defend Northern Ireland. The Government of Ireland Act (1920) empowered the northern regime to deal with security, which Westminster duly transferred in November 1921. The Minister of Home Affairs and the RUC Inspector General controlled deployment, size, management and training in a single command. The powers of the police were extensive, as on 15 March Dawson Bates, the Minister of Home Affairs, introduced the Special Powers Act, permitting the suspension of civil liberties, capital punishment, house searches, arrests and detention without warrants.

In addition to the regular RUC, Stormont could also rely on A-, B- and C-Special Constabulary – basically a Protestant militia established in September 1920 to counter the emerging IRA campaign. After the initial IRA threat subsided, and at the expense of millions in British taxpayers' money, the force was reduced to its part-time reserve or the B-Specials, a force firmly based on Carson's UVF. As Fergal McCluskey points out, 'despite the internal dynamics of Ulster unionist politics, the British state underwrote this entire relationship through financial, political and military support'.[5] Both the Cameron and Hunt reports referred to the overtly military character of the B-Specials and their political control by the Stormont government.[6] The nationalist minority experienced the full impact of their draconian powers.

From the outset – and for perfectly obvious reasons – few Catholics joined the RUC, and its overt unionism and partisan character quickly hardened opinion against the force. Yet this did not convert into support for IRA campaigns during the 1940s and 1950s, which quickly petered out. Conversely, these marginal expressions of republican resistance helped underpin the deeply embedded siege mentality within Northern Ireland, from a unionist perspective fully justifying the existence of a coercive apparatus directed solely against the disloyal nationalist community:

> The Specials were a formidable force ... They were armed with rifles, revolvers, bayonets and later sub-machine guns which they kept in their homes, and in the 1950s and 1960s they had access to Bren-guns and Shorland armoured cars ... with their intimate knowledge of local geography and the politics of their Catholic neighbours they were extremely effective in suppressing all resistance to Unionist rule ... They were also of course a constant irritant to the Catholic population and with their weapons at home they represented a constant threat of sectarian attack.[7]

After the violence of the previous two days, on 16 August 1969 James Callaghan sent two senior policemen, Douglas Osmond and Robert Mark, to Northern Ireland. Callaghan remarked, 'At that moment Jack Andrews, the Deputy Prime Minister [Northern Ireland], was touring police stations trying to rally morale, which was very low, and make the RUC feel that not all the world was against them.'[8]

Osmond and Mark lost little time in assessing the true – and shocking – nature of policing in the Orange State. Three days later, Callaghan, clearly disturbed by their initial briefings, advised Prime Minister Harold Wilson to commission an immediate report into the RUC. Osmond and Mark claimed that the Minister of Home Affairs, Porter, took 'second place to' Peacock, his sole source of information, and that 'the top leadership of the RUC was poor and that Peacock would have to be replaced'.[9] Incompetent, bigoted and ineffectual, the RUC leadership and the force in general was not fit for purpose. Osmond and Mark's report damningly continued that the RUC 'were a force apart': paramilitary in nature and by instinct, appearing immune to complaints and constituting a law unto themselves. Convinced that the rioting emerged from an IRA plot, the police possessed little useful information about the civil rights movement, the Paisleyites or the UPV, and had no intelligence at all inside the Bogside. Regarding the B-Specials, Osmond and Mark described the USC as an independent paramilitary Protestant reserve army.[10] Their findings would form the basis of the Hunt Report.

Ten days after the devastation in nationalist areas, on 26 August 1969 the RUC Central Representative Body publicly denied police involvement in the pogroms on the Falls, in Clonard and Ardoyne:

> We the RUC … feel very concerned at the gross inaccuracy and apparent bias of the reporting by certain sections of the Press and other news media of events which have occurred since 5th October, 1968. Often the position of the RUC has not been appreciated and frequent allegations have been made without factual foundation.[11]

Indeed, despite overwhelming evidence to the contrary, they continued that 'allegations have been made of police "attacking these unarmed and innocent rioters" or of "invading" their areas. Such emotive reporting only increases the problem.' Nevertheless, these retrospective denials didn't mask the failure of police officers to protect citizens, or explain the numerous instances when Stormont's uniformed men had directly participated in the violence.

Clearly engaged in a rearguard action, the RUC then appointed a senior police officer to investigate specific incidents that supported the police narrative – for instance, the testimony of a Protestant textile worker who claimed to have witnessed republicans moving firearms in the early hours of 15 August on the Falls Road. On 23 September, he told two detectives that men removed weapons from a vehicle there. 'The foreman told somebody about it and he knew a couple of detectives who approached me to see whether I would make a statement and they said they wanted to find enough evidence to have the [Nationalist] MPs [shut] up – it would never come to

Court.'[12] The eyewitness could not, however, identify the make or colour of the vehicle, and he failed to properly identify the streets in question. Furthermore, he delivered his statement to detectives in a private home in Dundee Street, off the Shankill Road, and not at a police station. More interestingly, the textile worker claimed that the police wanted:

> ... evidence so that they could fight against what Nationalist MPs were saying, that the Protestants were to blame for everything. They wanted evidence so that they could have the story true ... The way they put it to me was that they [Nationalists] were going to blame all the shooting on the Shankill on the Protestant people, and they wanted something to hit back, enough evidence so that they could do the same thing on the other side. The police wanted evidence to counter this allegation being made by Mr Fitt and his like ... That was what I was told.[13]

The Hunt Report, its findings announced on 10 October 1969, only increased unionist anxieties. Robert Porter had asked Hunt to 'examine the recruitment, organisation, structure and composition of the Royal Ulster Constabulary and the Ulster Special Constabulary ... and to recommend as necessary what changes are required to provide for the efficient enforcement of law and order in Northern Ireland'.[14] While the inquiry operated under Stormont's authority, in reality, British ministers applied pressure (as had been the case with the Cameron Commission), a situation that influenced the forty-seven recommendations. RUC Inspector General Anthony Peacock submitted his resignation – just ahead of the Hunt Report recommending the abolition of his role. The report also recommended a central recruiting system; closer links with British police forces, including the adoption of their rank and promotion structure; an independent complaints tribunal; and a representative

Police Authority to essentially by-pass Stormont's Minister of Home Affairs. More controversially Hunt recommended disarming the RUC, but the real body blow for loyalism arrived with the disbandment of the B-Specials.

While many of its findings appeared innocuous, the proposed changes to the RUC and the disbandment of the USC sent unionism into apoplexy. 'The RUC members, to a man, refused to change the colour of their uniforms. But the issue of disbanding the 'B' Specials caused the greatest furore and created the biggest problem for Chichester-Clark who had always the greatest regard for the Ulster Special Constabulary.'[15] At 10 Downing Street, Minister of Defence Denis Healey noted that the B-Specials (485 in Belfast and 250 in Derry) had used excessive force, echoing the GOC's recommendations that the USC's arms be centrally controlled, to which Chichester-Clark replied: 'Well, there would be a lot of difficulty about that. He was not at all sure we would get the arms out of their hands.'[16]

As well as commissioning the Hunt Report, the British government also called on the services of several British senior police officers, including Commander Jack Remnant, Deputy Chief Constable Robert Boyes and Wilson Hill. Boyes carried out a survey of the establishment, organisation and structure of the RUC. His January 1970 report recommended root-and-branch reorganisation on the lines of a provincial police force. On 1 June 1970 the Police Act (Northern Ireland) changed the rank structure from inspector general to chief constable, chief superintendent and chief inspector. The recommendations also envisaged a police force representative of the six counties' entire community. Recruitment into the RUC by the time of the Hunt Report was 3,400, with Catholics making up just 9.4 per cent; the 8,481 strong USC was entirely Protestant.[17]

In February 1969 Harold Wolseley had secured the role of RUC Belfast Commissioner; he left that position in November. As a constable Wolseley had experienced the 1932 Belfast riots, when

Rolls Royce armoured vehicles mounted with Vickers machine guns attacked the working classes of Belfast. In 1939 he became a district inspector before joining Special Branch in Belfast. After a period as deputy inspector general of the British Zone in Germany, he boasted that, 'I was the first British officer to handle the Hamburg riots and that is on the record.'[18] During the 1956–62 IRA campaign, Wolseley established a force within Special Branch to protect buildings and installations and monitor major incidents. While commander of Belfast, he led approximately 400 men, including B-Specials. He admitted that many of the security forces were in the Orange Order, but refused to 'see why it should' affect their relationship with the nationalist community. During the riots in early August, Wolseley had deployed hundreds of B-Specials onto the Shankill at the behest of McKeague, and he continued to defend the USC as 'a disciplined force … Anything I saw of the Specials in Belfast, any time I saw them, their behaviour was above reproach.'[19]

On 1 August 1969, 300 B-Specials had been mobilised into the RUC and its Reserve Force. This was a significant factor in the escalation of state violence, beginning with the attack on the Unity Walk flats which led to the death of pensioner Patrick Corrie. Similarly, 'the Reserve Force led the "Rossville Street incursion" into the Bogside on 12 August and provided the armed Shorlands which were used in the Belfast riots'.[20] All-in-all, in terms of history, structure and political outlook, the B-Specials not only represented the least well-equipped force imaginable for policing a deeply divided community, but they directly caused much of the destruction.

THE SHORLAND ARMOURED VEHICLE

Ordered by the home affairs minister at Stormont as a weapon against republican mobilisation in border areas, the Shorland armoured vehicle wreaked havoc in the claustrophobic warren of urban side streets that traversed the Falls and Shankill. Equipped with a Land Rover chassis and heavily armoured, Short Brothers and Harland Belfast constructed the first prototype in 1964. It was delivered during Easter 1966 and immediately deployed. By 1968 the RUC had ten Shorlands, with five based near the border, three under the control of the Reserve Force and the remaining two held in reserve. By August 1969 Anthony Peacock had deployed all Shorlands to Belfast.[21] Moreover, on 15 August, just hours after a machine gun mounted on a Shorland had killed a nine-year-old child, the RUC received a further consignment, each equipped with battlefield .30 Browning machine guns. The vehicles held a crew of three, with a commander acting as observer, a gunner and a driver.

When violence escalated on 13 August, chosen members of the Reserve Force and B-Specials assembled at Musgrave Street in Central Belfast. On 14 August, none of the crews that ranged through nationalist streets had previously operated together. Furthermore, one officer (Mr U) had never seen either a Shorland or a Browning before, and another (Mr X) had not done any duty in a Shorland previously.[22] After a brief demonstration on both the vehicle and machine gun, the police unleashed the Shorlands, manned by inexperienced personnel from a partisan sectarian force into a defenceless community crammed into tightly packed terraces.

The Browning has a killing range of one mile and is not designed to engage individual targets. Firing ten rounds per second, it sprays bullets over a wide area. According to ballistic experts the gun is a very unsteady weapon, despite being bolted in position. This spray causes a main point of impact known as the 'beaten zone' with a fringe of lighter strikes around the point of main concentration. 'It follows, whether it is being fired by day or night, it is in practice necessary to fire a sustained burst in order to be sure of hitting the target. At night it was sometimes difficult to see the graticule [lines] on the sight and its position had to be guessed. For this reason tracer bullets are used to enable the gunner to line up his target.'[23] Disregarding orders, the Shorland gunners fired their Brownings on the move in Divis Street, the Falls Road and Ardoyne, spraying large amounts of rounds recklessly into homes and other buildings. Scarman commented on one of the many incidents regarding Shorlands and their Browning machine guns: 'The expert ballistic evidence of bullet damage to Brookfield Street houses illustrates the menace of the weapon.'[24]

THE BALLISTIC EVIDENCE

On Friday 25 June 1971, an RUC sergeant from the Arms Section of Police Central Stores at Sprucefield appeared before the Tribunal to give evidence on the Reserve Force Browning .30 ammunition. He stated that the Reserve Force held 27,000 rounds of .30 ammunition from a total of 164,660 held in store in August 1969. The 27,000 rounds were 'supplied by Sprucefield in bulk' and held by various Reserve Force platoons in Belfast. The ammunition came in sealed boxes with two types of belts, one containing 240 and the other 250 rounds. He claimed that officers returned 26,604 rounds in September 1969, leaving only 381 rounds unaccounted for, and remarked that he was 'completely 100 per cent satisfied' with the number returned. However, the officer then admitted that he had not been in charge of the store in August 1969, that his evidence relied on hearsay from another officer and that he had no knowledge of whether checks were made at the time.[25] Nevertheless, at the Tribunal, counsel for nationalist residents insisted that a closer scrutiny of the records actually revealed that police fired 3,581 rounds on 14–15 August, and that eyewitness accounts made the figure of 381 appear ridiculous. Journalist Max Hastings personally claimed to have witnessed thousands of rounds fired from Shorlands.

Counsel for the Divis Street residents claimed that the police attempted to cover up the enormous number of rounds fired by producing records from Reserve Force members and evidence from some of the Shorland commanders and gunners, which they provided in 'Secret Session'. They claimed to have received only 500 rounds, with ammunition limited in supply. In reality, counsel for the Divis residents claimed, the Shorland crews that operated across three nights received 32,936 rounds of .30 ammunition. Hastings had observed police restocking the armoured cars and identified an RUC armoured vehicle which 'looked like a sort of mobile arsenal ... stacked to the roof with cases of ammunition and assorted weaponry'.[26] In the early hours of 15 August, police officers had spent all ammunition for their sub-machine guns and received in Percy Street additional rounds of Sterling 9mm rounds distributed to both the RUC and B-Specials in the Divis Street area. It was generally accepted by the Scarman Tribunal that a Reserve Force commander was in charge, having been spotted carrying an SLR issued exclusively to that force. Despite Hastings' eyewitness account, police consistently denied the extent of the arsenal at their disposal.

Scarman's neutrality came into question when he rejected dozens of eyewitness accounts detailing how the police fired Browning machine guns into homes, shops and businesses on the Falls Road and its interlocking streets. Scarman largely accepted police evidence, while dismissing other sources, professional or otherwise. He concluded:

All the Shorland [i.e. police] witnesses denied any responsibility for these alleged shootings; it was their evidence that at no time did they move south of Divis Street into Albert Street or any of the neighbouring side streets. In the absence of any Browning bullet damage in this area the Tribunal accepts these denials and finds that the Shorlands did not move south of Divis Street/Falls Road and could not, therefore, have discharged their weapons there. The evidence does not justify a finding that there was firing into side streets from the Falls Road or Divis Street.[27]

Scarman claimed there was no ballistic evidence to justify a further search, yet forensic teams which examined Divis Street and the area of the Divis complex discovered overwhelming evidence of gunfire from Shorlands during the night and early morning of 14 and 15 August 1969. The Tribunal also dispatched teams to investigate the shootings in and around the Clonard and Ardoyne areas, where experts noted significant discharge from Shorlands. Nevertheless, Scarman failed to send teams to the Falls Road from Northumberland Street to the junction of the Falls, Springfield and Grosvenor roads. Apparently, the police received partial exoneration due to the absence of ballistics evidence from streets that were not actually examined.

Forensic scientist Dr John Martin gave evidence that inadvertently points to this conclusion. Martin informed the Tribunal that the police were unable to accompany him in the Divis area where his team spent the afternoon under the supervision of the British Army. His colleague, Mr Beavis, examined the substantial damage to St Comgall's primary school. Martin then recounted how:

> We never attempted to get into Raglan Street. When we eventually started our investigation on behalf of the Tribunal we had a document signed by the Secretary, Mr Green, giving us authority to carry out these investigations and it was on the strength of this document and on the authority of this that we did these investigations. We confined our activities to these areas or buildings on the list provided by the Tribunal.[28]

Counsel challenged Martin, insisting that buildings and homes in the area of Conway/Norfolk Street and Falls Road suffered high-velocity damage, an account of events supported by multiple eyewitness accounts from residents. In addition, bullet holes remained in the walls of a co-operative shop and the Bank of Ireland at the corner of Balaclava Street and the Falls Road, while residents noted damage and bloodstains at Bell's dry cleaning shop at the corner of Conway Street and the Falls. Nevertheless, Martin reaffirmed that the Falls Road and surrounding streets were not his responsibility. Moreover, before forensic scientists arrived to examine the vehicles, the Browning machine guns were removed from all vehicles: 'When I examined the Shorland vehicle,' one of the ballistics experts recounted, 'I was informed then that these were not available, in fact that they were not even available at the armoury.'[29] The Tribunal thus heard no forensic evidence to confirm the indiscriminate firing of Browning machine guns, thereby justifying Scarman's inaccurate conclusion.

Throughout the Tribunal, police officers attempted to conceal the amount of rounds fired, although they did admit to firing into Divis Street, Dover Street, Percy Street and Conway Street. And yet, many eyewitnesses stated they came under sustained fire from Shorlands firing into Albert Street, Sultan Street (where residents were being treated for gunshot wounds), Plevna Street and throughout the Lower Falls Road. In addition, the occupants of the Shorlands already knew the deadly capacity of the Browning machine guns and yet apparently also fired on innocent residents in Raglan, Lemon, Peel, Alma, Balaclava, Leeson and Derby streets. Entering the Grosvenor Road, they fired into Osman and Theodore streets.

Before 14 August, the Reserve Force had received direction to only fire Brownings over the heads of the nationalist crowds, whether they were armed or not, or indeed engaged in offensive action against police. However, after a Shorland opened fire in Conway Street, police fired every available weapon at their disposal. Independent journalists confirmed how police had fired indiscriminately into Divis Street and towards Divis Tower. Two Shorland commanders (out of the five vehicles in Divis) claimed to have come under automatic fire, after which they returned fire for effect, i.e. to kill.

The commanders and gunners of the Shorlands (Mr X, Y, V and U) were granted anonymity and their testimony was given in private sessions.[30] Serious inconsistencies appeared in these men's four statements. Scarman said of one episode: 'Witness U's account of what appears to be the same incident is, however, quite different. Contrary to the evidence of all other witnesses ... It will be noted that the chief difference between the evidence of Mr Y and Mr U is that the latter describes the incident as taking place when their vehicle was travelling away from the city, whereas Mr Y recollects it having taken place on the trip *towards* the city. But both witnesses denied firing into the flats.'[31] Counsel for the Divis residents pointed out to the Tribunal: 'Two of the Commanders and a gunner also claim that a hand grenade exploded under one of the vehicles. There is absolutely no evidence of this and it clashes with evidence that the Shorland had no protection underneath. No damage of any kind was suffered.'

Forensic evidence confirms that the Shorland gunners fired indiscriminately and recklessly, striking at least thirteen homes. This represents a minimum estimate considering the heights of the flats and the inability of forensic scientists to locate the bullet holes, and the destruction of homes and buildings in the area by loyalist firebombers. Alice Bell claims that Brownings raked countless homes on Divis Street before firebombs destroyed the buildings, leaving no forensic evidence. 'The RUC used the machine guns on the Shorlands to shoot into my aunt's shop, they couldn't get out to put the petrol bombs out because they were shooting in all the time.'[32] Forensics established that there was evidence of short bursts and substantial bursts of concentrated and raking Browning machine-gun fire, fired from a minimum of eight to nine different places. In Whitehall Path, rounds struck Nos 2, 3, 4, 5 and 11.[33]

Meanwhile in Ardoyne, Shorland gunners attacked several streets and the Holy Cross boys' primary school, strafing homes while residents lay on the floors. In Brookfield Street, off the Crumlin Road, Mr Y, a Shorland gunner under the instructions of his commander, fired several bursts indiscriminately down the street and into nationalist homes. There ballistic experts found damage to the front of six houses.[34] Loyalists later burned down a substantial part of the street while a Shorland remained in the street.

The Brownings were not the only police weapons wreaking havoc. Reporting on the damage to St Comgall's school in Divis Street, ballistics recorded that police used various weapons, including low-velocity rounds from both automatic weapons and revolvers, which caused:

> … extensive bullet damage to the entire front of the school … On this wall there are fifty-two sites of damage that can be equated to the damage caused by high-velocity bullets. In addition to this damage on the exterior of the building there were ten sites of damage inside the building where bullets have passed through the windows and struck the interior walls … eleven bullets had come through the slate roof.[35]

On 14 August, police had deployed two 'marksmen', an RUC officer and an RUC reservist, onto the roof of Hastings Street Barracks. While one of these must have been responsible for the death of Trooper McCabe, both inflicted numerous casualties in the vicinity of Divis Tower and the surrounding area. Senior police officers claimed that they deployed marksmen to protect the barracks from gunfire, yet forensics later found no evidence of an attack. DI Lagan eventually conceded that an examination revealed that there was no damage.[36]

The refusal to accept culpability, and the attempts to conceal the true nature of events, chimed with Osmond and Mark's critical observations regarding senior officers. Inspector General Anthony Peacock attempted to distance himself from the responsibility of deployment of armed Shorlands, claiming that he was not consulted.[37]

He insisted this was not his policy and had no recollection of the arming of the Shorlands: 'a Browning gun is part of the vehicle, and it would be a decision for the operational commander as to whether he would mount the gun or not'.[38] Later he relented and conceded that he could 'not fully recall whether I decided it or whether the commissioner told me he had done it and I approved it, but whichever way it was, my Lord, it basically comes back to being my decision'.[39] Belfast's RUC Commissioner likewise attempted to evade responsibility, but had also been party to the decision to arm the Shorlands.[40] He freely told Scarman:

> I am just thinking this one out, my Lord, for the moment. What your Lordship is saying, in effect I think, is that this would be a Government decision … This again is where my memory lets me down, but looking at it logically I would say that there must have been a high-level policy decision.[41]

Robert Porter, the Minister of Home Affairs, claimed that he was not consulted about the arming or firing of the Brownings, nor did he direct that he should have been be consulted.[42] Deputy Commissioner for Belfast S. J. Bradley, in charge of operations 'on the ground' in the Falls and Divis, distanced himself from the shootings when he claimed he had no knowledge of their arming, while stating it was a policy decision.[43] District Inspector of B Division Francis Lagan was aware of the arming of the Shorlands when they reported to Hastings Street at 7 p.m. on 14 August, but denied responsibility, claiming that the decision was taken at government level. 'I do not know who made the decision but I assume it was done at very high level as far as the RUC was concerned; certainly not at Mr Bradley's level or my level.'

Senior officers knew the likely consequences of deploying Shorlands for the old, young and disabled living in small terraced kitchen houses and high-rise dwellings, and the danger of death and injury to innocent residents by the firing of Brownings in a heavily populated area. He added, 'Yes, certainly a danger, but one had to also consider the circumstances under which the police were operating in that area ... Bullets had been fired on the previous night in Leeson Street'.[44] In effect, the unionist government and their police failed to accept responsibility for the murderous decision to deploy Shorlands; worse still, they continued to legitimise the subsequent violence by citing an imaginary republican insurrection.

While Scarman chose to accept police claims regarding nationalist gunfire, despite sufficient independent contrary evidence, he could not ignore the report of forensic and ballistic scientists:

> The evidence adduced puts beyond doubt that during the period that three vehicles were in Divis Street a considerable number of rounds of Browning ammunition were discharged in the direction of the flats on the south side of Divis Street ... the Tribunal finds that this firing, from Browning machine guns mounted on Shorland armoured cars, fatally injured Patrick Rooney, a boy of 9, in his home [in] Divis Street flats.[45]

Sterling machine-gun fire from police wounded nationalist residents from Conway, Cupar and Balaclava streets. Eyewitness Max Hastings stated that it 'seemed extraordinary [that] anybody should be permitted to fire a Sterling without anybody saying this was damned ridiculous'.[46] Hastings reported how senior officers oversaw the use of Sterlings, revolvers and rifles in Percy, Dover and Divis streets. 'Fire went on for longer than I was there, I was there for about forty minutes.'[47] Fire continued without any orders or provocation, or, indeed, regard for police regulations. During the evening of 14 August, the RUC requested and received a further thirty rifles, plus 4,000 rounds of .303 ammunition, together with an additional four Bren machine guns.[48] One of the first British Army commanders to arrive in Belfast, Brigadier Hudson, recounted how the police had expended their ammunition after midnight, at 1.20 a.m. on 15 August, and were loaned 1,000 rounds of 9mm ammunition by the British Army.[49]

All RUC ranks maintained that they faced an IRA uprising. Yet Deputy Commissioner Bradley revealed that the majority of police officers went home after the first night's violence – hardly the actions of a police force under siege. While Conway Street and its vicinity blazed, 100 yards away the police arrested a republican at his home in Kane Street (Clonard). 'The operation that I performed commenced at 7 a.m. [15 August] and it was over, I presume, about 10 [a.m.]. The majority of them [police] went home ...' Bradley conceded that no IRA attack took place anywhere in Belfast.[50]

During the period police officers shot dead a nine-year-old child, they fired on and (according to doctors on the scene) injured hundreds of Falls Road residents, while providing safe passage to loyalist firebombers. Commissioner Wolseley recalled:

I was up all that night – you are referring to the night of the 14th/15th August – and early next morning *our main concern was to round up as many known IRA men as possible* [emphasis added]. Six IRA suspects were arrested in Belfast and detained under the Civil Authorities (Special Powers) Act.[51]

He added that plain-clothes men were operating on the Falls Road on the evening and night of 14 August.

Bradley calculated that there were about nine guns on the nationalist side, three automatic weapons and a few rifles and revolvers.[52] However, the CCDC later rightly concluded that the 'RUC Special Branch, whose main function was to keep files on Republican sympathisers, were in a position to know beyond any shadow of doubt that the IRA were not able to mount an armed uprising.'[53]

Shortly after 11 a.m. on 15 August, at police headquarters at Castlereagh, senior police officers, including RUC Inspector General Peacock, met British Army officers, Brigadier Hudson and Colonels Napier and Fletcher to discuss military deployment in Belfast. A senior police officer claimed that the British Army insisted on deploying its 600 men of the two battalions of Prince of Wales and Queen's Regiment along the Falls Road:

> The first decision made was that the Military would occupy the Falls Road area ... The next thing was where to deploy the Military, and when they saw the line known as the Orange/Green line the Military Officers were not satisfied with this because of the maze of narrow streets ... they felt that if they took up position on Divis Street starting from Millfield right through to the traffic lights at the Falls Road/Springfield Road this would be their first deployment.[54]

Hudson, Fletcher and Napier recounted how 'they were satisfied that the border ran along the Falls Road/Divis Street, with this reservation, that there were enclaves of Catholics north of that line but the police view was that they would, by the time the Army came in, be evacuated.'[55] A senior police officer denied this. The meeting lasted less than two hours. While the police and army top brass took lunch, loyalist gunmen killed Gerard McAuley, wounded many other Clonard residents and burned dozens of homes in the Clonard area.

The crux of the police justification for their actions hinged on the assertion that nationalists had fired first. However, in the immediate aftermath of the pogrom, Hunt had little compunction in identifying the partisan nature of the police, and recommended that 'the RUC should be relieved of all duties of a military nature as soon as possible and its contribution to the security of Northern Ireland from subversion should be limited to the gathering of intelligence, the protection of important persons and the enforcement of the relevant laws'.[56] Yet by 1972 the objective of the British state in Ireland had changed. In the wake of the British Army deployment into Belfast on 15 August, General Freeland rightly prophesied that the army's honeymoon period with the nationalist community would not last long. After a change in British government in June 1970, Ted Heath's Tory government effectively allowed the Stormont regime to employ the army as a hammer against the nationalist working class. The Falls curfew, the introduction of internment, the Ballymurphy massacre, Bloody Sunday and the Widgery whitewash that followed all suggested that the Scarman Report would omit the harsh criticism of police actions that the evidence demanded when it was published in April 1972.

There is unequivocal evidence that the RUC drove Shorlands down a series of streets on 14 August and that they employed overwhelming and deadly force against an unarmed civilian population, and that loyalists followed in their wake and expelled thousands of people from their homes. Remarkably, Scarman largely accepted the factual basis of this account with the crucial proviso that police and loyalist actions were not co-ordinated, and that the RUC had responded to nationalist aggression. Despite a complete lack of real evidence, Scarman took police claims of a nationalist attack at face value, and systematically disregarded voluminous accounts by victims and, more crucially, independent witnesses. The existence of an actual republican insurrection in 1972 meant that the British establishment could hardly provide their antagonists with a propaganda boon by acknowledging in an official report the truth of what had occurred in August 1969. Scarman trotted out what would become an all too familiar line – namely that 'a few bad apples' had besmirched the reputation of a fine police force. Scarman concluded that:

> In a very real sense our inquiry was an investigation of police conduct … Undoubtedly mistakes were made and certain individual officers acted wrongly on occasions. But the general case of a partisan force

co-operating with Protestant mobs to attack Catholic people is devoid of substance and we reject it utterly.[57]

In 1973 the CCDC published a pamphlet entitled *The Black Paper: Northern Ireland – the Story of the Police*. Established in August 1969 as a West Belfast nationalist defence organisation, the CCDC originated during the immediate aftermath of the burnings of the Falls and Clonard. After four years of army and police brutality, they published this scathing report, which stated unequivocally that the nationalist community rejected the deeply sectarian RUC:

> It was rejected only when people witnessed in their own streets or on the television screen the brutality of the Royal Ulster Constabulary. The present upheaval which has engulfed Northern Ireland started with the killing of innocent people by police guns, the burning of homes while police stood idly by or joined the arsonists, and the utter partiality of police deployment and control when minority areas were invaded by hostile mobs.[58]

The CCDC admitted that the Hunt recommendations and Wilson's reforms were well conceived, but argued that they had not been fully implemented. On his appointment to the role of chief commissioner, Robert Mark of the London Metropolitan Police stated, 'that police depended entirely for their successful operation on their acceptability by the community, and that this in turn depended entirely on their accountability for their actions'.[59] Indeed, the CCDC noted: 'Only when that is seen to be happening will the laws gain the respect from the community upon which its validity rests. That respect has been lost in Northern Ireland. It must be regained and strengthened … When those who make the law break the law in the name of the law there is no law.'[60]

CONCLUSION

At midnight on 27 September 2017, almost fifty years after the tragic summer of 1969, PSNI officers entered Catholic homes in Cantrell Close, East Belfast, to inform residents that they would have to leave their homes immediately due to UVF death threats.[1] In the first week of August 1969 Gerry Fitt had responded to similar death threats against a Catholic mother and her children, labelling the RUC as UVF messenger boys. 'Here we have two members of the RUC whose duty is to protect the citizens, standing by and hearing a murder threat without taking any action whatever against either men.'[2] Despite four decades of violence, and twenty years after the signing of the Good Friday Agreement, the reactionary character of loyalism survives, only now attacks extend to newly settled foreign nationals and ethnic minorities.

Almost 3,500 lives have been lost since McKeague and his mobs began their sectarian campaign against Belfast's nationalist community. Hours after the pogrom, barricades mushroomed across nationalist districts in anticipation of further loyalist incursions, and West Belfast's population swelled under the weight of thousands of incoming refugees. Days after the murderous attacks, shocked journalists sent reports about the enormity of the problem from makeshift refugee centres in schools. 'Everywhere there were signs of the refugee problem. Cars with red stickers, lorries loaded with belongings and doctors with their professions clearly marked in red across the car window.'[3]

Yet the wistful prophetic comments of one elderly refugee pointed to the dragon's teeth sown by those who orchestrated the pogrom over two bloody nights in Belfast. He pointed to a boy in the centre and remarked to a reporter: 'That wee boy is the next generation and the way he has been treated he will be a rebel. It is your children I feel sorry for. The way things are going there are fifty-one per cent of his kind and he is going to be a rebel. That's the tragedy of all this.'[4] Young nationalists quickly sought means of protection from sectarian state forces and loyalist marauders, and a new militant republican group emerged from the ashes of Bombay Street.[5] Ironically, McKeague and his cohorts had breathed life into the bogeyman of their perverted imaginations – the Provisional IRA. The unionist regime's determination to employ the British Army to hammer working-class nationalist communities, whether through curfew, internment or massacre, only lengthened the recruitment lines.

Several weeks after the arrival of the British Army into nationalist areas, owners and employees of occupied premises tried to pressure authorities for the army's removal to permanent bases. Joe McCann, superintendent of the Falls Road Baths, pressed his manager for the army's removal so that he might reopen the bathing facilities to the public. After intense talks, the army relocated to a disused nearby factory at the corner of North Howard Street and First Street. The barracks replaced the barbed wire 'peace-line' erected by the army days after the initial burnings. The military did not want to withdraw from certain vantage points within nationalist areas, but persistent and at times heated petitions from the Clonard clergy convinced them to withdraw from church grounds shortly afterwards. Many in the nationalist community came to view the military presence as an intelligence-gathering operation. This marked the beginning of the end of General Freeland's oft-quoted honeymoon period between the nationalist community and the army.

Arguably, the continued loyalist violence and the change of government in London had convinced Whitehall that the army could not fight on two fronts. The squaddies quickly morphed from defenders of the Falls Road to tools of unionist reaction. More concerning was the establishment of British Army surveillance units and death squads that operated across nationalist Belfast. A short time after the opening sessions of the Scarman Tribunal, Brigadier Frank Kitson assembled a counter-insurgency unit, integrated into his 39 Brigade, which he employed as a weapon against the nationalist population. The Military Reaction Force (MRF) contained members of the Special Air Service, Special Boat Service, Royal Marines and Parachute Regiment, and comprised forty men and several women.[6] Operating from army barracks in Belfast and Hollywood, these surveillance units drove unmarked cars, carried sub-machine guns, wore civilian clothes and carried false identities. They were responsible for a catalogue of deaths and injuries, including a Catholic woman on the Glen Road in West Belfast.

Kitson's counter-insurgency policy, honed through bloody experience in Britain's colonies, aimed to instigate an all-out war between loyalists and republicans, the key objective being to engage the newly emerging IRA. Apparently, the MRF conspired with the UVF in the bombing of McGurk's Bar in North Belfast on 4 December 1971, which killed seventeen Catholics – including two children – and injured fifteen others.[7] The role of the state in the subsequent loyalist campaign does not form part of the current analysis, but the interested reader should be aware of Margaret Urwin's *A State in Denial: British Collaboration with Loyalist Paramilitaries* and Anne Cadwallader's *Lethal Allies: British Collusion in Ireland*.

The main aim of my book is to highlight the relationship produced between reactionary loyalism, state forces and the unionist regime in the conflagration that erupted in the summer of 1969, which arguably generated three decades of subsequent violence. I have concentrated on two individuals, John McKeague and Ian Paisley, in order to examine the wider nature of loyalism and the state. Before Whitehall dirtied its own hands in Ireland, it had essentially indicted the Stormont regime as culpable for the devastating violence of August 1969. Yet by the time Scarman reported, Britain had once again assumed its traditional position of copper-fastening reactionary loyalism. Scarman lightly chastised John McKeague for his participation in the summer of evictions and burnings. More astonishingly, while Scarman deliberated, McKeague's cohorts were permitted to drive more families from their homes, while his *Loyalist News* published vile anti-Catholic rhetoric and sectarian songs celebrating the deaths of nationalists. McKeague had clear links to the loyalist bombing campaign that had forced Terence O'Neill from office. Furthermore, his SDA operated as the template and inspiration for a network of similar vigilante organisations – most notably the 50,000 loyalists in the UDA that also contained the hard-core Ulster Freedom Fighters (UFF), who indiscriminately, and at times gruesomely, murdered hundreds of Catholics and Protestants.

Within a year of the 1969 pogrom, the UDA were patrolling Protestant areas alongside the British Army. Army foot patrols often hurled Catholics into Land Rovers, dumping them in loyalist areas, shouting, 'There's another Fenian for you.'[8] Members of the Parachute Regiment, in particular, carried out these abductions in the Ballymurphy district of West Belfast.[9] In addition, as Scarman sat, the Paras carried out two mass killings: the Ballymurphy massacre and Bloody Sunday, shooting dead twenty-five innocent Catholic civilians.

In 1971, during a dispute between the UDA and McKeague, members of the UDA attacked McKeague's family shop in East Belfast, burning his mother alive. McKeague subsequently established the Red Hand Commandos. This gang, also associated with the UVF, was ultimately responsible for the murder of hundreds of innocent nationalists. McKeague allegedly participated in a number of sectarian murders, and in torture and mutilations. This reactionary and fascistic culture found expression first in the Tartan gangs and reached its nadir in the heinous campaign of Lenny Murphy and the Shankill Butchers, which lasted several years, amounting to thirty deaths.

Yet McKeague also had the ear of powerful unionist politicians. He joined the Vanguard, for example, led by ex-Stormont minister William Craig.[10] Craig organised mass loyalist rallies threatening to liquidate the enemies of 'Ulster', a call that found predictable expression in the death of more innocent nationalists. In 1974 McKeague played a leading part in a paramilitary umbrella group – the Ulster Loyalist Central Co-ordinating Committee. British military intelligence used McKeague's proclivities for young boys to blackmail him into informing.[11] During police questioning in 1982, he threatened to go public about the role of British intelligence in blackmailing others, such as William McGrath, the housemaster at Kincora Boys' Home in East Belfast.[12] A short time after his release, two Irish National Liberation Army members shot him dead in his shop. It has been reported that one gunman was an RUC Special Branch agent, the other linked to British military intelligence.[13]

Ian Paisley lit the long sectarian fuse, destabilised the unionist elite and intensified hatred by his sectarian speeches and actions. He stood back as his incendiary rhetoric exploded into violence against the Bogside on 12 August. As hundreds of nationalist homes burned in Belfast two days later, Paisley spewed further venom, accusing Catholic survivors of burning their own homes. Yet Paisley's vitriol set the tone for the wider unionist response. In short, the unionist political establishment has always been a prisoner to the powerful reactionary forces conjured by Carson and Craig before the Great War in order to breathe life into the Orange State. Moreover, their inherent antipathy to the Catholic community found its most raucous expression amongst the rump of loyalist bigots on the Shankill Road in April 1969.

The costs of loyalist ideology were catastrophic. Extreme loyalism destroyed the social fabric of the Shankill and surrounding districts by attempting to eradicate the minority Catholic community. The RUC singularly failed to stop McKeague from establishing a sectarian army in the spring of 1969 and thereby avert the slide towards violence. Yet the police were not equipped to do so: both the officers and the regime they defended shared many of McKeague's views. A partisan, paramilitary force, many were members of the Orange Order: quite naturally, the police chose to either ignore or connive in the pogrom.

Academic accounts since August 1969 have failed to recognise McKeague's role in the violence, even though he was no backwoodsman. McKeague had the ear of senior policemen; he had connections with Special Branch, and later operated as an informer for military intelligence. A false narrative, constructed to excuse the Stormont regime and characterise the Troubles as a republican plot, has instead dominated the discourse. The actions of student radicals in Derry and then at Burntollet seeking civil rights are held up as deliberately provocative acts that undermined a reformist prime minister who may have turned Northern Ireland in a different direction at the fatal crossroads of 1969. This convenient fable ignores the fact that institutionalised sectarianism reigned at every level of government and state in the six counties of Northern Ireland at the time.

This study has demonstrated that the origins of armed conflict had a long gestation in fifty years of discriminatory Orange rule, and that the violence itself emerged from the aggressive actions of paramilitary state forces, many of whom acted in conjunction with murderous sectarian mobs in August 1969. Nevertheless, against a mountain of contrary evidence, many still choose to blame the violence on the commemoration of the Easter Rising in 1966 and the inadequate, yet courageous, efforts of the nationalist community to defend themselves on two hellish August nights in the late summer of 1969.

NOTES

FOREWORD

1 Tommy McKearney is a lifelong republican and socialist from Tyrone. He spent sixteen years imprisoned at Long Kesh, where he spent fifty-three days on hunger strike in 1980. He was a founding member of, and remains active in, the Independent Workers' Union of Ireland (IWU) and is a frequent commentator on Irish politics.

2 During July and August 1969, ten people died. Eight died of gunshot wounds: seven in Belfast, one in Armagh. The other two died of head injuries, one in Belfast, the other in Dungiven.

INTRODUCTION

1 Farrell, Michael, *Arming the Protestants: The Formation of the Ulster Special Constabulary and the Royal Ulster Constabulary, 1920–27* (Pluto Press, London, 1983), p. 1.

2 *The Times*, 22 August 1969.

3 *The Irish Times,* 3 October 1988.

1   ORANGE STATE IN CRISIS

1 Whelan, Kevin, 'Bew's Ireland', *Saothar*, vol. 33, 2008, pp. 126–31; available at www.jstor.org/stable/i23199887.

2 Wichert, Sabine, *Northern Ireland Since 1945* (Longman, London, 1991), p. 96.

3 Hennessey, Thomas, *Northern Ireland: The Origins of the Troubles* (Gill & Macmillan, Dublin, 2005), p. 114.

4 *Ibid.*, p. 118. Craig was responsible for banning the 5 October 1968 march in Derry, often regarded as a watershed in the path towards violence. Marchers refused to abide by the government order and television images of their being batoned off the streets by the RUC were some of the earliest images of the Troubles to be viewed internationally.

5 Hanley, Brian and Millar, Scott, *The Lost Revolution: The Story of the Official IRA and the Worker's Party* (Penguin Books, London, 2010), p. 21.

6 Author interview with Witness A (Belfast: 7 February 2008).

7 Author interview with Witness B (Belfast: 7 February 2008).

8 *Belfast Telegraph*, 11 July 1966.

9   Belfast *News Letter*, 2 July 1966.

10   Hennessey (2005), pp. 95–106.

11   Scarman, *Violence and Civil Disturbances in Northern Ireland in 1969*, Report of Tribunal of Inquiry (hereafter Scarman Report), Cmd 566 (HMSO Belfast, 1972) pp. 45–54.

12   Hennessey (2005), p. 103; Scarman Report, p. 50.

13   Hennessey (2005) pp. 67, 69.

14   Elliott, Marianne, *The Catholics of Ulster: A History* (Penguin Books, London, 2001), p. 411.

15   *The Times*, 11 April 1966.

16   Farrell, Michael, *Northern Ireland: The Orange State* (Pluto Press, London, 1983), p. 235.

17   The London *Sunday Times* Insight Team, *Northern Ireland: A Report on the Conflict* (Vintage Books, New York, 1972), p. 41.

18   *Ibid*, p. 43.

19   O'Neill, Terence, *The Autobiography of Terence O'Neill: Prime Minister of Northern Ireland 1963–1969* (Rupert Hart-Davis, London, 1972), p. 137.

20   Brewer, John D., *Anti-Catholicism in Northern Ireland, 1600–1998: The Mote and the Beam* (Macmillan, London, 1998), p. 104.

21   Patterson, Henry, *Ireland Since 1939: The Persistence of Conflict* (Penguin Books, Dublin, 2006), p. 191.

22   Callaghan, James, *A House Divided: The Dilemma of Northern Ireland* (Collins, London, 1973), p. 2.

23   Farrell, *Northern Ireland: The Orange State*, p. 92.

24   Darby, John, *Conflict in Northern Ireland: The Development of a Polarised Community* (Gill & Macmillan, Dublin, 1976), p. 83.

25   *Ibid.*, p. 88.

26   Boyd, Andrew, *Brian Faulkner and the Crisis of Ulster Unionism* (Anvil Books, Tralee, 1972), p. 57.

27   Mulholland, Marc, *Northern Ireland at the Crossroads: Ulster Unionism in the O'Neill Years, 1960–9* (Macmillan Press, London, 2000), p. 158.

28   Boyd, Andrew, *Holy War in Belfast* (Pretani Press, Belfast, 1987), p. 223.

29   Boyd (1972), pp. 56–7.

30   Mulholland (2000), p. 141.

31   *Daily Telegraph*, 4 July 1966.

32   The London *Sunday Times* Insight Team (1972), p. 46.

33 Farrell *Northern Ireland: The Orange State*, p. 243.

34 Patterson (2006), p. 198.

35 Robert Lundy is reviled to the present day by loyalists for his perceived treachery during the Siege of Derry in 1688–89. His effigy is burned each year during loyalist celebrations to mark the shutting of the gates of Derry in 1688 against the army of King James II. A by-word for 'traitor' among unionists and loyalists, Ian Paisley used the term frequently against those he perceived as soft on the nationalist threat, including PMs Terence O'Neill and Margaret Thatcher and NI First Minister David Trimble.

36 Brewer (1998), pp. 57, 69.

37 *Ibid.*, p. 69.

38 Farrell, *Arming the Protestants*, p. 192.

39 Buckland, Patrick, *A History of Northern Ireland* (Gill & Macmillan, Dublin, 1981), p. 51.

40 Brown, William, *An Army with Banners: The Real Face of Orangeism* (Beyond the Pale, Belfast, 2003), p. 90.

41 Author interview with Lily Fitzsimmons (Belfast: 26 May 2008).

42 Farrell, *Northern Ireland: The Orange State*, p. 144.

43 Budge, Ian and O'Leary, Cornelius, *Belfast: Approach to Crisis. A Study of Belfast Politics, 1613–1970* (Macmillan, London, 1973), p. 151.

44 Author interview with John McGreevy (Belfast: 12 June 2008).

45 Wallace, Martin, *Drums and Guns: Revolution in Ulster* (Geoffrey Chapman, London, 1970), p. 82.

46 Nelson, Sarah, *Ulster's Uncertain Defenders: Protestant Political, Paramilitary and Community Groups and the Northern Ireland Conflict* (Appletree Press, Belfast, 1984), p. 34.

47 Darby (1976), p. 90.

48 Moloney, Ed and Pollak, Andy, *Paisley* (Poolbeg Press, Swords, 1986), pp. 89–90.

49 Farrell, *Northern Ireland: The Orange State*, p. 234.

50 *The Revivalist*, February 1966.

51 Moloney and Pollak (1986), p. 125.

52 *Ibid.*, p. 136

53 *Ibid.*, p. 138.

54 Boulton, David, *The UVF 1966–73: An Anatomy of Loyalist Rebellion* (Torc Books, Dublin, 1973), p. 53.

55 *Ibid.*, p. 34.

56 Taylor, Peter, *Loyalists* (Bloomsbury, London, 2000), p. 36.

57 Boulton (1973), p. 42.

58 Taylor (2000), p. 39.

59 *Belfast Telegraph*, 18 July 1966.

60 Farrell, *Northern Ireland: The Orange State*, p. 235.

61 Bruce, Steve, *God Save Ulster! The Religion and Politics of Paisleyism* (Oxford University Press, Oxford, 1989), p. 85.

62 Brewer (1998), p. 107.

63 Buckland (1981), p. 120.

64 Moloney and Pollak (1986), p. 143.

65 Belfast *News Letter*, 4 July 1966.

66 *Belfast Telegraph*, 13 July 1966.

67 *Daily Mirror*, 13 July 1966.

68 *Daily Telegraph*, 3 July 1966.

69 Belfast *News Letter*, 13 July 1966.

70 Cooke, Dennis, *Persecuting Zeal: A Portrait of Ian Paisley* (Brandon, Dingle, 1996), p. 144.

71 O'Neill (1972), p. 75.

72 *Belfast Telegraph*, 24 September 1966.

73 *The Irish News*, 1 July 1966.

74 *Ibid.*

75 Belfast *News Letter*, 5 July 1966.

76 *Belfast Telegraph*, 5 July 1966.

77 *Ibid.*, 15 July 1966.

78 *Ibid.*, 6 July 1966.

79 Author interview with Owen McDonald (Belfast: 2 February 2008).

80 Author interview with Eamon McGonigle (Belfast: 25 May 2012).

81 Author interview with Paddy Carlin (Belfast: 14 April 2008).

82 Author interview with Kevin Kennedy (Belfast: 9 April 2008).

83 Bell, Geoffrey, *The Protestants of Ulster* (Pluto Press, London, 1976), pp. 49–50.

84 Moloney, Ed, *Voices from the Grave: Two Men's War in Ireland* (Faber and Faber, London, 2010), p. 31.

85 Author interview with Paddy Carlin (Belfast: 14 April 2008).

86 Taylor (2000), pp. 49–50.

87 *Belfast Telegraph,* 10 May 1969.

88 Elliott (2001), p. 418. On 15 August 1969 loyalist mobs attacked nationalist homes in the Clonard area, including Bombay Street, burning many to the ground. At the beginning of the assault loyalists shot dead a fifteen-year-old Catholic boy.

2 THE EVICTIONS COMMENCE

1 Ardoyne Commemoration Project, *Ardoyne: The Untold Truth* (Beyond the Pale, Belfast, 2002), p. 20.

2 The march supported by NICRA was protesting discrimination against the majority nationalist, mainly Catholic, population in Derry by the Protestant, unionist-controlled local authority. The baton attack by police on the peaceful marchers was broadcast by television crews, bringing international attention to Northern Ireland's brutal practices. Thirty people were injured, including Gerry Fitt, MP, when the RUC used batons and water cannons against the crowd.

3 The Reverend S. E. Long, a member of the Order, quoted in Feargal Cochrane, 'Meddling at the Crossroads: The decline and fall of Terence O'Neill within the Unionist Community' in English, Richard and Walker, Graham (eds.), *Unionism in Modern Ireland: New Perspectives on Politics and Culture* (Macmillan Press, London, 1996), p. 157.

4 Stewart, A. T. Q., *The Narrow Ground: the Roots of Conflict in Ulster* (Faber and Faber, London, 1989), p. 14.

5 *Ibid.,* p. 153.

6 Foster, Roy F., *Modern Ireland: 1600–1972* (Penguin Books, London, 1989), p. 588.

7 Bruce, Steve, *The Red Hand: Protestant Paramilitaries in Northern Ireland* (Oxford University Press, Oxford, 1992), p. 28.

8 *Disturbances in Northern Ireland* (hereafter Cameron Commission), Cmd 532 (HMSO, Belfast, 1969), p. 64.

9 Farrell, *Northern Ireland: The Orange State*, p. 247.

10 Cameron Commission, p. 72.

11 *Ibid.,* p. 9.

12 Bruce (1989), p. 95.

13 Boyd (1972), p. 50. The Cameron Commission's report was published on 12 September 1969. Cameron's conclusions were, among a number of issues,

gerrymandering of local authority boundaries, discrimination in housing allocation, resentment among Catholics to the B-Specials and the continuance of the Special Powers Act.

14 O'Neill (1972), p. 116.

15 Cameron Commission, p. 36.

16 Boulton (1973), p. 79.

17 Cameron Commission, pp. 42–3.

18 Cooke (1996), p. 156.

19 Cameron Commission, pp. 40–1.

20 Belfast *News Letter*, 29 January 1969.

21 Farrell, *Northern Ireland: The Orange State*, p. 250.

22 Devlin, Paddy, *Straight Left: An Autobiography* (Blackstaff Press, Belfast, 1993), p. 95.

23 Mulholland (2000), pp. 175–6. Partisan condemnation of PD has been reinforced by the work of some historians, including Henry Patterson and Joseph Lee. Daniel Finn offers a well-argued response to this trend in 'The point of no return? People's Democracy and the Burntollet march', *Field Day Review* (Sept. 2013), pp. 5–21.

24 Belfast *News Letter*, 27 January 1969.

25 Hezlet, Arthur, *The 'B' Specials: A History of the Ulster Special Constabulary* (Pan Books, London, 1973), p. 212.

26 Egan, Bowes and McCormack, Vincent, *Burntollet* (LRS Publishers, London, 1969), p. 56.

27 *Ibid.*

28 O'Neill (1972), p. 111.

29 Moloney and Pollak (1986), p. 169.

30 Cameron Commission, p. 73.

31 Callaghan (1973), p. 12.

32 Rose, Richard, *Governing Without Consensus: An Irish Perspective* (Faber and Faber, London, 1971), p. 121.

33 Belfast *News Letter*, 6 February 1969.

34 *The Times*, 6 February 1969.

35 *The Irish News*, 7 February 1969.

36 Rose (1971), p. 124.

37 *Ibid.*

38 *Ibid.*

39 *The Times,* 21 February 1969.

40 Taylor (2000), p. 59.

41 *Protestant Telegraph,* 5 April 1969.

42 Boulton (1973), pp. 106–7.

43 O'Neill (1972), p. 123.

44 Holland, Jack and McDonald, Henry, *INLA: Deadly Divisions. The Story of One of Ireland's Most Ruthless Terrorist Organisations* (Torc, Dublin, 1994), p. 199.

45 Dillon, Martin, *The Trigger Men* (Mainstream Publishing, Edinburgh, 2003), p. 109.

46 *Ibid.,* p. 104.

47 Boulton (1973), pp. 46–7.

48 Bruce (1992), p. 33.

49 Kelley, Kevin, J., *The Longest War: Northern Ireland and the I.R.A.* (Zed Books, London, 1988), p. 116.

50 *The Irish News,* 28 April 1969.

51 'Testimony of John McKeague', Day 162, Scarman Transcripts, p. 13.

52 Moloney and Pollak (1986), p. 160.

53 Ardoyne Commemoration Project (2002), p. 20.

54 'Testimony of John McKeague', Day 162, Scarman Transcripts, pp. 1–88.

55 Bruce (1992), pp. 34–5. The Connolly Association derives the name from James Connolly, a socialist republican, born in Scotland and executed by the British Army for his part in the 1916 Easter Rising.

56 Scarman Tribunal, Schedule of known outbreaks of fire during civil disturbances in Belfast – July and August 1969, Exhibit 18 (Belfast).

57 Boulton (1973), p. 111.

58 Ardoyne Commemoration Project (2002), p. 20.

59 Boulton (1973), p. 112.

60 'Testimony of RUC Sergeant Gracey', Day 46, Scarman Transcripts, p. 11.

61 Author interview with Ethna Byrne (Belfast: 9 April 2009).

62 Author interview with Eileen McGonigle (Belfast: 25 May 2012).

63 Scarman Report, p. 27.

64 'Testimony of Head Constable C. W. Kyle', Day 35, Scarman Transcripts, p. 29.

65 Belfast *News Letter,* 18 July 1969.

66 Farrell, *Northern Ireland: The Orange State,* p. 258.

67 Belfast *News Letter*, 25 July 1969.

68 Nelson (1984), p. 64.

69 'Testimony of John McKeague', Day 162, Scarman Transcripts, pp. 1–88.

70 Boulton (1973), pp. 108–9.

71 Nelson (1984), p. 82.

72 'Testimony of Frank McCullagh', Day 38, Scarman Transcripts, pp. 37–72.

73 Belfast *News Letter*, 8 August 1969.

74 'Testimony of Mr J. Dineen', Day 50, Scarman Transcripts, pp. 55–62.

75 'Testimony of Anthony Dunham', Day 50, Scarman Transcripts, p. 63.

76 'Testimony of Frank McCullagh', Day 38, Scarman Transcripts, pp. 37–72.

77 Scarman Report, p. 54.

78 *Ibid.*, pp. 56–7.

79 Boulton (1973), p. 112.

80 Belfast *News Letter*, 8 August 1969.

81 Scarman Report, p. 56.

82 *Ibid.*, p. 59.

83 *Ibid.*, p. 58.

84 'Testimony of District Inspector James Gilchrist', Day 36, Scarman Transcripts, pp. 69–70.

85 'Testimony of John McKeague', Day 159, Scarman Transcripts, p. 44.

86 Boulton (1973), p. 114.

87 *Ibid.*

88 'Testimony of RUC Head Constable Kyle', Day 35, Scarman Transcripts, p. 26.

89 'Testimony of RUC Deputy Commissioner S. J. Bradley', Day 44, Scarman Transcripts, p. 32.

90 Belfast *News Letter*, 4 August 1969.

91 'Testimony of John McKeague', Day 159, Scarman Transcripts, p. 43.

92 Belfast *News Letter*, 4 August 1969.

93 *The Times*, 5 August 1969.

94 'Testimony of John McKeague', Day 163, Scarman Transcripts, p. 1.

95 Boulton (1973), p. 115.

96 'Testimony of John McKeague', Day 163, Scarman Transcripts, p. 10.

97 *The Times*, 5 August 1969.

98 *Belfast Telegraph*, 5 August 1969.

99 Belfast *News Letter*, 8 August 1969.

100 The Unionist Party voted Chichester-Clark into office on 1 May 1969 by a majority of one. He was from landed gentry and served in the British Army. He was the penultimate Prime Minister of Northern Ireland and eighth leader of the Ulster Unionist Party.

101 'Testimony of John McKeague', Day 159, Scarman Transcripts, p. 45.

102 Downing, Taylor (ed.), *The Troubles: The Background to the Question of Northern Ireland* (Thames MacDonald, London, 1980), p. 149.

103 *The Irish News*, 29 August 2012.

104 Nelson (1984), p. 53.

105 *Protestant Telegraph*, 12 July 1969.

106 *Ibid.*, 2 August 1969.

107 Boulton (1973), p. 110.

108 *The Irish News*, 6 August 1969.

109 *Ibid.*, 5 August 1969.

110 *Ibid.*, 6 August 1969.

111 *Ibid.*, 7 August 1969.

112 Belfast *News Letter*, 8 August 1969.

113 *Ibid.*

114 *Belfast Telegraph*, 6 August 1969.

115 Bruce (1992), pp. 44–5.

116 *Belfast Telegraph*, 8 August 1969.

117 *Ibid.*, 9 August 1969.

118 Scarman Report, p. 119.

119 Farrell, *Northern Ireland: The Orange State*, p. 259.

120 Callaghan (1973), p. 32.

121 Boulton (1973), p. 116.

3   DERRY IN THE EYE OF THE STORM

1   'Testimony of Seán Keenan', Day 18, Scarman Transcripts, p. 7.

2   'Testimony of John Hume', Day 26, Scarman Transcripts, p. 2.

3   Derry Development Commission was established on 5 February 1969 by Derry Corporation and Derry Rural District Council to facilitate better community relations, housing and employment in the city and surrounding area.

4   'Testimony of Father V. A. Mulvey', Day 6, Scarman Transcripts, p. 58.

5   *Ibid.*

6   'Testimony of John Hume', Day 26, Scarman Transcripts, p. 4.

7   'Testimony of Patrick L. Doherty', Day 30, Scarman Transcripts, p. 59.

8   'Testimony of Mr Kevin McNamara', Day 5, Scarman Transcripts, p. 4.

9   'Testimony of Miss J. B. Devlin', Day 20, Scarman Transcripts, p. 13.

10 'Testimony of RUC County Inspector Gerald S. Mahon', Day 11, Scarman Transcripts, p. 3.

11 Scarman Report, p. 67.

12 'Testimony of RUC District Inspector (in charge of Reserve Force), William J. Hood', Day 13, Scarman Transcripts, p. 15.

13 Cameron Commission, p. 73.

14 Scarman Report, p. 68.

15 'Testimony of Mr R. Hodson, *Financial Times*', Day 4, Scarman Transcripts, p. 90.

16 'Testimony of Seán Keenan', Day 18, Scarman Transcripts, p. 36.

17 Scarman Report, p. 70.

18 *Ibid.*, p. 69.

19 'Testimony of Lt Kevin Francis Robbin', Day 3, Scarman Transcripts, p. 62.

20 Scarman Report, p. 71.

21 Limpkin, Clive, *The Battle of Bogside* (Penguin Books, Harmondsworth, 1972), p. 11.

22 Scarman Report, p. 74.

23 'Testimony of Miss J. B. Devlin', Day 20, Scarman Transcripts, p. 10.

24 'Testimony of RUC County Inspector Gerald S. Mahon', Day 11, Scarman Transcripts, p. 6.

25 The London *Sunday Times* Insight Team (1972), p. 116.

26 'Testimony of Miss J. B. Devlin', Day 20, Scarman Transcripts, p. 11. The 'Billy Boys' is a sectarian song adopted by some members of the Orange Order and played during the summer marching season. Offensive and intimidating to the Catholic minority population, one of its lines projects its sectarianism: 'We're up to our knees in Fenian blood'.

27 'Testimony of Mr H. Jackson', Day 4, Scarman Transcripts, p. 62.

28 Scarman Report, p. 74.

29 'Testimony of Patrick L. Doherty', Day 30, Scarman Transcripts, p. 67.

30 *Ibid.*

31 'Testimony of Miss J. B. Devlin', Day 20, Scarman Transcripts, p. 10.

32 Limpkin (1972), p. 20.

33 'Testimony of Mr J. G. O'Boyle', Day 13, Scarman Transcripts, pp. 8–10.

34 Scarman Report, p. 74.

35 'Testimony of RUC Sergeant A. J. Taylor', Day 33, Scarman Transcripts, p. 5.

36 Scarman Report, p. 38.

37 CS gas was a toxic chemical compound used as a riot control agent, known to cause a burning sensation and uncontrollable tearing of the eyes, rendering victims difficulty with sight and breathing.

38 'Testimony of RUC District Inspector General R. E. G. Shillington', Day 11, Scarman Transcripts, p. 36.

39 G. W. Target, *Bernadette: the story of Bernadette Devlin* (Hodder and Stoughton, London, 1975), p. 241.

40 'Testimony of Miss J. B. Devlin', Day 20, Scarman Transcripts, p. 14.

41 'Testimony of Mr Dennis Harley', Day 32, Scarman Transcripts, p. 27.

42 Scarman Report, p. 76.

43 *Belfast Telegraph,* 13 August 1969.

44 Scarman Report, p. 77.

45 McClean, Raymond, *The Road to Bloody Sunday* (Ward River Press, Swords, 1983), p. 76.

46 *Ibid.*

47 'Testimony of Bernard Hatfield', Day 29, Scarman Transcripts, p. 19.

48 *Ibid.*, p. 42.

49 Target (1975), p. 240.

50 *The Observer,* 24 August 1969.

51 *Ibid.*

52 'Testimony of County Inspector Gerard S. Mahon', Day 11, Scarman Transcripts, p. 1; Day 32, p. 14.

53 'Testimony of Dr Raymond McClean', Day 32, Scarman Transcripts, p. 13.

54 McClean (1983), p. 84.

55 'Testimony of Dr Raymond McClean', Day 32, Scarman Transcripts, p. 11.

56 *The Observer,* 24 August 1969.

57 Coogan, Tim Pat, *The Troubles: Ireland's Ordeal 1966–1996 and the Search for Peace* (Roberts Rinehart, Boulder, 1996), p. 99.

58 'Testimony of Dr D. McDermott', Day 23, Scarman Transcripts, p. 40.

59 'Testimony of Miss J. B. Devlin', Day 20, Scarman Transcripts, p. 17.

60 'Testimony of RUC Head Constable R. J. Wallace', Day 28, Scarman Transcripts, p. 78.

61 'Testimony of Mr Tim Jones', Day 5, Scarman Transcripts, p. 26.

62 'Testimony of RUC District Inspector McAtamney', Day 32, Scarman Transcripts, p. 78.

63 Scarman Report, p. 81.

64 *Ibid.*

65 'Testimony of John Porter', Day 28, Scarman Transcripts, p. 14.

66 McClean (1983), p. 77.

67 'Testimony of William Joyce', Day 28, Scarman Transcripts, p. 37.

68 Scarman Report, pp. 82–3.

69 'Testimony of ITN reporter Bernard Hatfield', Day 29, Scarman Transcripts, pp. 20–1.

70 Scarman Report, p. 81.

71 'Testimony of Aidan McKinney', Day 33, Scarman Transcripts, pp. 67–8.

72 *Ibid.*, p. 66.

73 'Testimony of Denis Coghlan', Day 6, Scarman Transcripts, p. 39.

74 Farrell, *Northern Ireland: The Orange State*, p. 260.

75 The Fountain is a predominately Protestant area located close to Derry's Walls on the city side of Derry.

76 Scarman Report, p. 99.

77 'Testimony of B-Special Adjutant Edward H. O'Neill', Day 16, Scarman Transcripts, p. 39.

78 'Testimony of RUC Constable Cameron', Day 30, Scarman Transcripts, p. 18.

79 'Testimony of Dermot O'Shea', Day 28, Scarman Transcripts, pp. 2–3.

80 'Testimony of Michael McLoughlin', Day 29, Scarman Transcripts, pp. 89–94.

81 'Testimony of William Hippesley', Day 28, Scarman Transcripts, pp. 102–3.

82 'Testimony of RUC Constable Cameron', Day 30, Scarman Transcripts, pp. 12–35.

83 Scarman Report, p. 84.

84 'Testimony of B Special Sergeant A. M. Cole', Day 33, Scarman Transcripts, p. 24.

85 *Ibid.*, p. 29.

86 'Testimony of Tim Jones', Day 5, Scarman Transcripts, p. 28.

87 'Testimony of B Special Sergeant Joseph Moore', Day 17, Scarman Transcripts, pp. 8–9.

88 Scarman Report, p. 84.

89 Limpkin (1972), p. 30.

90 'Testimony of RUC District Inspector, Francis Armstrong', Day 11, Scarman Transcripts, pp. 73–4. The Creggan estate was built on the hills overlooking Derry city in the 1950s by unionists determined to contain the city's nationalist majority in a single electoral ward. It was the scene of some of the most bitter violence of the Troubles. Six of the fourteen victims of Bloody Sunday were from the area, as was hunger striker Mickey Devine.

91 Cameron Commission, p. 55.

92 'Testimony of Philomena Harkin', Day 30, Scarman Transcripts, pp. 39–47.

93 *Ibid.*, p. 48.

94 Ryder, Chris, *The RUC: A Force under Fire* (Mandarin Paperbacks, London, 1990), p. 112.

95 'Testimony of British Army Officer, Lt Kevin Francis Robbin', Day 3, Scarman Transcripts, p. 81.

96 'Testimony of Eddie McAteer', Day 7, Scarman Transcripts, p. 31.

97 'Testimony of British Army Officer, Lt Colonel Todd', Day 3, Scarman Transcripts, p. 45.

98 'Testimony of RUC District Inspector General R. E. G. Shillington', Day 11, Scarman Transcripts, p. 45.

99 *Ibid.*, pp. 48–9.

100 'Testimony of British Army Officer, Lt Colonel W. A. E. Todd', Day 3, Scarman Transcripts, p. 31.

101 *Ibid.*, p. 75.

102 Belfast *News Letter*, 14 August 1969.

4 ASHES TO ASHES: POGROM ON THE FALLS

1 Scarman Report, p. 151.

2 *Belfast Telegraph*, 11 August 1969.

3 *Ibid.*

4 Brown (2003), p. 100.

5 Scarman Tribunal, RUC Commissioner's Headquarters control room, 13–16 August 1969, Exhibit 43 (Belfast).

6 'Testimony of Father Patrick Egan', Day 134, Scarman Transcripts, p. 67.

7 'Testimony of RUC Belfast Commissioner, Mr Alfred Harold Wolseley', Day 136, Scarman Transcripts, pp. 1–54.

8 'Testimony of Witness A', Day 72, Scarman Transcripts, p. 32.

9   'Testimony of RUC Belfast Commissioner, Mr Alfred Harold Wolseley', Day 136, Scarman Transcripts, p. 50.

10   Scarman Report, p. 122.

11   *Ibid.*, p. 124.

12   *Ibid.*, p. 125.

13   'Testimony of John McKeague', Day 159, Scarman Transcripts, pp. 60–1.

14   *Ibid.*, Day 162, Scarman Transcripts, p. 18.

15   'Testimony of John M. McRitchie', Day 50, Scarman Transcripts, p. 37.

16   *Ibid.*, pp. 40–1.

17   'Testimony of RUC Belfast Commissioner, Mr Alfred Harold Wolseley', Day 136, Scarman Transcripts, p. 17.

18   Scarman Tribunal, RUC Commissioner's Headquarters control room, 13–16 August 1969, Exhibit 43 (Belfast).

19   Scarman Report, p. 126.

20   *Ibid.*

21   Moloney and Pollak (1986), p. 197.

22   Boulton (1973), p. 116.

23   Hastings, Max, *Ulster 1969: The Fight for Civil Rights in Northern Ireland* (Gollancz, London, 1970), p. 142.

24   'Testimony of Mr James Sloan', Day 71, Scarman Transcripts, p. 74.

25   Author interview with Owen McDonald (Belfast: 2 February 2008).

26   Author interview with Eileen McGonigle (Belfast: 25 May 2012).

27   Scarman Tribunal, RUC Commissioner's Headquarters control room, 13–16 August 1969, Exhibit 43 (Belfast).

28   Author interview with James Steenson (County Armagh: 16 October 2009).

29   Devlin (1993), p. 105.

30   Scarman Report, p. 145.

31   'Testimony of John McKeague', Day 163, Scarman Transcripts, p. 6.

32   Scarman Report, p. 139.

33   *Ibid.*, p. 137.

34   *Ibid.*, p. 139.

35   *Ibid.*, p. 143.

36   Devlin (1993), p. 106.

37   Muldoon, Jim, *Belfast Legionaries Remember: The Story of the Legion of Mary in Belfast* (Trimprint, Armagh, 2011), p. 145.

38 *Andersonstown News*, 15 August 2009.

39 Author interview with Kevin Kennedy (Belfast: 9 April 2008).

40 Scarman Report, p. 144.

41 Author interview with Patrick McAteer (Belfast: 25 February 2016).

42 Author interview with Eileen Devlin (Belfast: 19 March 2008).

43 'Testimony of RUC District Inspector Francis Lagan', Day 134, Scarman Transcripts, p. 32; Scarman Report, p. 168.

44 'Testimony of RUC Belfast Commissioner, Mr Alfred Harold Wolseley', Day 136, Scarman Transcripts, p. 39.

45 Scarman Tribunal, RUC Commissioner's Headquarters control room, 13–16 August 1969, Exhibit 43 (Belfast).

46 Author interview with Patrick McAteer (Belfast: 25 February 2016).

47 Hastings (1970), pp. 143–4.

48 During the mid-1960s redevelopment took place in Divis Street, where twelve blocks of eight-storey flats were constructed. In addition to and next to the flats, Divis Tower was constructed, consisting of twenty floors stretching sixty-one metres high. The tower and the flats were named the Divis Flats Complex. Divis Tower, located in Divis Street, was across the street from Dover Street.

49 Scarman Report, p. 137.

50 Hastings (1970), p. 143.

51 Scarman Report, p. 141.

52 'Testimony of RUC Sergeant McPhillips', Day 79, Scarman Transcripts, p. 32.

53 *Ibid.*, p. 34.

54 Witness statement by Felix McCaughley, submitted to McCloskey & Co. Solicitors, Belfast, 27 September 1969.

55 Author interview with Desi Kennedy (Belfast: 23 September 2009).

56 Scarman Report, p. 142.

57 Witness statement by Felix McCaughley, submitted to McCloskey & Co. Solicitors, Belfast, 27 September 1969.

58 Scarman Report, p. 146.

59 'Testimony of Max Hastings', Day 85, Scarman Transcripts, p. 8.

60 Hastings (1970), p. 13.

61 Author interview with Seán McErlean (Belfast: 25 March 2011).

62 Author interview with John Toner (Belfast: 26 November 2013).

63 'Testimony of Max Hastings', Day 85, Scarman Transcripts, p. 9.

64 Scarman Tribunal, RUC Commissioner's Headquarters control room, 13–16 August 1969, Exhibit 43 (Belfast).

65 'Testimony of RUC District Inspector Francis Lagan', Day 134, Scarman Transcripts, p. 28.

66 Scarman Report, p. 165.

67 Author interview with Eileen Devlin (Belfast: 19 March 2008).

68 Author interview with Alice Bell (Belfast: 15 February 2011).

69 Scarman Report, p. 156.

70 *Ibid.*, pp. 155–6.

71 Author interview with Brendan Wilson (Belfast: 6 May 2008).

72 'Testimony of John McKeague', Day 162, Scarman Transcripts, p. 43.

73 'Testimony of Mr James Sloan', Day 72, Scarman Transcripts, p. 2.

74 Author interview with Thomas Daly (Belfast: 31 July 2008).

75 Scarman Tribunal, Ballistics Report by Mr G. Price, Senior Experimental Officer and Head of Ballistics Department, Exhibit 8 (Belfast).

76 'Testimony of Max Hastings', Day 85, Scarman Transcripts, p. 48.

77 Hastings (1970), p. 144.

78 Scarman Report, p. 167.

79 *The Irish News,* 15 August 2009.

80 Scarman Report, p. 169.

81 Swan, Seán, *Official Irish Republicanism, 1962 to 1972* (Lulu Press, Morrisville, 2008), p. 300

82 'Testimony of Max Hastings', Day 85, Scarman Transcripts, p. 39.

83 Author interview with Billy McKee (Belfast: 26 February 2010).

84 Moloney (2010), pp. 17–18.

85 Scarman Tribunal, RUC Commissioner's Headquarters control room, 13–16 August 1969, Exhibit 43 (Belfast).

86 Author interview with Billy McKee (Belfast: 26 February 2010).

87 Scarman Tribunal, Ballistics Report by Mr G. Price, Senior Experimental Officer and Head of Ballistics Department, Exhibit 8 (Belfast).

88 'Testimony of RUC District Inspector, Francis Lagan', Day 134, Scarman Transcripts, p. 60.

89 Scarman Report, p. 148.

90 'Testimony of Max Hastings', Day 85, Scarman Transcripts, p. 40.

91 *Ibid.*, p. 13.

92 Hastings (1970), p. 145.

93 Scarman Report, p. 170.

94 Scarman Tribunal, RUC Commissioner's Headquarters control room, 13–16 August 1969, Exhibit 43 (Belfast).

95 Scarman Report, p. 174.

96 Author interview with Lily Fitzsimons (Belfast: 26 May 2008).

97 Hastings (1970), p. 144.

98 Scarman Transcripts, Day 88, pp. 61–2; Day 98, pp. 63–4.

99 'Testimony of Paddy J. Devlin, MP', Day 98, Scarman Transcripts, p. 65.

100 McKearney, Tommy, *The Provisional IRA: From Insurrection to Parliament* (Pluto Press, London, 2011), p. 48.

101 'Testimony of Mr James Sloan', Day 71, Scarman Transcripts, p. 78.

102 Scarman Report, p. 159.

103 *Ibid.*, p. 152.

104 Scarman Tribunal, RUC Commissioner's Headquarters control room, 13–16 August 1969, Exhibit 43 (Belfast).

105 Scarman Report, p. 150.

106 *Ibid.*

107 *Ibid.*, p. 159.

108 Scarman Tribunal, Belfast Fire Brigade records, Exhibit 18 (Belfast).

109 'Testimony of Mr S. Wallace', Day 137, Scarman Transcripts, p. 23.

110 Smith, William, *Inside Man: Loyalists of Long Kesh – The Untold Story* (Blackstaff Press, Newtownards, 2014), p. 21.

111 Scarman Report, p. 154.

112 Author interview with Brendan Wilson (Belfast: 6 May 2008).

113 Author interview with Eamon McGonigle (Belfast: 25 May 2012).

114 Scarman Report, p. 154.

115 'Testimony of RUC Inspector Francis Lagan', Day 134, Scarman Transcripts, p. 8.

116 Author interview with Brendan Wilson (Belfast: 6 May 2008).

117 *The Irish News*, 19 August 2009.

118 *Ibid.*, 29 August 2009.

119 Author interview with Patrick Stott (Belfast: 4 March 2008).

120 Scarman Report, p. 160.

121 *Ibid.*, p. 161.

122 Devlin (1993), p. 106.

123 Scarman Report, p. 161.

124 Author interview with Eamon McGonigle (Belfast: 25 May 2012).

125 Author interview with Pat McGrath (Belfast: 8 September 2011).

126 Boulton (1973), p. 120.

127 *The Times*, 16 August 1969.

128 Author interview with Billy Barrett (Belfast: 3 June 2008).

5 FROM EPICENTRE TO PERIPHERY: CLONARD AND ARDOYNE

1 Scarman Report, p. 190.

2 Author interview with Joe Robinson (Belfast: 31 March 2009).

3 Author interview with Brendan Wilson (Belfast: 6 May 2008).

4 Author interview with Alice Bell (Belfast: 15 February 2011).

5 Author interview with Brian Conlon (Belfast: 10 June 2010).

6 'Testimony of Mrs Scott', Day 158, Scarman Transcripts, p. 48.

7 Scarman Report, p. 190.

8 'Testimony of RUC Belfast Commissioner, Mr Alfred Harold Wolseley', Day 136, Scarman Transcripts, p. 23.

9 *Ibid.*, p. 39.

10 Scarman Report, p. 193.

11 *The Times*, 16 August 1969.

12 'Testimony of Mr Charles Hemsworth', Day 146, Scarman Transcripts, p. 19.

13 Author interview with Noel Devine (Belfast: 1 March 2008).

14 'Testimony of RUC Belfast Commissioner, Mr Alfred Harold Wolseley', Day 136, Scarman Transcripts, p. 18.

15 'Testimony of RUC Deputy Commissioner S. J. Bradley', Day 97, Scarman Transcripts, p. 13.

16 'Testimony of RUC District Inspector Francis Lagan', Day 134, Scarman Transcripts, p. 21.

17 'Testimony of RUC Belfast Commissioner, Mr Alfred Harold Wolseley', Day 136, Scarman Transcripts, p. 18.

18 Scarman Report, p. 198.

19 Collins, Gerry, *Bombay Street: Taken from the Ashes* (Red Barn Gallery, Belfast, 2009) p. 40.

20 Scarman Report, p. 198.

21 Conroy, John, *Belfast Diary: War as a Way of Life* (Beacon Press, Boston, 1995), pp. 29–30.

22 Scarman Report, p. 200.

23 *IRIS*, Summer/Autumn 2009, p. 21.

24 Scarman Report, pp. 198–9.

25 *IRIS*, Summer/Autumn 2009, p. 13.

26 Scarman Report, p. 199.

27 'Testimony of Father Patrick Egan', Day 135, Scarman Transcripts, p. 5.

28 Scarman Report, p. 200.

29 *Ibid.*

30 'Testimony of Father Patrick Egan', Day 135, Scarman Transcripts, p. 6.

31 Bruce (1992), p. 37.

32 Author interview with Witnesses A and B (Belfast: 7 February 2008).

33 Scarman Report, p. 201.

34 Author interview with Witness C (Belfast: 29 March 2010).

35 *Andersonstown News*, 15 August 2009.

36 Scarman Tribunal, Ballistics Report by Mr G. Price, Senior Experimental Officer and Head of Ballistics Department, Exhibit 8 (Belfast).

37 Scarman Report, p. 191.

38 Devlin (1993), p. 107; Murphy, Michael A., *Gerry Fitt: Political Chameleon* (Mercier Press, Cork, 2007), p. 135.

39 Callaghan (1973), p. 49.

40 Scarman Tribunal, General Exhibit 2.

41 Scarman Tribunal, RUC Commissioner's Headquarters control room, 13–16 August 1969, Exhibit 43 (Belfast).

42 'Testimony of RUC Belfast Commissioner, Mr Alfred Harold Wolseley', Day 136, Scarman Transcripts, pp. 45–6.

43 Author interview with Joseph Robinson (Belfast: 31 March 2009).

44 'Testimony of Max Hastings', Day 85, Scarman Transcripts, p. 44.

45 Scarman Report, p. 192.

46 Author interview with Alice Bell (Belfast: 15 February 2011).

47 Author interview with Patrick McAteer (Belfast: 25 February 2016).

48 *IRIS*, Summer/Autumn 2009, p. 35.

49 'Testimony of Father Patrick Egan', Day 135, Scarman Transcripts, p. 7.

50 Scarman Report, pp. 203–4.

51 'Testimony of Father Patrick Egan', Day 135, Scarman Transcripts, pp. 9–10.

52 *Ibid.*, p. 10.

53 Author interview with Paddy Stott (Belfast: 4 March 2008).

54 'Testimony of Max Hastings', Day 85, Scarman Transcripts, p. 47.

55 *Ibid.*, p. 46.

56 Author interview with Paddy Stott (Belfast: 4 March 2008).

57 'Testimony of Father Patrick Egan', Day 135, Scarman Transcript, p. 11.

58 *IRIS*, Summer/Autumn 2009, p. 15.

59 O'Riordan, Flo, *A Shattered Silence: The Burning of Bombay Street and How it Changed my Life* (Multimedia Heritage, Belfast, 2016), p. 25.

60 'Testimony of Mr James Murray', Day 48, Scarman Transcripts, p. 35.

61 Scarman Tribunal, RUC Commissioner's Headquarters control room, 13–16 August 1969, Exhibit 43 (Belfast).

62 *Ibid.*

63 'Testimony of Dick Walsh', Day 59, Scarman Transcripts, pp. 10–25.

64 Scarman Report, p. 180.

65 'Testimony of Mr William Joseph Elwood', Day 57, Scarman Transcripts, p. 64.

66 'Testimony of Dick Walsh', Day 59, Scarman Transcripts, pp. 10–25.

67 'Testimony of Head Constable Daniel Blair Wallace', Day 63, Scarman Transcripts, pp. 48–9.

68 'Testimony of Head Constable Cecil William Kyle', Day 56, Scarman Transcripts, p. 29.

69 'Testimony of Mr Robert McCargo', Day 61, Scarman Transcripts, p. 52.

70 *Ibid.*, pp. 51–3.

71 Ardoyne Commemoration Project (2002), p. 23.

72 'Testimony of Head Constable James Herbert Seay', Day 61, Scarman Transcripts, p. 4.

73 'Testimony of Mr Robert Lannigan', Day 52, Scarman Transcripts, pp. 83–4.

74 'Testimony of Head Constable James Herbert Seay', Day 61, Scarman Transcripts, p. 11.

75 Scarman Tribunal, Police strengths on Crumlin Road 13–16 August, Exhibit 53 (Belfast).

76 'Testimony of Father Ailbe Delaney', Day 54, Scarman Transcripts, p. 58.

77 'Testimony of Head Constable Kerr Patterson', Day 55, Scarman Transcripts, p. 18.

78 *Ibid.*, p. 21.

79 'Testimony of Mr Peter M. Toal', Day 51, Scarman Transcripts, pp. 17–21.

80   'Testimony of Mr Edward R. Deeds', Day 58, Scarman Transcripts, p. 55.

81   Scarman Report, p. 183.

82   'Testimony of Mr Thomas McMullan', Day 56, Scarman Transcripts, pp. 65–9.

83   'Testimony of Sergeant George Bernard St John', Day 64, Scarman Transcripts, p. 3.

84   *Ibid.*, p. 8.

85   McKeown, Michael, *The Greening of a Nationalist* (Murlough Press, Dublin, 1986), p. 65.

86   'Testimony of Sergeant George Bernard St John', Day 64, Scarman Transcripts, p. 9.

87   Scarman Report, p. 187.

88   'Testimony of Head Constable Cecil Wilfred Kyle', Day 55, Scarman Transcripts, p. 78.

89   'Testimony of Sergeant George Bernard St John', Day 64, Scarman Transcripts, p. 10.

90   Ardoyne Commemoration Project (2002), pp. 31–2.

91   Scarman Report, p. 187.

92   Scarman Tribunal, Ballistics Report by Mr G. Price, Senior Experimental Officer and Head of Ballistics Department, Exhibit 8 (Belfast).

93   'Testimony of Mr Thomas McMullan', Day 56, Scarman Transcripts, p. 69.

94   'Testimony of Mr Robert McCargo', Day 62, Scarman Transcripts, p. 3.

95   'Testimony of Mr Leo Morris', Day 56, Scarman Transcripts, pp. 32–3.

96   Scarman Report, p. 188.

97   McKeown (1986), p. 66.

98   Scarman Report, p. 188.

99   'Testimony of Sergeant George Bernard St John', Day 64, Scarman Transcripts, p. 11.

100 'Testimony of Mr Hugh Alexander Megarry', Day 63, Scarman Transcripts, p. 70.

101 Scarman Report, p. 189.

102 *Ibid.*, p. 209.

103 'Testimony of Mr William Joseph Elwood', Day 57, Scarman Transcripts, p. 76.

104 'Testimony of Mr Thomas McMullan', Day 56, Scarman Transcripts, p. 70.

105 'Testimony of Mr Peter M. Toal', Day 50, Scarman Transcripts, p. 78.

106 *Ibid.*

107 'Testimony of RUC Head Constable Daniel Blair Wallace', Day 63, Scarman Transcripts, p. 4.

108 'Testimony of RUC Head Constable Cecil Wilfred Kyle', Day 56, Scarman Transcripts, p. 1.

109 Scarman Report, p. 214.

110 'Testimony of Mr Ernest George Mills, Associate Member of the Royal Institution of British Architects', Day 66, Scarman Transcripts, pp. 57–8.

111 Scarman Report, p. 214.

112 'Testimony of Mr Francis Martin Foster', Day 64, Scarman Transcripts, pp. 41–51.

113 Scarman Report, p. 215.

114 Scarman Tribunal, Ballistics Report by Mr G. Price, Senior Experimental Officer and Head of Ballistics Department, Exhibit 8 (Belfast).

115 Scarman Tribunal, RUC Commissioner's Headquarters control room, 13–16 August 1969, Exhibit 43 (Belfast).

116 'Testimony of Head Constable Anthony Owens', Day 48, Scarman Transcripts, pp. 68–9.

117 'Testimony of Mr William Joseph Elwood', Day 57, Scarman Tribunal, p. 82.

118 'Testimony of Head Constable Cecil Wilfred Kyle', Day 55, Scarman Transcripts, p. 85.

119 'Testimony of Mr William Joseph Elwood', Day 57, Scarman Transcripts, p. 51.

120 Scarman Report, p. 215.

121 Scarman Tribunal, Ballistics Report by Mr G. Price, Senior Experimental Officer and Head of Ballistics Department, Exhibit 8 (Belfast).

122 *Ibid.*

123 Scarman Report, pp. 215–16.

124 *Ibid.*, p. 215.

125 Scarman Tribunal, Ballistics Report by Mr G. Price, Senior Experimental Officer and Head of Ballistics Department, Exhibit 8 (Belfast).

126 Scarman Tribunal, RUC Commissioner's Headquarters control room, 13–16 August 1969, Exhibit 43, (Belfast).

127 *Ibid.*

128 'Testimony of Mr Thomas McMullan', Day 56, Scarman Transcripts, p. 73.

129 Scarman Report, p. 216.

130 *Ibid.*

131 'Testimony of Mr Peter M. Toal', Day 51, Scarman Transcripts p. 12.

132 Author interview with Comgall McNally (Belfast: 8 May 2008).

133 'Testimony of Mr Peter M. Toal', Day 51, Scarman Transcripts, p. 3.

6 PICKING UP THE PIECES

1 *The Irish News*, 19 August 1969.

2 Callaghan (1973), p. 52.

3 *The Times*, 18 August 1969.

4 *The Observer*, 18 August 1969.

5 Belfast *News Letter*, 16 August 1969.

6 *Ibid.*, 18 August 1969.

7 Moloney and Pollak (1986), p. 198.

8 *Belfast Telegraph*, 20 August 1969.

9 Moloney and Pollak (1986), p. 196

10 Smyth, Rev. Martin, *In Defence of Ulster* (County Grand Orange Lodge of Belfast, Belfast, 1969), p. 14.

11 Belfast *News Letter*, 18 August 1969.

12 O'Brien's attitudes changed during the 1970s in response to the outbreak of the Troubles. In 1996 he joined the United Kingdom Unionist Party (UKUP) and was elected to the Northern Ireland Forum in 1997.

13 *The Times*, 19 August 1969.

14 *Ibid.*, 22 August 1969.

15 *Belfast Telegraph*, 19 August 1969.

16 A letter retained by his son Noel Devine and shared with the author: precise date unknown.

17 *The Times*, 27 August 1969.

18 'Testimony of Father Patrick Murphy', Day 170, Scarman Transcripts, pp. 68–70.

19 *The Irish News*, 18 August 1969.

20 'Testimony of Dr Poole', Department of Geography, Queen's University, Belfast, Day 158, Scarman Tribunal, pp. 1–16.

21 Darby (1976), p. 43.

22 'Testimony of Father Patrick Murphy', Day 158, Scarman Transcripts, p. 76.

23 *Ibid.*, p. 71.

24 Scarman Tribunal, Report of the service provided by headquarters transport A/N division of St John Ambulance brigade during civil disturbances in Belfast, Exhibit 44 (Belfast).

25 *Protestant Telegraph,* 30 August 1969.

26 *The Irish News,* 23 August 1969.

27 Author interview with Joseph Doyle (Belfast: 10 September 2007).

28 *Belfast Telegraph,* 20 August 1969.

29 *Ibid.*, 27 August 1969.

30 *The Irish News,* 4 September 1969.

31 *Belfast Telegraph,* 28 August 1969.

32 *Ibid.*

33 *Andersonstown News,* 15 August 2009.

34 Author interview with Owen McDonald (Belfast: 2 February 2008).

35 *Belfast Telegraph,* 17 October 1969.

36 *The Irish News,* 5 September 1969.

37 Author interview with Paddy Stott (Belfast: 4 March 2008).

38 Author interview with Patrick McAteer (Belfast: 25 February 2016).

39 Author interview with John McGreevy (Belfast: 12 June 2008).

40 *Ibid.*

41 Author interview with Paddy Carlin (Belfast: 14 April 2008).

42 It has been established that a total of ten people were killed during the summer of 1969. Scarman documents a total of 745 people injured, 154 by gunshot. This is a very modest estimate, however, considering the countless numbers who did not attend hospitals or first-aid stations, but sought help elsewhere. The number of police injured by gunfire was established at six, one of which, it was claimed, received a slight nick to his earlobe in Ardoyne.

43 *The Irish News,* 20 August 1969.

44 *Ibid.*, 19 August 1969.

45 Callaghan (1973), p. 62.

46 Hamill, Desmond, *Pig in the Middle: The Army in Northern Ireland 1969–1985* (Methuen, London, 1986), p. 27.

47 Bruce (1992), p. 37.

48 The London *Sunday Times* Insight Team (1972), p. 142.

49 *The Guardian*, 18 August 1969.

50 Nelson (1984), pp. 57–9.

51 Walsh, Andrew, *Belfast '69: Bombs, Burnings and Bigotry* (Fonthill, Oxford, 2015), p. 144.

52 *Belfast Telegraph*, 22 August 1969.

53 *The Irish News*, 18 August 1969.

54 *Belfast Telegraph*, 21 August 1969.

55 *The Irish News*, 22 August 1969.

56 *Belfast Telegraph*, 21 August 1969.

57 Scarman Tribunal, Schedule of statements by His Eminence Cardinal Conway and joint statement made by Cardinal Conway and Bishops, Exhibit 2c (Belfast).

58 Cooke (1996), p. 164.

59 *The Observer*, 24 August 1969.

60 *Belfast Telegraph*, 26 August 1969.

61 Devlin (1993), pp. 116–17.

62 Author interview with Brian Conlon (Belfast: 10 June 2010).

63 *Belfast Telegraph*, 26 August 1969.

64 *Ibid.*, 23 August 1969.

65 Callaghan (1973), p. 66.

66 *The Irish News*, 27 August 1969.

67 *Ibid.*, 29 August 1969.

68 *Ibid.*, 27 August 1969. The NUM was a moderate group, non-sectarian. It was established to help support Terence O'Neill in the election of 24 February and went on to help form the Alliance Party of Northern Ireland in 1970.

69 *The Times*, 2 September 1969.

70 *Ibid.*, 29 August 1969.

71 *The Irish News*, 1 September 1969.

72 Quoted in the *Belfast Telegraph*, 1 September 1969.

73 *The Irish News*, 2 September 1969.

74 *Ibid.*, 3 September 1969.

75 *Ibid.*, 4 September 1969.

76 Hastings (1970), p. 197.

77 *The Irish News*, 4 September 1969.

78 Author interview with Ethna Byrne (Belfast: 9 April 2009).

79   *Belfast Telegraph*, 5 September 1969.

80   *The Irish News*, 5 September 1969.

81   *Ibid.*, 6 September 1969.

82   *Ibid.*, 8 September 1969.

83   Sweetman, Rosita, *On our Knees: Ireland 1972* (Pan Books, London, 1972), pp. 225–6.

84   *Ibid.*, p. 229.

85   *The Irish News*, 8 September 1969.

86   *The Times*, 8 September 1969. CS gas had previously been used once by the British Army against loyalists, on the evening of 15 August 1969. However, the use of gas appeared to have little effect on the loyalists as they burned down more homes in Clonard.

87   *The Irish News*, 8 September 1969.

88   *Ibid.*

89   Hastings (1970), pp. 197–8.

90   Belfast *News Letter*, 8 September 1969.

91   Author interview with Joe Law (Belfast: 4 March 2014).

92   Sweetman (1972), p. 234.

93   *The Irish News*, 8 September 1969.

94   *Ibid.*, 9 September 1969.

95   *The Times*, 8 September 1969.

96   Author interview with Joseph Fitzpatrick (Belfast: 10 December 2016).

97   *The Irish News*, 8 September 1969.

98   Belfast *News Letter*, 9 September 1969.

99   The London *Sunday Times* Insight Team (1972), p. 158.

100 *The Irish News*, 9 September 1969.

101 *Ibid.*, 10 September 1969.

102 Belfast *News Letter*, 30 September 1969.

103 *The Irish News*, 9 September 1969.

104 *Ibid.*, 27 September 1969.

105 Target (1975), p. 286.

106 Belfast *News Letter*, 13 September 1969.

107 *Ibid.*, 15 September 1969.

108 *Ibid.*, 16 September 1969.

109 *Ibid.*, 15 September 1969.

110 *Ibid.*, 16 September 1969.

111 *Ibid.*, 25 September 1969.

112 Scarman Report, p. 246.

113 'Testimony of RUC Belfast Commissioner, Mr Alfred Harold Wolseley', Day 136, Scarman Transcripts, p. 40.

114 Scarman Report, p. 218.

115 *Ibid.*

116 Author interview with a member of McCambridge family (Belfast: 25 October 2016).

117 Belfast *News Letter*, 29 September 1969.

118 *Ibid.*, 30 September 1969.

119 Winchester, Simon, *In Holy Terror: Reporting the Ulster Troubles* (Faber and Faber, London, 1974), p. 124.

120 Callaghan (1973), p. 118.

121 Boulton (1973), p. 127.

122 Smith (2014), p. 23.

123 The London *Sunday Times* Insight Team (1972), pp. 164–5.

124 Coogan (1996), p. 93.

125 Smith (2014), p. 24

126 Hastings (1970), p. 183.

127 Hamill (1986), p. 28.

128 Rose (1971), pp. 152–3.

129 Target (1975), p. 287.

130 Nelson (1984), p. 87.

131 Callaghan (1973), p. 128.

132 Moloney and Pollak (1986), p. 203.

7   ABSOLVING THE ESTABLISHMENT

1   Ardoyne Commemoration Project (2002), p. 23.

2   Callaghan (1973), p. 49.

3   *Ibid.*, p. 73.

4   Scoular, Clive, *James Chichester-Clark: Prime Minister of Northern Ireland* (Scoular, Killyleagh, 2000), p. 90.

5   McCluskey, Fergal, *The Irish Revolution, 1912–23: Tyrone* (Four Courts Press, Dublin, 2014), p. 127.

6   Darby (1976), p. 61.

7   Farrell, *Northern Ireland: The Orange State*, pp. 95–6.

8   Callaghan (1973), p. 54.

9   *Ibid.*, pp. 54–6.

10 *Ibid.*, p. 58.

11 RUC statement submitted to the Scarman Tribunal.

12 'Testimony of Mr Gourley', Day 79, Scarman Transcripts, p. 52.

13 *Ibid.*, pp. 69–70.

14 *Report of the Advisory Committee on Police in Northern Ireland* (hereafter Hunt Report), Cmd 535 (Belfast, 1969), p. 2.

15 Scoular (2000), p. 94.

16 Callaghan (1973), p. 60.

17 Hunt Report, p. 49.

18 'Testimony of RUC Belfast Commissioner, Mr Alfred Harold Wolseley', Day 136, Scarman Transcripts, p. 31.

19 *Ibid.*, p. 14.

20 Scarman Report, p. 19.

21 Anthony Peacock, Inspector General of the RUC, resigned 10 October 1969 and died 14 August 2001.

22 Scarman Report, p. 174.

23 *Ibid.*, p. 173.

24 *Ibid.*, p. 216.

25 'Testimony of RUC Sergeant Dawson', Day 170, Scarman Transcripts, pp. 54–7.

26 'Testimony of Max Hastings', Day 85, Scarman Transcripts, p. 14.

27 Scarman Report, p. 175.

28 'Testimony of Dr J. Martin', Day 92, Scarman Transcripts, p. 23.

29 'Testimony of Mr G. Price', Day 92, Scarman Transcripts, p. 58.

30 Scarman Report, Volume 2, p. 2.

31 Scarman Report, p. 164.

32 Author interview with Alice Bell (Belfast: 15 February 2011).

33 'Testimony of Mr J. Martin', Day 92, Scarman Transcripts, pp. 32–4.

34 Scarman Report, p. 215.

35 'Testimony of Mr G. Price', Day 92, Scarman Transcripts, p. 60.

36 'Testimony of RUC District Inspector Francis Lagan', Day 134, Scarman Transcripts, p. 34.

37 'Testimony of RUC Inspector General Peacock', Day 142, Scarman Transcripts, p. 191.

38 *Ibid.*, pp. 21, 54.

39 Scarman Report, p. 173.

40 'Testimony of RUC Belfast Commissioner, Mr Alfred Harold Wolseley', Day 136, Scarman Transcripts, p. 5.

41 *Ibid.*, p. 20.

42 'Testimony of Mr Robert Porter', Minister of Home Affairs, Day 161, Scarman Transcripts, pp. 9, 51–2.

43 'Testimony of RUC Deputy Commissioner S. J. Bradley', Day 90, Scarman Transcripts, p. 44.

44 'Testimony of RUC District Inspector Francis Lagan', Day 134, Scarman Transcripts, p. 27.

45 Scarman Report, p. 148.

46 'Testimony of Mr Max Hastings', Day 85, Scarman Transcripts, p. 51.

47 *Ibid.*, pp. 6–8.

48 'Testimony of Mr G. Price', Day 92, Scarman Transcripts, p. 58.

49 'Testimony of Brigadier P. Hudson', Day 140, Scarman Transcripts, p. 21.

50 'Testimony of RUC Deputy Commissioner S. J. Bradley', Day 90, Scarman Transcripts, pp. 68–9.

51 'Testimony of RUC Belfast Commissioner, Mr Alfred Harold Wolseley', Day 136, Scarman Transcripts, p. 39.

52 'Testimony of RUC Deputy Commissioner S. J. Bradley', Day 90, Scarman Transcripts, p. 77.

53 Central Citizens' Defence Committee, *The Black Paper: Northern Ireland – The Story of the Police* (Central Citizens' Defence Committee 1973), p. 14.

54 'Testimony of RUC District Inspector Francis Lagan', Day 134, Scarman Transcripts, p. 12.

55 *Ibid.*, p. 35.

56 Hunt Report, p. 44.

57 Scarman Report, pp. 14–15.

58 Central Citizens' Defence Committee (1973), p. 1.

59 *Ibid.*, p. 39.

60 *Ibid.*, pp. 39–40.

CONCLUSION

1 *Belfast Telegraph*, 28 September 2017.

2 *The Irish News*, 5 August 1969.

3   *Belfast Telegraph*, 20 August 1969. Red stickers were available to anyone who wanted to get access to areas behind the barricades.

4   *Ibid.*

5   Despite thousands of nationalists being attacked and burnt from their homes during August 1969, the burnt-out images of Bombay Street are an everlasting reminder to the Catholic population of what happened. While declaring that such attacks would never be tolerated again, the Provisional IRA was born here.

6   Urwin, Margaret, *A State in Denial: British Collaboration with Loyalist Paramilitaries* (Mercier Press, Cork, 2016), pp. 15–16.

7   See Police Ombudsman report of February 2011 into the bombing of McGurk's Bar, Belfast, on 4 December 1971.

8   Ian Cobain, 'Ballymurphy shootings: 36 hours in Belfast that left 10 dead' *The Guardian*, 26 June 2014.

9   The violence of the Parachute Regiment is seared into the memory of older residents of Ballymurphy.

10 The Vanguard Unionist Party was a political unionist party in Northern Ireland between 1972–8. It emerged from a split within the Ulster Unionist Party and was closely linked to several loyalist paramilitary groups.

11 Dillon (2003), p. 104.

12 *Ibid.*, pp. 104, 113–8, 174–5, 181.

13 Holland and McDonald (1994), pp. 199–200.

BIBLIOGRAPHY

Ardoyne Commemoration Project, *Ardoyne: The Untold Truth* (Beyond the Pale, Belfast, 2002)

Bardon, Jonathan, *A History of Ulster* (Blackstaff Press, Belfast, 2005)

Bell, Geoffrey, *The Protestants of Ulster* (Pluto Press, London, 1976)

Bew, Paul, *Ireland: The Politics of Enmity 1789–2006* (Oxford University Press, Oxford, 2007)

Bew, Paul, Gibbon, Peter and Patterson, Henry, *Northern Ireland: Political Forces and Social Classes* (Serif, London, 1995)

Boulton, David, *The UVF 1966–73: An Anatomy of Loyalist Rebellion* (Torc Books, Dublin, 1973)

Boyd, Andrew, *Brian Faulkner and the Crisis of Ulster Unionism* (Anvil Books, Tralee, 1972)

— *Holy War in Belfast* (Pretani Press, Belfast, 1987)

Brewer, John D., *Anti-Catholicism in Northern Ireland, 1600–1998: The Mote and the Beam* (Macmillan, London, 1998)

Bruce, Steve, *God Save Ulster! The Religion and Politics of Paisleyism* (Oxford University Press, Oxford, 1989)

— *The Red Hand: Protestant Paramilitaries in Northern Ireland* (Oxford University Press, Oxford, 1992)

— *The Edge of the Union: The Ulster Loyalist Political Vision* (Oxford University Press, Oxford, 1994)

Brown, William, *An Army with Banners: The Real Face of Orangeism* (Beyond the Pale, Belfast, 2003)

Buckland, Patrick, *A History of Northern Ireland* (Gill & Macmillan, Dublin, 1981)

Budge, Ian and O'Leary, Cornelius, *Belfast: Approach to Crisis: A Study of Belfast Politics, 1613–1970* (Macmillan, London, 1973)

Cadwallader, Anne, *Lethal Allies: British Collusion in Ireland* (Mercier Press, Cork, 2013)

Callaghan, James, *A House Divided: The Dilemma of Northern Ireland* (Collins, London, 1973)

Carlton, Charles, *Bigotry and Blood: Documents on the Ulster Troubles* (Nelson-Hall, Chicago, 1977)

Central Citizens Defence Committee, *The Black Paper: Northern Ireland – the Story of the Police* (Central Citizens Defence Committee, Belfast, 1973)

Collins, Gerry, *Bombay Street: Taken from the Ashes* (Red Barn Gallery, Belfast, 2009)

Conroy, John, *Belfast Diary: War as a Way of Life* (Beacon Press, Boston, 1995)

Coogan, Tim Pat, *The Troubles: Ireland's Ordeal 1966–1996 and the Search for Peace* (Roberts Rinehart, Boulder, 1996)

— *Ireland in the Twentieth Century* (Hutchinson, London, 2003)

Cooke, Dennis, *Persecution Zeal: A Portrait of Ian Paisley* (Brandon, Dingle, 1996)

Crawford, Colin, *Inside the UDA: Volunteers and Violence* (Pluto Press, London, 2003)

Cusack, Jim and McDonald, Henry, *UVF* (Poolbeg Press, Dublin, 1997)

Darby, John, *Conflict in Northern Ireland: The Development of a Polarised Community* (Gill & Macmillan, Dublin, 1976)

De Paor, Liam, *Divided Ulster* (Penguin Books, Harmondsworth, 1970)

Devlin, Bernadette, *Bernadette Devlin: The Price of my Soul* (Pan Books, London, 1972)

Devlin, Paddy, *Straight Left: An Autobiography* (Blackstaff Press, Belfast, 1993)

Dillon, Martin, *The Shankill Butchers: A Case Study of Mass Murder* (Arrow, London, 1990)

— *Stone Cold: The True Story of Michael Stone and the Milltown Massacre* (Arrow, London, 1993)

— *The Trigger Men* (Mainstream Publishing, Edinburgh, 2003)

— *Crossing the Line: My Life on the Edge* (Merrion Press, Newbridge, 2017)

Downing, Taylor (ed.), *The Troubles: The Background to the Question of Northern Ireland* (Thames MacDonald, London, 1980)

Doyle, Mark, *Fighting like the Devil for the Sake of God: Protestants, Catholics and the Origins of Violence in Victorian Belfast* (Manchester University Press, Manchester, 2009)

Egan, Bowes and McCormack, Vincent, *Burntollet* (LRS Publishers, London, 1969)

Elliott, Marianne, *The Catholics of Ulster: A History* (Penguin Books, London, 2001)

English, Richard and Walker, Graham (eds), *Unionism in Modern Ireland: New Perspectives on Politics and Culture* (Macmillan Press, London, 1996)

Evelegh, Robin, *Peacekeeping in a Democratic Society: The Lessons of Northern Ireland* (C. Hurst and Publishers, Montreal, 1978)

Farrell, Michael, *Arming the Protestants: The Formation of the Ulster Special Constabulary and the Royal Ulster Constabulary 1920–27* (Pluto Press, London, 1983)

— *Northern Ireland: The Orange State* (Pluto Press, London, 1983)

Ferriter, Diarmaid, *The Transformation of Ireland 1900–2000* (Profile Books, London, 2004)

Finn, Daniel, 'The point of no return? People's Democracy and the Burntollet march', *Field Day Review* (Sept. 2013), pp. 5–21

Foster, Roy F., *Modern Ireland: 1600–1972* (Penguin Books, London, 1989)

Geraghty, Tony, *The Irish War: The Military History of a Domestic Conflict* (Harper Collins, London, 2000)

Greaves, C. Desmond, *The Irish Crisis* (Lawrence & Wishart, London, 1972)

Hamill, Desmond, *Pig in the Middle: The Army in Northern Ireland 1969–1985* (Methuen, London, 1986)

Hanley, Brian and Millar, Scott, *The Lost Revolution: The Story of the Official IRA and the Worker's Party* (Penguin Books, London, 2010)

Hastings, Max, *Ulster 1969: The Fight for Civil Rights in Northern Ireland* (Gollancz, London, 1970)

Hennessey, Thomas, *Northern Ireland: The Origins of the Troubles* (Gill & Macmillan, Dublin, 2005)

Hezlet, Arthur, *The 'B' Specials: A History of the Ulster Special Constabulary* (Pan Books, London, 1973)

Holland, Jack and McDonald, Henry, *INLA: Deadly Divisions. The Story of One of Ireland's Most Ruthless Terrorist Organisations* (Torc, Dublin, 1994)

Jackson, Alvin, *Ireland 1798–1998: Politics and War* (Blackwell, Oxford, 1999)

Kelley, Kevin, J., *The Longest War: Northern Ireland and the I.R.A.* (Zed Books, London, 1988)

Limpkin, Clive, *The Battle of Bogside* (Penguin Books, Harmondsworth, 1972)

London *Sunday Times* Insight Team, *Northern Ireland: A Report on the Conflict* (Vintage Books, New York, 1972)

Marrinan, Patrick, *Paisley: Man of Wrath* (Anvil Books, Tralee, 1973)

McClean, Raymond, *The Road to Bloody Sunday* (Ward River Press, Swords, 1983)

McCluskey, Fergal, *The Irish Revolution, 1912–23: Tyrone* (Four Courts Press, Dublin, 2014)

McDermott, Jim, *Northern Divisions: The Old IRA and the Belfast Pogroms 1920–22* (First Edition, Belfast, 2012)

McKay, Susan, *Northern Protestants: An Unsettled People* (Blackstaff Press, Belfast, 2000)

McKearney, Tommy, *The Provisional IRA: From Insurrection to Parliament* (Pluto Press, London, 2011)

McKeown, Michael, *The Greening of a Nationalist* (Murlough Press, Dublin, 1986)

McKittrick, David and McVea, David, *Making Sense of the Troubles* (Blackstaff Press, Belfast, 2001)

Mitchel, Seán, *Struggle or Starve: Working Class Unity in Belfast's 1932 Outdoor Relief Riots* (Haymarket Books, Chicago, 2017)

Moloney, Ed and Pollak, Andy, *Paisley* (Poolbeg Press, Swords, 1986)

Moloney, Ed, *Voices from the Grave: Two Men's War in Ireland* (Faber and Faber, London, 2010)

Muldoon, Jim, *Belfast Legionaries Remember: The Story of the Legion of Mary in Belfast* (Trimprint, Armagh, 2011)

Mulholland, Marc, *Northern Ireland at the Crossroads: Ulster Unionism in the O'Neill Years 1960–9* (Macmillan Press, London, 2000)

— *The Longest War: Northern Ireland's Troubled History* (Macmillan Press, London, 2002)

Murphy, Michael, A., *Gerry Fitt: Political Chameleon* (Mercier Press, Cork, 2007)

Murray, Raymond, *State Violence: Northern Ireland 1969–1977* (Mercier Press, Cork, 1998)

Nelson, Sarah, *Ulster's Uncertain Defenders: Protestant Political, Paramilitary and Community Groups and the Northern Ireland Conflict* (Appletree Press, Belfast, 1984)

O'Neill, Terence, *The Autobiography of Terence O'Neill: Prime Minister of Northern Ireland 1963–1969* (Rupert Hart-Davis, London, 1972)

O'Riordan, Flo, *A Shattered Silence: The Burning of Bombay Street and How it Changed my Life* (Multimedia Heritage, Belfast, 2016)

Patterson, Henry, *The Politics of Illusion: Republicanism and Socialism in Modern Ireland* (Hutchinson Radius, London, 1989)

— *Ireland Since 1939: The Persistence of Conflict* (Penguin Books, Dublin, 2006)

Prince, Simon and Warner, Geoffrey, *Belfast and Derry in Revolt: A New History of the Start of the Troubles* (Irish Academic Press, Dublin, 2011)

Purdie, Bob, *Politics in the Streets: The Origins of the Civil Rights Movement in Northern Ireland* (Blackstaff Press, Belfast, 1990)

Rose, Richard, *Governing Without Consensus: An Irish Perspective* (Faber and Faber, London, 1971)

Ryder, Chris, *The RUC: A Force under Fire* (Mandarin Paperbacks, London, 1990)

Scoular, Clive, *James Chichester-Clark: Prime Minister of Northern Ireland* (Scoular, Killyleagh, 2000)

Smith, William, *Inside Man: Loyalists of Long Kesh – The Untold Story* (Blackstaff Press, Newtownards, 2014)

Smyth, Rev. Martin, *In Defence of Ulster* (County Grand Orange Lodge of Belfast, Belfast, 1969)

Stewart, A. T. Q., *The Narrow Ground: The Roots of Conflict in Ulster* (Faber and Faber, London, 1989)

Swan, Seán, *Official Irish Republicanism, 1962 to 1972* (Lulu Press, Morrisville, 2008)

Sweetman, Rosita, *On our Knees: Ireland 1972* (Pan Books, London, 1972)

Target, G. W., *Bernadette: The Story of Bernadette Devlin* (Hodder and Stoughton, London, 1975)

Taylor, Peter, *Provos: The IRA and Sinn Fein* (Bloomsbury, London, 1997)

— *Loyalists* (Bloomsbury, London, 2000)

Thompson, E. P., *The Making of the English Working Class* (Penguin Books, London, 1978)

Urwin, Margaret, *A State in Denial: British Collaboration with Loyalist Paramilitaries* (Mercier Press, Cork, 2016)

Wallace, Martin, *Drums and Guns: Revolution in Ulster* (Geoffrey Chapman, London, 1970)

Walsh, Andrew, *Belfast '69: Bombs, Burnings and Bigotry* (Fonthill, Oxford, 2015)

Whelan, Kevin, 'Bew's Ireland', *Saothar*, vol. 33, 2008

Wichert, Sabine, *Northern Ireland Since 1945* (Longman, London, 1991)

Winchester, Simon, *In Holy Terror: Reporting the Ulster Troubles* (Faber and Faber, London, 1974)

GOVERNMENT REPORTS

Disturbances in Northern Ireland (Cameron Commission Report) Cmd 532, HMSO, Belfast, 1969

Report of the Advisory Committee on Police in Northern Ireland (Hunt Report), Cmd 535, HMSO, Belfast, 1969

Violence and Civil Disturbances in Northern Ireland in 1969 (Scarman Report), Cmd 566, HMSO, Belfast, 1972

Scarman Transcripts

NEWSPAPERS

Andersonstown News

Belfast Telegraph

Daily Mirror

Daily Telegraph

(Belfast) *News Letter*

Protestant Telegraph

The Guardian

The Irish News

The Irish Times

The Observer

The People

The Revivalist

The Times

PAMPHLETS

In Defence of Ulster

IRIS

The Battle for Northern Ireland

Ulster Assailed

Ulster Must Fight

ACKNOWLEDGEMENTS

The motivation for undertaking the research for this book began with my disappointment – bordering on outrage, at times – that the voices of those who suffered the most from the violence in 1969 were excluded from accounts of the period produced by university-based historians, and are mostly absent from the retrospective attempts by journalists and others to explain the start of the Troubles.

Born and raised in an area that in August 1969 became the epicentre of sectarian confrontation, like many of my friends and neighbours I naturally became interested in modern Irish history. Beginning about ten years ago I decided to conduct my own interviews with victims and survivors, some of whom remained in West Belfast but many of whom had scattered far and wide. I am deeply indebted, first and foremost, to those who shared their experiences of the time and agreed to share their personal accounts with a wider audience. It says something about the precariousness of democratic life twenty years after the Belfast Agreement (and about the gaps in the documentary record that future historians will have to work from) that even then many others felt unable to speak freely. I am very grateful to Noel Devine, Owen McDonald, Alice Bell, Eileen Devlin, Desi Kennedy, Kevin Kennedy, James Steenson, Paddy Carlin, Pat McGrath, Billy Barrett, Seán McErlean, Joseph and Pauline Fitzpatrick, Thomas Daly, Joseph Doyle, Paddy and Richard Stott, Brian Conlon, Ethna Byrne, Eileen and Eamon McGonigle, Joe Law, Brendan Wilson, John McGreevy, Comgall McNally, John Toner, Billy McKee, Joe Robinson and Owen McKenna, as well as several others who wished to remain anonymous, for their generosity in sharing their reflections. Sadly, many of these courageous people have passed away in the time since our interviews took place: may they find the peace that eluded too many of them in life.

I am grateful also to a number of people – local historians, selfless and hard-working community stalwarts and ordinary citizens – who helped provide me with a greater understanding of the period: to Patrick Armstrong, Patricia Armstrong, Paul Courtney, Dermot Campfield, Jimmy McDermott, Mary Enright, Oliver Hanratty, Dermot Hannaway, Tony Hughes, Colm Mac Giolla Bhéin, Patricia and Joe McCann, Gerry McCann, Jim McClean, Desi McGlue, Seán Murray, Arthur O'Hare and Dan Turley. I am indebted also to Brian Kelly and Fearghal Mac Bhloscaidh, both outstanding scholars in their own fields. Their critical advice has made this work immeasurably stronger. Over several years a group of dedicated West Belfast Gaels have encouraged my work, and I'm grateful to Fearghal Mac Ionnrachtaigh, Ciaran Ó Brolchain, Dónal Ó Dálaigh and Ciarán Mac Giolla Bhéin for their friendship and support.

I want to extend a special thanks to Michael C. Lavery, QC, and to Dr Eamon Phoenix for unlimited access to their personal collections of the Scarman Tribunal transcripts and exhibits; to Gerry and Michael Collins, Hugh McKeown and his family; to the Belfast Archive Project at belfastarchiveproject.com for permission to include their historic images of the aftermath of the burnings, and to photographer Gilles Caron and Francisco Aynard at Clermes Paris for permission to use their stunning photo for the book cover. I owe thanks also to the ever-helpful staff at Belfast's Central Library – especially the Heritage Department – to the team at Glór na Móna/ Gael Ionad Mhic Goill, and finally to my publishers at Mercier Press for their commitment to this project. I'm grateful to all involved in helping this project along, though of course its strengths and any remaining weaknesses are my own.

INDEX

A

Ahoghill 44

Andrews, Jack 249

Andrews, J. M. 35

Apprentice Boys 18, 19, 28, 80, 87, 92, 93, 96–100, 103, 112, 114, 123, 209

Arbuckle, Victor 243

Armagh 40, 62, 211

B

Ballymena 230

Ballymoney 44

Barrett, Billy 161

Bates, Dawson 33, 35, 248

Battle of the Bogside 19, 106, 117, 120, 122, 233, 247

Beattie, Rev 169, 175, 176

Belfast

Abercorn Street 130, 157

Admiral Bar 202, 236

Agnes Street 81, 204, 234, 239, 241

Albert Street 48, 133, 139, 145, 149, 214, 216, 217, 220, 256, 258

Albertbridge Road 68, 236

Alderman Bar 86, 202

Alloa Street 237

Alma Street 149, 258

Andersonstown 50, 90, 92, 165, 176, 218

Andrews' Flour Mill 139, 140, 177, 180, 210

Antigua Street 200

Antrim Road 236

Ardmoulin Avenue 45, 130, 137, 141, 163, 164, 177, 229, 232

Ardoyne 8, 35, 71, 72, 84, 89, 95, 124, 125, 141, 162, 186–208, 221, 224, 226, 229, 236, 238, 246, 250, 255, 257, 259

Argyle Street 123, 127, 130, 151, 152, 181, 209, 238

Ashmore Street 123, 151–153, 158, 169, 175

Balaclava Street 46, 47, 149, 150, 159, 165, 228, 257, 258, 262

Ballygomartin Road 200

Ballymena Street 90

Beechmount 150, 220

Bellevue Street 151, 183, 184

Berlin Street 171

Beverley Street 130, 148, 163, 177, 180

'Black Pad' 149

Blackwater Street 49

Bombay Street 54, 168, 170–174, 176, 182, 183, 185, 186, 207, 213, 237, 268

Boundary Street 45, 130, 229

Boyne Bridge 234

Bray Street 85, 204

Briton's Parade 165

Broadway 231, 232

Broadway Cinema 217

Brompton Park 203

Brookfield Mill 200, 201

Brookfield Street 192, 200, 201, 203–205, 255, 259

Broughan Street 238

Brussels Street 45

Burnaby Street 47

Butler Street 187, 188, 191–196, 203, 205

Byron Street 85

Cambrai Street 56, 85, 200

Canmore Street 151

Cargill Street 130

Carlisle Street 226, 230

Carlow Street 130

Carrick Hill 76

Castle Street 161

Castlereagh Road 161

Castlereagh RUC Station 92, 264

Chadolly Street 230

Chatham Street 189, 191, 193, 203

Chief Street 78, 85, 187, 197, 198

Church Street 235
Clarwood 235
Clonard 6, 39, 54, 146, 159, 162, 167–187, 199, 213, 231, 237, 250, 257, 263, 264, 266, 268
Clonard Gardens 174, 176, 237
Clonard Monastery 54, 123, 124, 129, 168, 169, 171, 172, 174, 180–183, 231
Coates Street 237, 241
Colin Street 149
Colligan Street 125
Columbia Street 85, 91, 187
Conway Street 6, 46, 122, 128, 129, 138, 143, 150–163, 164, 167, 168, 187, 209, 218, 257, 258, 262, 263
Corby Way 50
Cosgrove Street 85
Cranmore Street 45, 169
Cromwell Street 74
Crosby Street 130
Crossland Street 151
Crumlin Road 56, 70–72, 78, 80, 83, 85, 86, 123, 125, 131, 186–189, 191, 192, 194–205, 208, 226, 259
Crumlin Road Gaol 41, 245
Cullingtree Road 220
Cumberland Street 130
Cupar Street 127–130, 138, 151–154, 158, 163–166, 168, 169, 171, 173–176, 181–184, 187, 220, 232, 262
David Street 46, 128, 129, 152, 153, 158, 220
Dee Street 232
Delaware 230
Derby Street 148, 150, 258
Devonshire Street 225
Disraeli Street 72, 75, 84, 85, 126, 187, 188, 190, 191, 197, 199, 204, 236
Distillery football ground 46, 48
Divis Street 9, 18, 37, 38, 87, 122, 124, 128, 130–151, 155, 157, 161, 179, 181, 187, 196, 199, 214, 219, 222, 230, 234, 255–262, 264
Divis Tower 136, 140, 141, 143, 144, 147, 258, 260
Donegall Pass 148, 229, 230

Donegall Road 45, 48, 73, 230–232
Dover Street 70, 124, 127, 130–138, 140, 141, 145, 147, 148, 151, 153, 156, 157, 163, 164, 177, 180, 214, 219, 229, 232–235, 258, 262
Duffy Street 130, 229
Dundee Street 251
Dunville Street 156
Durham Street 147, 219, 234
Earl Street 90
Eastland Street 129, 151
Edenderry Inn 187, 188, 199
Eighth Street 151
Elm Street 230
Elmfield Street 153, 196
Ernie Street 151, 164
Etna Drive 230
Ewart's Mill 200
Excise Street 47
Fairfield Street 203
Fairview Street 226
Falls Road 27, 34, 39, 45–48, 66, 83, 84, 88, 89, 122, 124, 126–128, 130, 133, 135–137, 142, 143, 145–150, 152–157, 159–161, 163–165, 168, 177–181, 187, 199, 202, 209, 210, 213–216, 221–224, 226, 232, 234, 236–238, 243, 250, 254–258, 261, 263–266, 268
Falls Road Lower 19, 24, 56, 123, 124, 135, 150, 151, 153, 157, 160, 163, 164, 222, 258
Falls Road Baths 129, 168, 217, 268
Fifth Street 128, 129, 151
Finbank Gardens 75
First Street 151, 152, 268
Fisherwick Place 41
Foreman Street 171
Forsythe Street 130
Fortwilliam Parade 232
Fourth Street 151
Frenchpark Street 45
Garnet Street 129
Geoffrey Street 72, 74
Gibraltar Bar 238
Gilford Street 138, 141
Glen Road 222, 269

Glenard 35
Glenbank Place 226
Glenbryn 38
Glencairn 200
Granville Street 48
Grosvenor Road 45, 47–49, 147, 150, 225, 230, 231, 257, 258
Hastings Street 25, 124, 131, 134, 135, 137, 138, 142, 144, 147, 156, 237, 260, 261
Herbert Street 188–195, 197, 199, 200, 203, 204, 205
Hillview Street 85, 238
Holy Cross 186, 192, 193, 197, 198, 200, 203, 259
Hooker Street 80, 84, 187, 188, 190, 191, 193, 199, 200, 202–204
Jamaica Street 204
James Street 171
Kane Street 167, 171, 174, 176, 182, 183, 263
Kashmir Road 168–171, 174–176, 182, 183, 185, 237
Kent Street 78
Keswick Street 171
Kilfeather's pub 158, 169
Lanark Street 184
Lawnbrook Avenue 183, 184
Leeson Street 46, 47, 48, 124, 146, 150, 154, 156, 258, 262
Lemon Street 124, 149, 258
Leopold Street 78, 85, 90, 91, 187
Linen Hall Library 71
Little Distillery Street 45
London Street 230
Lorton Street 130
Louden Street 130
Louisa Street 74
Lucknow Street 146, 175, 237
Malvern Street 39, 171
Manor Street 70, 226, 236, 237
Marlborough Street 82
Mary Street 34, 124, 149, 161
McDonnell Street 48
McGurk's bar 269
McQuillan Street 125

Melbourne Street 130
Midland Street 151
Millfield Technical College 135, 142
Milligan Street 159
Moltke Street 232
Monarch Parade 232
Montreal Street 197
Morning Star Hostel 132
Morpeth Street 130
Musgrave Street 254
New Barnsley 225
New Northern Mill 135, 142, 145
Newtownards Road 45, 74, 230, 232, 235
Ninth Street 151
Nixon Street 151
Norfolk Street 129, 150, 152–154, 157, 159, 163, 168, 220, 222, 257
North Howard Street 127, 129, 143, 268
North Queen Street 236
North Thomas Street 36
Northland Street 151
Northumberland Street 45, 143, 145, 180, 210, 215, 216, 236, 257
Oakfield Street 203
Ohio Street 78, 85, 187, 197, 204
Oldpark 70, 74, 75, 202, 216, 236
Oldpark Road 74
Omar Street 149
Oregon Street 85, 90, 187
Osman Street 150, 258
Ottawa Street 187
Palmer Street 74, 85, 187, 188, 199
Panton Street 128, 155, 158
Patton Street 149
Peel Street 124, 149, 150, 258
Penrith Street 45, 130
Percy Street 130–134, 136, 137, 139–141, 143, 145, 147, 148, 151, 156, 157, 163, 177, 178, 180, 181, 210, 214, 229, 233, 234, 236, 256, 258, 262
Peter's Hill 76, 78
Plevna Street 149, 258
Pound Street 143
Princes Street 112

Queen's Bridge 221
Queen's University 22, 58, 60, 66, 139, 211, 215
Raglan Street 149, 257, 258
Rathlin Street 90
Ravenhill Road 41, 42, 230
Rockland Street 232
Rockview Street 232
Roden Street 47, 231
Rosebank Street 85, 90, 188, 202, 204
Ruth Street 90
Sackville Place 241
Sackville Street 130, 241
Sandhill Parade 236
Sandy Row 41, 45, 48, 73, 234
Seaforde Street 225
Selby Street 230
Seventh Street 129, 151
Shankill Road 30, 32, 37–40, 45, 46, 48, 49, 56, 57, 68–71, 73, 75–78, 80–89, 91–94, 98, 106, 119, 122–132, 134–136, 142, 143, 145–147, 149, 151, 152, 158, 160, 168, 178, 179, 181, 184, 187, 198, 210, 215, 216, 222–224, 227, 232–235, 238, 241–245, 251, 253, 254, 271
Shannon Street 72
Short Strand 123, 235
Sixth Street 129, 151
Snugville Street 171, 226
Southland Street 151
Springfield Road 124, 125, 180, 181, 225, 231, 257, 264
St Brendan's Path 143, 148
St Brendan's Walk 143
St Comgall's Row 147
St Comgall's school 137, 141, 145–148, 180, 257, 260
St Comgall's Walk 147
Sugarfield Street 151, 153, 175
Sultan Street 135, 142, 149, 155, 258
Summer Street 226
Tavanagh Street 232
Templemore Avenue 232
Tennent Street 68, 69, 79, 84, 85, 89, 127, 190, 197, 200–202, 241
Tenth Street 151

Theodore Street 150, 258
Third Street 129, 142, 143, 151
Torrens Crescent 221
Townsend Street 130, 147, 217, 232, 236
Twaddell Avenue 200
Twickenham Street 226
Unity Walk 57, 73, 74, 76–83, 86, 87, 89, 94, 106, 119, 164, 230, 238, 241–243, 245, 253
Upper Library Street 76
Urney Street 151
Warkworth Street 130
Waterville Street 172, 181, 182
Wesley Street 204
West Circular Road 229
Westmoreland Street 130
Whitehall Path 259
Whitehall Row 144, 147
Wigton Street 130
William Street 66, 93, 100, 104
Wilton Street 45, 84, 93, 123, 151, 161, 184
Woodstock Road 235
York Street 35, 36, 237
Bell, Alice 141, 164, 259
Bell, Anthony 164, 165
Bessbrook 88
Boyes, Robert 252
Bradford, Roy 44
Bradley, Samuel J. 77, 80, 81, 83, 167, 168, 261, 263
Brooke, Basil 27, 28, 35
Browne, Mina 68, 69, 86
B-Specials 25, 27, 32, 40, 53, 63, 65, 66, 75, 78, 79, 82–84, 89, 112–116, 119, 120, 125–128, 130, 131, 133–138, 141, 143, 147–149, 156, 160, 165, 166, 171, 174–177, 184, 189, 191, 192, 195, 197, 200, 201, 203, 204, 207, 208, 212, 214, 222, 228, 233, 236, 241–243, 245, 246, 248–250, 252, 253, 254, 256
Bunting, Ronald 61–63, 65, 67, 81, 127

Bushmills 68
Byrne, Ethna 73, 231

C

Callaghan, James 28, 65, 75, 87, 177,
 208, 223, 229, 236, 242, 245, 247,
 249
Cameron Commission 26, 59, 60–62,
 65, 99, 116, 223, 238, 247, 248,
 251
Campbell, Edward 201
Campbell, John 105
Canavan, Rita 171, 185
Carlin, Paddy 47, 50, 221
Carrickfergus 70
Central Citizens Defence Committee
 (CCDC) 236, 241, 263, 266
Chichester-Clark, James 65, 86–88,
 92, 94, 108, 127, 128, 167, 208,
 212, 222, 234, 236, 247, 252
Claudy 44
Coalisland 109
Coleraine 29
Conlon, Brian 165
Corrie, Patrick 79, 253
Craig, James 28, 29, 271
Craig, William 23, 29, 31, 60, 271

D

Davison, Joseph 35
Delaney, Fr Ailbe 191
Derry city 5, 13, 17–19, 28, 29, 53, 57,
 60, 62, 63, 65, 66, 74, 75, 80, 87,
 92–94, 96–121, 123, 127, 136, 208,
 209, 211, 219, 226, 246, 252, 272
 Bishop Street 93, 114, 116
 Bogside 19, 65, 66, 74, 92–94, 96–122,
 124, 151, 208, 250, 253, 271
 Burntollet 63–66, 272
 Butcher's Gate 99, 100
 Carlisle Road 115
 Clarendon Street 97
 Creggan 96, 97, 116, 117

 Eglinton 115
 Eglinton Place 97
 Fahan Street 115
 Fountain 112–116
 Fountain Street 114, 116
 Foyle Road 98
 Great James Street 100, 103, 110, 112
 Guildhall 65
 Guildhall Square 100, 120
 Lecky Road 101
 Little James Street 100, 103, 110, 112
 Long Tower Road 114
 Naylor's Row 97
 Nixon's Corner 115
 Rossville Street 100–104, 253
 Sackville Street 100, 103, 104, 111
 Shipquay Street 109
 Waterloo Place 93, 100, 113, 115
 Waterside 109
 Westland Street 102, 105, 151
Devenney, Samuel 66, 101, 117
Devlin, Bernadette 75, 98, 102, 104,
 108, 109, 220
Devlin, Joe 36
Devlin, Paddy 63, 130, 132, 150, 158,
 177, 227, 236
Dickie, George 244
Doherty, Jack 110
Doherty, Noel 39, 40, 69
Doherty, Paddy 102, 109
Donegal 115, 210, 214, 219
Donegan, John 45
Donnelly, Robert 45
Downing Street Declaration 222, 228
Doyle, Joseph 209
Dublin 13, 26, 67, 144, 214, 224, 225
Dungannon 61, 109, 113, 219
Dungiven 75, 88, 109
Dunham, Anthony 78

E

Egan, Fr Patrick 123, 172, 173, 181–
 183
Elwood, William 188, 202

Enniskillen 42, 109

F

Farrell, Michael 17, 27, 35, 38, 60
Faulkner, Brian 29, 30, 61, 87, 222
Finner Camp 219
Fitt, Gerry 66, 90, 177, 222, 236, 251, 267
Fitzpatrick, Joseph 235
Fitzsimmons, Lily 34, 149
Freeland, Ian 232, 234, 244, 247, 265, 268

G

Girvan, Theresa 156
Gormanston Camp 219
Gormley, Bernard 85, 86
Gormley, Thomas 25
Goulding, Cathal 144
Gould, Matilda 39
Government of Ireland Act 17, 248

H

Hastings, Max 135, 136, 138, 140, 143, 145, 148, 150, 184, 230, 234, 243, 255, 256, 262
Hawe, Herbie 244
Healey, Denis 252
Heath, Ted 246, 265
Helliwell, Arthur 215
Hemsworth, Charles 168, 169
Hill, Wilson 252
Himsworth, Harold 247
Hippesley, William 114
Holland, Mary 17
Hudson, Brigadier P. 263, 264
Hughes, Brendan 49, 145
Hughes, Sam 46
Hume, John 75, 97, 99, 104
Hunt Report 26, 119, 223, 242, 245, 248, 250–252, 264, 266

I

Irish Republican Army (IRA) 13, 16, 20, 22–25, 30, 38, 49, 51, 53, 54, 62, 65–68, 70, 84, 87, 101, 124, 127, 137, 138, 144–146, 148, 149, 163, 166, 167, 173, 174, 178, 179, 181, 205, 207–209, 212–214, 225, 226, 233, 248, 249, 253, 263, 268, 269

J

James Mackie and Sons 170, 171, 175, 231
Johnston, Rev. F. M. K. 211
Joyce, William 110

K

Keenan, Seán 96, 99
Kennedy, Kevin 48, 133
Kennedy, Paddy 148, 158, 177, 222, 236
Keown, Annie 234
Kilkeel 44
Kitson, Frank 269

L

Lagan, Francis 156, 234, 260, 261
Larne 114
Leebody, Alec 221
Lemass, Seán 29, 42, 44
Linton, David 199
Loughgall 40
Loughran, Terence 45
Lurgan 109
Lynch, Jack 108, 210, 211
Lynch, Michael 195, 196

M

MacAirt, Proinsias 144, 167
Mark, Robert 247, 249, 250, 260, 266
Martin, John 257, 258
Martin, Leo 45
McAteer, Eddie 99, 101, 118

McAteer, Patrick 133, 134, 180, 181, 221
McAuley, Gerard 172, 264
McCabe, John 144, 145, 222, 260
McCambridge, Patrick 239–241
McCann, Joe 129, 268
McCargo, Robert 189, 195
McCaughley, Felix 136
McClean, Hugh 39
McClean, Raymond 105, 107, 110
McCloskey, Francis 75
McCrossan, Edward 75
McCullagh, Frank 77, 79
McDaid, Gerald 110
McDonald, Owen 46, 128, 153, 220
McErlean, Seán 139
McGonigle, Eamon 46
McGonigle, Eileen 73, 128
McGreevy, John 35, 221
McGuire, Thomas 45
McKeague, John Dunlop 20, 57, 68–73, 76–78, 80–84, 86–91, 93, 94, 119, 123, 125–127, 130, 131, 133, 136, 141, 142, 144, 146, 151, 154, 161, 165, 167, 186–188, 198, 204, 207, 216, 224, 225, 227, 233–235, 242, 245, 253, 267–272
McKeating, Alexander 232
McKee, Billy 145, 175
McKeown, Gerard 226
McKeown, Michael 196
McKinney, Aidan 112
McLarnon, Sammy 194–196
McLaughlin, Fr 168, 169, 171, 172, 181
McMullan, Thomas 192, 193
McNamara, Kevin 97
McParland, Patrick 171
McPhillips, Sergeant 136, 138, 153
McQuade, John 36, 72, 131, 132, 136, 142, 169, 209, 226, 228
Megarry, Hugh 197, 198

Minford, Nat 44, 69
Mitchell, Billy 16, 40, 51
Morris, Leo 195, 196
Murphy, Fr Patrick 214, 215, 217, 229, 236
Murray, James 187

N

Newry 87, 88, 225
Northern Ireland Civil Rights Association (NICRA) 30, 31, 57, 60, 62, 65, 68, 99, 212, 223

O

O'Brien, Conor Cruise 211
O'Hanlon, Paddy 238
O'Kane, Kathleen 189
Omagh 109
O'Neill, Edward 113
O'Neill, Phelim 44
O'Neill, Terence 15, 18, 22, 23, 26–31, 38, 39, 42–44, 51–53, 61–63, 65–67, 212, 223, 270
Orange Order 16–18, 27–33, 35, 42–45, 49, 58, 64, 68, 74–80, 83, 86, 88, 92, 96, 99, 210, 212, 227, 233, 234, 238, 253, 272
O'Rawe, Richard 150, 151
O'Rourke, Catherine 79
Osmond, Douglas 247, 249, 250, 260
Owens, Anthony 80, 152, 202

P

Paisley, Ian 11, 18, 20, 23, 27, 29–32, 36–45, 51, 53, 56, 57, 60–62, 65, 67–69, 71, 75, 76, 81, 82, 84, 87–89, 93, 108, 127, 128, 148, 165, 207, 209, 210, 217, 222, 224–232, 238, 242–245, 269, 271
Peacock, Anthony 65, 66, 128, 177, 178, 249, 251, 254, 260, 264
People's Democracy (PD) 60, 61, 63, 65

Porter, John 110
Porter, Robert 82, 104, 128, 209, 222, 249, 251, 261

R

Randalstown 44
Remnant, Jack 252
Robinson, Alex 176
Robinson, Joe 164
Rooney, Patrick 20, 144, 145, 148, 153, 160, 166, 262
Royal Black Preceptory 18, 27, 68, 83
Roy, Herbert 138

S

Saintfield 70
Scarman Tribunal 11, 25, 71, 74, 76, 78, 79, 81, 83, 84, 93, 102, 112, 114, 117, 120, 166, 170, 172, 176, 192, 196, 197, 203, 205, 215, 239, 246, 256–258, 262, 265, 269
Scullion, John Patrick 39
Shankill Butchers 270
Shankill Defence Association (SDA) 20, 57, 68–72, 76–79, 81–84, 86–89, 93, 94, 98, 119, 120, 123, 125, 126, 130, 131, 133, 136, 142, 151, 152, 161, 187, 190, 198, 202, 204, 207, 227, 270
Shankill Redevelopment Association (SRA) 77
Shankill UVF 40, 44, 68, 69, 71
Shillington, Robert Graham 103, 104, 106, 117–119
Sloan, James 128, 142
Smyth, Martin 80, 211
Special Powers Act 17, 33, 39, 58, 167, 237, 248, 263
Steenson, James 129, 130, 157
St John, George Bernard 193, 194, 197, 198
Stott, Paddy 220

Strabane 109

T

Taylor, John 29, 30, 31
Taylor, Mary 45
Toal, Peter 191, 192, 199, 202, 205, 206
Toner, Charlie 56
Toner, John 139
Turner, Rev. John 123
Tyler, Private 182

U

Ulster Constitution Defence Committee (UCDC) 18, 39, 40, 42, 57, 67, 69, 82, 83, 209, 227
Ulster Defence Association (UDA) 173, 241, 270
Ulster Protestant Volunteers (UPV) 18, 39, 40, 57, 60, 67–69, 71, 83, 93, 108, 207, 245, 250
Ulster Special Constabulary (USC) 13, 25, 32, 33, 39, 64, 70, 83, 105, 112–116, 122, 126, 131, 133, 134, 141–143, 160, 209, 228, 248, 250–253. *See also* B-Specials
Ulster Volunteer Force (UVF) 16, 18, 33, 36, 38–40, 45, 51, 53, 62, 64, 67–71, 75, 89, 90, 207, 228, 230, 237, 238, 267, 269, 270

W

Ward, Peter 39
Wilson, Brendan 142, 156, 164
Wilson, Harold 22, 27, 29, 93, 208, 222, 223, 249, 266
Wolseley, Arthur Harold 78, 90, 124, 126, 130, 135, 150, 166, 167, 239, 252, 253, 263

Y

Young, Arthur 242
Young, Robert 220